STEPPINGSTONES TOWARD AN ETHICS FOR FELLOW EXISTERS

STEPPINGSTONES TOWARD AN ETHICS FOR FELLOW EXISTERS

Essays 1944–1983

HERBERT SPIEGELBERG

1986 **MARTINUS NIJHOFF PUBLISHERS**
a member of the KLUWER ACADEMIC PUBLISHERS GROUP
DORDRECHT / BOSTON / LANCASTER

Distributors

for the United States and Canada: Kluwer Academic Publishers, 190 Old Derby Street, Hingham, MA 02043, USA
for the UK and Ireland: Kluwer Academic Publishers, MTP Press Limited, Falcon House, Queen Square, Lancaster LA1 1RN, UK
for all other countries: Kluwer Academic Publishers Group, Distribution Center, P.O. Box 322, 3300 AH Dordrecht, The Netherlands

Library of Congress Cataloging in Publication Data

```
Spiegelberg, Herbert.
   Stepping stones toward an ethics for fellow
existers.

   1. Ethics--Addresses, essays, lectures.  2. Social
ethics--Addresses, essays, lectures.  I. Title.
BJ1012.S59  1984      170      84-4114
ISBN 90-247-2963-7
```

ISBN 90-247-2963-7

PRINTED IN THE NETHERLANDS

The unleashed power of the atom has changed everything save our mode of thinking, and we thus drift toward un-paralleled catastrophe.

Albert Einstein

as quoted by Ralph E. Lapp in an article on "The Einstein Letter That Started it All" in *The New York Times Magazine*, August 2, 1964*

TO MY FELLOW-HIBAKUSHA* OF THE EARTH
PRESENT — AND FUTURE?

* "Hibakusha" is the Japanese name for A-bomb and H-bomb victims and survivors.

PREFACE

In releasing the text of this volume, originally set aside as a collection for possible posthumous publication, during my lifetime, I am acting in a sense as my own executor: I want to save my heirs and literary executors the decision whether these pieces should be printed or reprinted in the present context, a decision which I wanted to postpone to the last possible moment. As to the reasons why I changed my mind I can refer to the Introduction.

Here I merely want to make some acknowledgments, first to the copyright holders for the reprinted pieces and then to some personal friends who had an important influence on the premature birth of this brainchild.

The copyright holders to whom I am indebted for the permission to reprint here, in the original or in slightly amended form, the articles listed are, with their names in alphabetical order:

Ablex Publishing Company: 'Putting Ourselves into the Place of Others'

Atherton Press: 'Equality in Existentialism' and 'Human Dignity: A Challenge to Contemporary Philosophy'

Friends Journal: 'Is There a Human Right to One's Native Soil?'

Gordon Breach: 'Human Dignity: A Challenge to Contemporary Philosophy?'

Humanities Press: 'Ethics for Fellows in the Fate of Existence'

Journal of the History of Ideas: 'Accident of Birth: A Non-utilitarian Motif in Mill's Philosophy'

Philosophical Review: 'A Defense of Human Equality'

Review of Existential Psychology and Psychiatry: 'On the I-am-me Experience in Childhood and Adolescence'

The Monist: 'A Phenomenological Approach to the Ego'

Nomos Verlag: 'Equality in Existentialism'

Springer Verlag New York: 'On the Motility of the Ego'

The University of Chicago Press: 'Good Fortune Obligates: Albert Schweitzer's Second Ethical Principle'

Among the many friends who have taken encouraging interest in some of these essays I received a special boost for this collection from Osborne Wiggins and Richard M. Zaner, who even offered spontaneously their help in preparing it. Fortunately, I seem to have some time left to spare them this chore. All the more do I appreciate their support.

The main credit for efficient technical help in the preparation of the volume goes to the Administrative Assistant of the Department of Philosophy of Washington University, Dorothy Fleck, and to its secretary, Shaaron Benjamin.

In the proofreading I had the reassuring help of my friends Karl Schuhmann, Stanley L. Paulson and Bonnie Paulson.

TABLE OF CONTENTS

PART I
NEW ONTIC DIMENSIONS OF THE SELF

XII

INTRODUCTION

1 MY MAJOR CONCERN

This book does not offer a coherent philosophy of the self or of ethics. Rather it is my first attempt to present together the ideas which I consider as potentially my most substantial contribution to a new phenomenological philosophy. It is based on a new conception of the existing self on phenomenological foundations in a sense to be clarified through the doing of phenomenology in the following essays. This effort in all its inchoate character is to me the major justification for my philosophizing, if not my remaining *raison d'être*. I withheld it so long in the hope that by postponing its final formulation I could give it a better chance to mature and to speak to the condition of my fellow existers. But now the time has come when I no longer feel I have the right to wait.

My primary objective in this collection of essays is to open up and explore dimensions in our experience of ourselves which I believe will be new to most of my readers. I see the main function of this book in showing new perspectives and new phenomena which philosophy and even phenomenology have neglected. I believe that this neglect is responsible for their failure to provide the kind of insight and guidance which I consider to be essential for a genuine phenomenology of what I call 'the existing self'.

Such a phrase calls immediately for an explanation. Meaningful titles that are to speak first to an uninformed reader and are meant to awaken his curiosity for unfamiliar phenomena face at once the dilemma of either mystifying him by extraordinary neologisms or trivializing their themes through ordinary expressions. I am trying to escape between the horns of this dilemma by applying partially familiar words in new combinations like 'the existing self'.

But even so I feel some hestiation in view of the past inflationary use and misuse of the term 'self'. What I really mean by it in the combination with the adjective 'existing' is the phenomenon which I shall call later the 'I-am-me' or the 'I-myself' experience, in contrast to the traditional versions of the self as it occurs in phrases like 'self-love', 'self-determination', or 'self-realization'. By speaking of 'the existing self' I also want to announce that one of my objectives is to restore to the self the dimension of existence, i.e., of the 'I-am' in the new and intensified sense that Kierkegaard assigned to the late Latin word 'existence'. I consider it one of the main failings of most of the philosophies of existence and especially of existentialism that they have deprived the existing self of its central position and dissolved it, as it were, into transitory acts, events, processes or relations (between what?). Without returning to a rigid substantialism I want to give back to the self the weight of the original I-am-me experience, which eventually will have to be clarified in terms of an enlarged ontology.

In my title I am calling this book 'Steppingstones', rather than buildings blocks, as I contemplated at first, for several reasons. A negative reason is that I do not consider these essays as pieces that are to enter unchanged the eventual pattern, where they are to be replaced by new sections planned and executed from the start for the new structure I envisage. Positively these pieces are meant to be stones solid enough to support the weight of the reader and my own in moving across temporary supports to the other bank of the river. But they are not to be used as permanent platforms or resting places. Moreover they do not form a continuous solid flagstone walk with a smooth pavement. They leave gaps to be jumped across that later will have to be filled. I do not want to conceal that this way to my goal is still a rough road, and that to travel it requires the patience and courage of a sympathetic reader. My hope is that they will give him the necessary footholds for following me and for checking on me.

Finally, the phrase 'Toward an Ethics for Fellow-Existers' is to prepare the newcomer for several new features of my conception. The preposition 'toward' is obviously an admission that this book is not yet a developed ethics, of which it offers at best samples in Chapters 10-15 in connection with limited topics. Eventually these pieces will have to be complemented by connecting pieces and to be integrated into a more systematic frame. In talking about 'ethics' I am thinking of what is now mostly called 'normative ethics' and also of a concrete ethics dealing with specific and burning issues of living, and certainly not with a meta-ethics dealing merely with the basic concepts of ethics. Not that I reject such an enterprise. But enough has been said and written about it for my purposes. The urgent need for me as well as fortunately also for many of the younger generation of ethicists is to face the real issues of today's moral crisis like those of bioethics (birth control, abortion and euthanasia) or national and international ethics (civil disobedience and human rights).

The destination of this road is an ethics 'for fellow-existers'. I do not conceive of such an ethics as a full-fledged system of ethical norms for social existence. But it is to be a normative ethics addressed to fellow-existers. I hope that the use of the noun 'fellow-exister' will not only be intelligible from its components but convey a new idea about the addressees for such norms. In coining the term 'exister' I want to make it clear that what is at stake is more than a coreless and anonymous 'existence', as it is understood by so many existentialists, but a centered existing self. I also want to suggest a new type of social existentialism in the spirit of Maurice Merleau-Ponty, who uses the term 'co-existence' repeatedly, though without developing its meaning. 'Existence' is no longer to be confined to a solitary, let alone solipsistic, style of being. It is to include the dimension of a basic fellowship in existence among fellow beings which is neglected in the notorious Cartesian approach to the ego. I do not intend to join the chorus of contempt for the inventor of the phrase 'cogito, ergo sum' whose emphasis on the epistemological priority of the ego seems to me indispensable. Even ontologically the dimension of existential solitude is essential and needs to be intensified and deepened. But so are the dimensions of fellowship and solidarity which I consider cornerstones of a renewed ethics.

The components of this volume are not completely new. Most of them have appeared separately in scattered locations since 1944. I have united them here in a pattern in which they can serve as parts of an encompassing structure which is to make new and fuller sense of them.

In most of the essays, with the exceptions of no. 2, 4, and 5, I refer little to phenomenology explicitly as the main foundation for my assertions. This does not mean that I am abandoning phenomenology. I believe that eventually all my findings can be and will have to be buttressed phenomenologically. But such buttressing will have to wait until I can fill in the solid walk between the stepping stones which I am offering in the present collection.[1]

I do not pretend that the essays here assembled meet the challenge of Albert Einstein's words which I used as a motto for this volume. But I hope that they can contribute to the fundamental changes in thinking and feeling now needed. In particular, I hope that the essays on the new ethical dimensions (Part One Section 2) together with the added sample applications (Section 3) can provide stepping stones toward an ethics for the nuclear age. What they try to awaken is chiefly

a deeper sense for the uniqueness and depth of each self as the center of a world of his own, which also reflects the worlds of innumerable other selves;

a sense for the "moral accident" of the historical incarnation of each self into his contingent place; and

a more intense sense for the moral bonds among all fellow-selves.

My plan for the following sections of this Introduction is as follows: Section 2 contains an autobiographical account of the genesis of my conceptions, which is at the same time to explain its lateness.

1. In a preliminary way I can state my position about the potential contribution of phenomenology to ethics as follows:
On the one hand I do not share the approach implied in Max Scheler's and Nicolai Hartmann's ethics, who simply claim unconditional validity for their assertions about ethical phenomena. Such claims must remain conditioned on Husserl's original phenomenological suspension of belief in the validity of what presents itself to us first-hand beyond the range of immediate consciousness (cogito) (See my "Indubitables in Ethics: a Cartesian Medition" in ETHICS 58 (1947) 35-50.) On the other hand I submit that our first-hand findings about ethical phenomena, once they are critically scrutinized and examined, especially with regard to their modes and degrees of appearance, can provide prima facie evidence for ultimate ontological validity, even where they transcend the immediate phenomenal range. In other words, phenomenology can provide relevant, but not absolutely conclusive grounds for ontological claims. (See my "The 'Reality Phenomenon' and Reality" in *Doing Phenomenology* (1975) pp. 130-172.)

To this extent phenomenology can (1) open up better access to ethically relevant situations not yet sufficiently explored, (2) give deeper insight into the phenomena underlying fundamental concepts of normative ethics, (3) provide the fullest possible experiential grounds for claiming validity for normative ethics. (In formulating these claims I have been aided by my colleague Carl Wellman's probing suggestions.)

Section 3 is to show the relevance of my conception to today's human condition by lining up some of the new challenges to our civilization in the cosmic area as revealed by natural science, in the socio-economic area and in the cultural area. Section 4 will be a condensed statement of the new ideas which I consider relevant to this situation. Section 5 is to show how they can help to meet it concretely. Section 6 will appraise briefly what kind of meanings to our existence will remain if worse comes to worst. Finally in Section 7 I shall give a brief preview of the ingredients of this collection in the order in which I shall present them and indicate their functions in the new context.

2 WHY I WAITED SO LONG

Why offer such a patchwork solution now? To account for it requires a piece of philosophical autobiography over and above what I have offered thus far, especially in my 'Apologia Pro Bibliographia Mea'.[2]

The beginning of the ideas I am presenting goes back to some fundamental experiences I underwent long before I was in touch with academic philosophy and even with philosophical readings. I can still recall and relive some of the most gripping phases of my conscious awakening before my fifteenth year when I was still living in my native Alsace, then under German rule shortly before World War I. During these years I often felt invaded by an awesome sense of being I myself, accompanied inextricably with soliloquies (of course, in German): 'This I, with its curious name 'Herbert', is me myself, I am it, here and now; there is no escape from this inexorable being "it", born as I am into this particular family, country and time'. Actually I was the youngest of three brothers, three years younger than the second, of mixed stock (three quarters Jewish) but educated in a liberal Protestant church. My parents had immigrated from Central Germany after the annexation of 1871. As such they and the family, until then well-to-do, had to leave Strassburg after World War I, when Alsace was reunited with France. Already before the war I had become aware of the fact that Alsace

---

2. *Phenomenological Perspectives*, edited by Philip Bossert, The Hague: Martinus Nijhoff, 1975, pp. 261-274.

had been the bone of contention between France and Germany for centuries. When the war erupted in 1914 I was ten years old. During the following four years we lived in Strassburg, not far from the western front. More alarming than the rare sight of French planes overhead was the distant earthshaking rumble of the cannonades from the battlefront, especially from Verdun. The moral scandal of this war gradually undermined not only my nationalist self-righteousness of being born 'on the right side' of the slaughter; it also destroyed my faith in the all-loving God of the Church creed and made me toy with Zoroastrian dualism. The main lasting outcome was my growing distrust of all authorities in my native world, even before the collapse of Germany in 1918. This led to an inner revolt against the 'unfairness' of having been born unasked into all other 'accidental' circumstances of my existence. I also developed an increasing equalitarianism in the face of the elitist ideology of my native environment in school and church. Soon I opted for the still despised ideals of democracy and even socialism and pacifism.

After the expulsion of my family from Strassburg as 'enemy aliens' and resettlement in Heidelberg and later Munich, I was exposed to the atmosphere of resurgent German nationalism and incipient racism among my age- and class-mates, which added to my alienation. Certainly I felt isolated with my innermost sentiments and ideas, which I was too diffident and probably unable to articulate. So, except for occasional diary notes, I failed to put down my emerging pre-philosophical thoughts in writing. In spite of warm friendships with a few classmates, I felt that I had to find out first how my experiences and ideas related to those of the contemporary world in the lone hope that I could find some congenial climate for my emerging 'philosophy'.

Here begins the story of my fateful procrastinations. First they took the form of going through a university education in which I focussed on fields like history, the social sciences and law, in the hope that on the way I would also encounter anticipations of my primal reflections among my fellow students. I also set some hope on academic psychology. The outcome was almost complete disillusionment. Even though the name of the ego or rather the soul had a vanishing foothold in science, this was not my own gripping self-experience, but at best an abstraction, at worst a mere distortion of real existence. My only hope remained the serious study of academic and classical philosophy, first marginally, and then, after the completion of my law studies, exclusively. This led me into the Phenomenological Movement as the best hope for developing my original reflections. At least here I found a starting ground for my philosophizing. But first I allowed myself to be diverted into traditional problems of ontology, notably the essential nature of Platonic ideas, as the best way for establishing my scholarly credentials, but also as a possible base for approaching my fundamental questions more effectively. In my final German book manuscript on the philosophical foundations of moral rights and duties I outlined the conception of existential rights as a new anchor for a renewed ethics.

The Fascist-Nazi catastrophe meant for my personally the end of my academic prospects in Europe, largely, but not exclusively, because of the accident of my mostly Jewish ancestry. It also meant the need to transfer my life and philosophical work into the Anglo-American world. I therefore had to shelve all my previous literary plans for the near future. All I could still do with them before sailing for the United States from Southampton in February 1938 was to condense my basic existential beliefs into a short self-addressed creed which I called '*nux sapiendi*', i.e., sober wisdom in a nutshell. I formulated it in Latin since at this point I was cutting off my last German moorings. Here I shall insert them in an English translation, adding the Latin original in a note at the end of this Introduction.

Facts

Initial Mystery: I myself exist (*ipse sum*)

1. I am neither the actor of my life's drama, into which *I myself* am incarnated and with which I am habitually merged, nor my individual character, nor my personal physiognomy, nor my family, nation, tribe, nor any other specific difference from others. They are mine, given to me, but distinct from me — alien. The acting self becomes visible only to the one who turns back from his roles into the abyss of his selfhood.

2. I-myself *exist:* I do not play a role but am seriously and inexorably condemned to this particular existence.

3. I am a human being in the midst of the tremendous wonders of

this impure world (*mundus immundus*) presented to me. I am an infinitesimally small being among infinitely large ones.

4. I am a human among humans: There are other I-myselfs incarnated on the same terms as I myself. But although I am joined with them in social communion, I am segregated from them by an ultimate abyss.

Origins

1. I do not know and shall never know the origins of my selfhood and my incarnation.

2. The lot of my existence is an incomprehensible accident: a *metaphysical* accident since there is no intelligible physical cause for my becoming precisely me and being incarnated as I am, even though it would have been possible that someone exactly like me should have been born into being in my place; a *moral* accident since no merit or demerit for my becoming precisely me and for my incarnation are known or even conceivable. The same is the case with all my fellows in fate.

Moralia

1. Accept the accidents of your existence and incarnation insofar as they can serve the good.

2. Multiply the goodness that is mixed in with the impure world by vivification through enjoyment.

3. Transpose yourself into the positions of your fellow beings which are not yours only by accident, and consider the lots which are actually theirs as your own potentially.

This programmatic overcondensation of my conclusions at the time, jotted down on a little scrap of paper after I had embarked for America as a steerage passenger on the 'Queen Mary', remained for a long time the only installment of my basic philosophy. The necessity of a fresh start in the American world absorbed all my energies for some ten years. True, they meant a widening of my outlook which I have no reason to regret, all the more since this meant an additional emancipation from the provincialism of my native German background. Yet the need to express myself in an almost new language made a complete revision of my literary plans inevitable. For the immediate future it prevented more ambitious writing projects than occasional English essays. On the other hand, the upheaval of World War II, which I narrowly escaped, proved to me again the timeliness and urgency of some of my earlier ideas. Most of them, as I had conceived of them during these years, were shelved in an 'existential' diary. But I also managed to prepare and publish after much rewriting an article entitled 'A Defense of Human Equality', which contained a first installment of my existential ethics. However, the necessities of my precarious survival in the American academic world led to further detours. Thus I accepted the mandate suggested to me by my American colleagues at Ann Arbor to prepare a historical introduction to the entire Phenomenological Movement adjusted to the needs of the Anglo-American public. This task proved to be much more time-consuming than I had anticipated and diverted me for some twenty years. Yet I was able to eke out the time for a piece on the 'accident of birth', introduced under the guise of a study of J.S. Mill's political philosophy, and a first exploration, seemingly merely empirical, of what I called the 'I-am-me experience'. In 1961 a Fulbright lectureship at my German alma mater, Munich, gave me a first chance to supplement and integrate these beginnings in German lectures under the title *Phänomenologie des Ich*, in which I also contrasted my enterprise with major historical ego philosophies. But even this occasion did not leave enough time for developing the new ethical implications of what I call here the ontic dimensions of my undertaking. After my return to America an invitation to a symposium of the American Philosophical Association (Western Division) gave me a first chance to contrast my findings on the I-am-me experience with those of other analytic thinkers. My transfer to Washington University in St. Louis, where I could teach phenomenology at the graduate level, allowed me to experiment with the idea of a cooperative phenomenological workshop, in which I tried to introduce some of my new themes. I also was able to prepare such installments of my plan as the article on 'The Motility of the Ego' as a first exploration of the structure of the self, and the article on 'Human Dignity', dealing with a value problem that has become urgent since the phrase has moved to the forefront of the contemporary human rights movement. A major stimulus for developing the program of an 'Ethics for Fellows in the Fate of Existence' came from Peter Bertocci's invitation to participate in a collection of essays for a statement about what seemed to me most important in my unfinished work. The centennial of Albert Schweitzer's birth in 1975 offered an opportunity for developing his seminal idea of what I called 'Good Fortune Obligates'. The International Year of the Handicapped in 1981 was a stimulus for working out an implication of my philosophy of equality that had occupied me for many years, namely the connection between natural handicaps and the problem of compensatory justice. International crises were occasions for putting some of these ideas to more concrete tests.

During the years since my retirement from teaching I have not yet been able to extricate myself sufficiently from the consequences of my historiographical entrapment, which needed supplementing and updating. Also until about 1970 I felt that my raids on seemingly disconnected aspects of my existential ethics had remained completely ineffective. More recently, thanks to the interest of John Rawls,[2] William T. Blackstone,[3] Alan Gewirth[4] and Van Cleve Morris[5] I have become aware of some delayed responses to my earlier pieces.

Some time ago, I had already put aside most of the essays here united for the case of an 'emergency' when I would no longer be able to rewrite and integrate them in a new systematic pattern. I am afraid what I can present now together with this introduction does not yet amount to such an integration. But I hope it can at least meet an immediate need and serve as a kind of prolegomena to a fresh synthesis.

3 NEW CHALLENGES FROM TODAY'S HUMAN SITUATION

Why should the ideas I withheld for so long be relevant to my fellow existers at the present juncture? An adequate answer to this question would require a full-scale analysis of our present human situation. It would be preposterous for me to offer it here on a few pages.

2. *A Theory of Justice* (1970), pp. 100-101.
3. *Social Justice and Preferential Treatment* (1977), pp. 78-80, 83.
4. *Reason and Morality* (1978), p. 378.
5. *Existentialism in Education* (1966), p. 117.

Instead I shall merely single out some of the issues which seem to me particularly challenging and to which my answer may be pertinent. Even so, I cannot go beyond naming them without describing them fully. I shall divide them into cosmic, socio-economic and cultural challenges.

A. Challenges from Man's Cosmic Situation

I shall begin with some features of the new picture of the physical universe, stressing its most startling and disturbing aspects.

1. Time and space, once considered separate dimensions, have now been merged in accordance with Einstein's theory of relativity and are 'relative' to the observer's standpoint. Hence there is no longer any absolute 'hitching post' in the universe, and no ultimate orientation is even conceivable. This realization can induce a cosmic vertigo.

2. Matter, seemingly the inert and compact stuff of our everyday living, has turned out to consist of infinitely tiny teeming particles, some of extremely short duration, convertible into enormous amounts of energy. Thus what seemed to be a placid universe is actually filled with tremendous tensions. This realization can induce a sense of cosmic insecurity.

3. Energy, no longer separable from matter, is, according to the second law of thermodynamics and in spite of minor local exceptions such as the phenomena of biological life, 'running down' relentlessly toward a 'heat death' (entropy). This seems to spell the ultimate futility of all cosmic events.

4. The 'order of nature', once believed to be universal, has turned out to be restricted to macro-events, whereas the base level of micro-events is subject to the unpredictable chance of quantum jumps. This spells the end of the argument for a supernatural 'orderer'.

5. The 'expanding' of the universe at an accelerating rate from a point zero, the place of the 'big bang' fifteen billion years ago, promises to go on indefinitely without any concrete indication of a possible reversal. This prospect may induce a sense of cosmic agoraphobia.

6. Life, particularly human life, exists according to the latest evidence only on a minor planet of a minor sun off the center of a minor galaxy among the 300 billion galaxies, each consisting of 300

billion stars of which we know, and only for a limited period. Thus cosmically it is a minor sideshow. This may suggest the conclusion that life is an infinitesimally small phenomenon without cosmic significance.

B. Challenges from Man's Socio-Economic Situation

1. The inflation of the human species through exponential population growth, especially in the developing world, has resulted in a devaluation of the individual. Each human being becomes more expendable, less desirable and ultimately unwanted. This superfluousness accounts also for the growing indifference and callousness toward one's fellow beings and for the insanity of thinking the unthinkable (but not undoable) atrocity of wiping out or maiming billions through thermonuclear warfare. This spells the end of the sanctity of human life.

2. The individual is considered and treated increasingly as a mere Social Security number and as a point of intersection in the mesh of causal chains which have neither a beginning nor an end. This spells the loss of man's distinctive personal dignity.

3. The human environment, once the home of man's existence, has become a mere quarry for technological exploitation, polluted without any thought of future generations and stripped of unrenewable resources. This spells an increasing sense of alienation from nature.

4. By harnessing natural energies through giant technology man has finally emancipated himself from terrestrial gravity to the extent that he can not only travel in space but also colonize it through artificial islands. This spells more homelessness.

5. Man has appropriated enough nuclear power to destroy all life on earth within minutes. This means that man is potentially the universal destroyer of life.

6. Through genetic engineering man may be able to modify profoundly, though not yet to create, life. This means that man can be the corrupter, but never the creator of life.

7. In the new economy based on these new powers over nature man, the worker, has become himself a mere means of production, who is increasingly replaceable by robots and is indispensable only as a consumer. This superfluity of the worker has added to growing

alienation between man and his work through structural unemployment and market glut (stagflation).

8. Mankind has become increasingly interdependent to an extent that makes individual and group independence impossible.

9. While global solidarity has become imperative for survival, there is an intensifying trend toward more segregation promoted by a nationalism which claims ultimate authority (sovereignty) for smaller and smaller units, followed by racism which claims the prime importance of racial purity and the superiority of one's own stock, and by sexism, which asserts the superiority of the one sex, thus far mostly the male sex, by classism, stressing the all-importance of membership in an economic class, and identifying the individual with the social status of his ancestors.

10. No economic system, private capitalism, state capitalism or a mixed economy, has succeeded thus far in overcoming cyclical disturbances.

C. Challenges from Man's Cultural Situation

1. The 'explosion of knowledge', scientific as well as historical and cultural, has made it increasingly impossible for the individual to keep abreast of the culture of mankind. Specialization and the break-up of cultural unity threatens man with another alienation and the loss of his heritage in spite of all computerized memory aids.

2. The growing rapidity of social change has led to the belief that all 'values', not only the aesthetic and moral ones, are 'relative', including truth itself. This trend results in a relativism for which there are no more firm standards except within periods, groups and individuals. The continuing expansion of our acquaintance with other cultures through history and anthropology has reinforced this relativism.

3. Nihilism, the disbelief in all values, predicted by Nietzsche as the inevitable outcome of his age, has gained ground, if not prevailed and has cleared the road for a subjectivist decisionism, in which values are merely the results of arbitrary choices.

4 NEW DIMENSIONS OF HUMAN EXISTENCE

In order to make my responses to these challenges at least persua-
sive, if not yet convincing, I shall formulate here some anticipations
which are to buttress these responses. Eventually I hope I can present these as the results of insights into new dimensions of human
existence. In the meantime I am aware that they are not supported
by ordinary 'common sense' understood as our everyday consciousness. What I am trying to achieve is to expand and to deepen it. How
then can I introduce these anticipations in the present context without merely postulating them as arbitrary axioms, if not as dogmas?
My solution will be to present what I myself consider to be definite
insights as mere proposals in the form of 'suppositions' to the critical reader. In order to facilitate this development I shall add after
each 'supposition' directives that can focus his search and refer to
those essays in the following collection which can at least illustrate
them. I do not expect that they will make my proposals immediately self-evident in the sense of insights that are obvious and 'hit
you in the eye'. In most cases it will require sustained and repeated
efforts to develop them and make them sink in.

Supposition I:
I-myself exist as a unique unsubstitutable being.

   Focusing directive: Reinforce the sense of your being you yourself; compare this experience with parallel cases in others. (Essays
1 and 2)

Supposition II:
I-myself am a being for whose unique identity no general law of
science can account (cosmic accident of birth).

   Focusing directive: Consider the enormous improbability of you
yourself of all beings having been born here and now, in this family, this country, this century, etc. (Essay 6)

Supposition III:
No known moral reason (merit or demerit) can account for the fact
that you were born as you yourself (moral accident of birth).

   Focusing directive: Consider the impossibility of determining
why it was you yourself who were born here and now. (Essay 7)

Supposition IV:
I am confronted with other fellow I-myselfs.

Focusing directive: Reflect on the ways in which you become unmistably aware of the presence of others by their looks, gestures and by responsive exchanges. (Essay 10)

Supposition V:
I may be factually unequal to others, but morally my initial moral score is equal to theirs.

Focusing directive: Consider the 'unfairness' of differences based merely on the accidents of birth and circumstances. (Essay 6)

Supposition VI:
I myself can initiate instantaneous acts such as thinking, deciding, 'innervating' without being aware of any other determining causes.

Focusing directive: Mobilize in yourself the sense of power to start spontaneous action. (Essay 4)

Supposition VII:
I can break out of the cosmic 'imprisonment' of my initial position, through my power of imaginative self-transposal.

Focusing directive: Realize the power of your consciousness to reach out beyond itself and to transpose yourself into other standpoints. (Essay 5)

Supposition VIII:
I can communicate with fellow selves through 'putting myself into their shoes'.

Focusing directive: Watch what goes on in yourself when you 'make contact' with others through encounter. (Essays 5 and 10)

Supposition IX:
I can enter into the worlds of fellow beings, if only through vicarious imagination based on their communications.

Focusing directive: Watch what happens in yourself as you try to understand others by 'seeing through their eyes'. (Essay 5)

Supposition X:
I can unite with fellow beings by developing solidarity with them.

Focusing directive: Watch what goes on in you during genuine we-talk and we-experiences.

Supposition XI:
I experience a more or less constant influx of energies not of my own making in initiating and carrying out actions.

Focusing directive: Attend to the source of your energies and efforts within yourself at high and low ebb.

Supposition XII:
The meaningfulness of my experiences does not depend on their duration but on their qualitative richness.

Focusing directive: Observe how transitoriness is essential to the enjoyment of beauty especially in the temporal arts such as music.

Supposition XIII:
The meaningfulness of my experience is not dependent on the quantitative volume of their content, but on their novelty and depth.

Supposition XIV:
The emergence of the I-am-myself experience marks a major turning point in the evolution of the universe.

Focusing directive: Consider the break in the sequence of cosmic phenomena when one of them cay say 'I', reflect upon himself and open himself to the world around him through his consciousness.

Once we can fully assimilate and convert these suppositions into insights, what significance could they have for meeting the new challenges from today's human plight?

5 FIRST RESPONSES TO THE NEW CHALLENGES

In trying to determine the relevance of the 'new dimensions' of human existence outlined above for answering the most serious challenges to the human situation today I shall point out where they seem to be pertinent, referring to them by number. But I do not mean to imply that all will make a difference. For I do not want to minimize the gravity of the new challenges even in the light of the new approach I am suggesting.

A. Man's Cosmic Plight

1. The relativity of the spatio-temporal universe is irrelevant to

its qualitative significance. The preoccupation with space-time characteristics is an expression of our uncritical idolatry of mere quantity and bigness. What matters is not the where and when, but the what. Consider suppositions XII and XIII.

2.   The chaotic turmoil of matter-energy at the micro-level of our physical universe has no bearing on our chances for finding and creating harmonies and peaceful order at the macro-level and in our personal life-worlds. Consider supposition XIV.

3.   The 'running down' of the energy level in the physical universe (even if it were self-explanatory without a preceding uphill phase) is irrelevant as long as it leaves room for qualitative evolution and especially for the emergence of selves, no matter how temporary. Its ultimate end would not mean that it was all 'sound and fury signifying nothing'. Consider suppositions XII and XIV.

4.   'Order', a term of many meanings, is neither a sign of benevolent purpose nor of a cold impersonal straightjacket. What matters is that the universe leave room for spontaneous initiation. Consider supposition VI.

5.   The apparent dispersal of the expanding universe during the present phase of cosmic evolution is irrelevant to the meaningfulness of that part of its history at which human existence with its qualitative novelties predominates. Consider suppositions XII and XIII.

6.   The fact that our existence is merely an infinitesimally small sideshow in our galaxy and those surrounding it has no bearing on its intrinsic meaningfulness. The emergence of qualities such as life is thus far still unique according to our new knowledge of the solar system, and beyond it merely a matter of speculation about its possible duplication millions of light-years away. It is the existence of selves capable of embracing even galaxies through thought which determines human grandeur and dignity. Consider suppositions I, VII, and XIV.

B. Man's Socio-Economic Plight

1.   The thesis about the devaluation of the individual through the still uncontrolled inflation of the human species is based on the assumption that value is a function of scarcity. But is scarcity conclusive proof of human value rather than of economic price? Once it is realized that man's real value and dignity is based on his I-am-

me experience in its uniqueness, the question of how many or how few other individuals exist beside him becomes irrelevant. Hence, regardless of the size of the world population, the deliberate anni- hilation of each I-myself and his world is equally unpardonable. Consider suppositions I, II, and III.

2. The fact that man is increasingly treated as a mere number and a link in an endless chain of generations does not contradict his experience of being a unique unsubstitutable I-myself with initiat- ing powers. Consider suppositions I and VI.

3. While it is true that migratory, urbanized and mechanized man has become alienated from his environment through techno- logy, the I-myself has also the power of reaching beyond himself to nature and of recovering the sense of fellowship and equal rights with others. Consider suppositions VII, VIII, IX, and X.

4. Man's physical emancipation from gravity does not mean that he will become alienated from planet Earth as his home ground, but only from the provincialism of special groupings. Consider sup- positions IX and XIV.

5. Man's power to destroy all life on earth and by that possibly throughout the known universe can be matched by the spirit of reverent encounter, forbidding him the use of power for its own sake. Consider suppositions IV, IX, and X.

6. Genetic engineering can modify life in the interest of richer and more human existence. Consider suppositions VI, X, and XIV.

7. Automation carefully controlled can bring not only a libera- tion from drudgery but take care of the needs of the less qualified workers by social planning, aimed at preserving the equal dignity of each individual. Consider supposition V.

8. The growing interdependence of men and nations can also increase their emancipation from accidents of birth and circum- stances and promote a new world-wide solidarity. Consider suppo- sitions II and X.

9. The new segregationism expressed in the increased demand for sovereign independence in the 'Third World' can best be coun- terbalanced not only by the necessity of economic cooperation on a shrinking globe, but on a vaster scale by developing the sense of fellowship based on the common realization of the accident of birth. See suppositions V, VII, and X.

10. While the apparent inability of all present economic systems

to solve problems like unemployment, inflation, stagflation etc. has now become manifest, the only livable solution seems to lie in the direction of equalitarian respect and fellowship which can prepare the ground for more humane practical solutions. Consider suppositions V and X.

C. Man's Cultural Plight

1. While the accident of birth includes also our accidental incarnation in different cultures, we can transpose ourselves into those of our fellow-beings and enter into them by vicarious imagination. While this cannot overcome all barriers, breaking down some of the cultural walls should bridge some of the worst culture gaps and promote the kind of cultural humility which will make for intercultural tolerance. Consider suppositions VIII and IX.

2. 'Cultural Relativism' is a term which covers many virtues and more sins. It may be interpreted as an attitude which awakens us to the significance of cultural variety for the needs of different individual selves and groups of selves and can as such enrich our existence. But it may also be asserted dogmatically in claiming that all values are dependent in their being on the differences of different subjects, an assertion which is by no means self-evident. Such extreme relativism can be neutralized to some extent by the realization that relative positions depend on the accidents of birth and circumstance, a realization which implies that we also have a sense for non-accidental common essentials. Compare suppositions II, III, and IV.

3. Cultural nihilism blinds itself to the richness of our experienced world. Ultimately it represents a dogmatic negativism which flies in the face of the undeniable phenomena. Consider suppositions XII and XIII.

6 MINIMUM AND OPTIMUM MEANINGS
FOR HUMAN EXISTENCE

The preceding first answers to today's challenges for the meaning of human existence must not be interpreted as total solutions of the underlying cosmic, socio-economic and cultural problems. On the contrary, I do not think that such solutions are in sight, and I am far from sure that they are even possible. This may be even a good thing in the spirit of Gotthold Ephraim Lessing's preference for the search for truth over its possession as more meaningful to him. What I mainly object to is the all-or-nothing attitude of a sweeping see-no-evil, hear-no-evil, speak-no-evil optimism affirming that this is the best of all possible worlds and an equally sweeping see-only-evil, hear-only-evil, speak-only-evil pessimism of the worst of all possible worlds. Instead I have tried to introduce some limited counterweights to balance the crushing burdens of the initial challenges in today's human situation; I hope they offer minimum meanings in a universe that at first may seem indeed largely devoid of meanings, if not downright 'absurd'. My hope is that the new dimensions of human existence which I have tried to point out will allow a fundamental reappraisal of the situation comparable to another 'Copernican revolution', for which the I-am-me experience can provide a new focus or fulcrum. In this perspective the entire universe can acquire new sense. But this does not mean that by itself this universe has a sense of its own, apart from existing selves that make sense of it. The universe by itself may still be 'absurd'. But man can make sense of it both by finding it in relation to himself and other foci of meaning and by introducing new sense through adding new dimensions to it.

Thus far I have talked only about minimum meanings which remain if worse comes to worst. But what if it does not? There is indeed no good reason for always expecting the worst, even if it is at least prudent to be always prepared for it. But it would certainly be foolish or cowardly to abandon sight unseen all possibilities for the better. This need not mean fooling oneself or indulging in the pragmatist will, or better, right to believe in the absence of evidence to the contrary. What I propose instead is not to close one's eyes to the possibilities of additional meanings in areas where there are strong, if not conclusive, reasons for a brighter outlook. I myself have hinted at some evidence in supposition XI of the 'New Dimensions of Human Existence' to the effect that we experience constantly influxes of energy not of our own making. But in the subsequent section I have not taken any advantage of this particular clue. I would like to leave it to each reader to decide how far he cares to interpret these clues more or less in the direction of religion or even theology. Without denying him the right to believe even in the absence of evidence, I would part company with any options in contradiction to the evidence as expressed in Tertullian's and even Kierkegaard's *credo quia absurdum*. But I see a possible case for solutions like finite theism or some dualistic metaphysics. Personally, I am trying to live without them and prefer simply to abide by the uninterpreted evidence pointing to a 'power, not ourselves, which makes for righteousness' (Matthew Arnold, his 'Dover Beach' notwithstanding) or rather, less moralistically, which makes for greater harmony in the midst of conflict, and light in the midst of darkness.

7 THE STEPPINGSTONES: A PREVIEW

Finally, I shall try to show how the pieces of the present collection fit into the new framework. The first five deal mostly with new ontic dimensions, the following nine with ethical dimensions.

'On the I-am-me Experience in Childhood and Adolescence' was a first attempt to make sure of the key phenomenon of the 'I-myself', which I had feared was completely private and inaccessible to others, undertaken largely on the basis of a questionnaire study among undergraduate students. As such it is to serve as an empirical entering wedge for the phenomenological and philosophical study of the basic phenomenon in the new approach to existential and ethical questions of this book.

'A Phenomenological Approach to the Ego' was written as the first paper in a philosophical symposium designed to compare the results of a phenomenological approach to the ego with those of analytic philosophy in the Anglo-American style, an experiment which was a failure largely because the other partners did not abide by the rules I had suggested in my original proposal. The paper contains a first application of phenomenology proper (in my sense) to the field, beginning with an exploration of the old dimensions of ego-philosophy and then turning to new dimensions of the ego-phenomenon. This paper was also a first example of a 'Phenomenology of the Ego' which I had outlined in my German lecture course in 1962 at the University of Munich on a Fulbright grant.

'On the Motility of the Ego' is an example of a descriptive ontology of the I-myself, focusing on a previously neglected aspect of the ego-phenomenon and yielding a new structural pattern of the ego. The choice of this particular aspect of the ego was due to the occasion of a *Festschrift* for Erwin Straus, the phenomenological psychologist interested particularly in the role of motility in perception.

'The Phenomenological Analysis of Initiating' is a new piece whose development seemed to me particularly urgent in order to justify the transition from the conception of the I-myself as mostly a static victim of his incarnation to his potential as a starter for an active recentering of human existence. Focusing on this phenomenon in the active self seems to me also a new way of approaching the stale problem of free will.

'Putting Ourselves Into the Places of Others', is a sketch of a phenomenological analysis of a neglected social potential of the ego. It was undertaken on the occasion of the International Congress of Philosophy in Brussels in 1953, when for the first time I felt free to do phenomenology after years of elementary philosophy teaching in the American college style.

'Accident of Birth: A Non-utilitarian Motif in J.S. Mill's Philosophy' may at first sight appear to be merely a piece of historical excavation. Actually it was my antecedent interest in a conception which I considered basic for social ethics that had attracted me to Mill as an unexpected illustration of this conception and as an occasion for clarifying the deeper meaning of this colloquial phrase. It also was meant to buttress the earlier piece which follows next.

'A Defence of Human Equality' was my first attempt after leaving Europe to formulate my answer to the Fascist-Nazi menace to human equality. It was based on the concept of 'accident of birth', which, however, I was not yet able to develop at the time. The essay first seemed to have fallen by the wayside until it re-emerged in the seventies, especially through John Rawls' use of it in his *Theory of Justice.*

'Equality in Existentialism' is, among other things, an attempt to relate the ethics of the moral accident of birth to the philosophies of French contemporary existentialism, which were still unknown to me at the time of the preceding piece.

' "Human Dignity": A Challenge to Contemporary Philosophy' was originally the topic for the Pacific Philosophy Forum founded by Professor William Nietman of the Pacific College at Stockton,

California, taken over by Professor Rubin Gotesky. I had suggested this theme to him and he had asked me to prepare at once the main thesis, which according to the pattern of these forums was to be matched by a counter-thesis and finally by a synthesis of a third participant. However, at the time, for reasons of priorities, I found myself unable to meet his deadline, at which point William T. Blackstone stepped in with the offer of his paper, dealing almost exclusively with human rights. This is the reason why my contribution took the form of a counterthesis on human dignity. The live symposium which was to follow these papers at Monterey never took place because not enough student participants registered for the occasion. Hence only a printed volume containing our papers and several related essays appeared in a series entitled *Human Dignity: This Century and the Next.* Here the sections answering Blackstone's thesis are omitted. 'Human Dignity', a phrase of surprisingly recent origin and popularity (just as the phrase 'human rights') and propelled to the fore by its violation rather than by its observance, was meant as a challenge to all types of contemporary philosophy in view of its vagueness, but not yet as my own final answer. The present context should make it clear that my main justification of this conception can be found in the ontic dimensions of selfhood, which I tried to explore in the first five essays.

'Ethics for Fellows in the Fate of Existence' is my boldest, but least substantiated proclamation of the ethical implications of the accident of birth for social ethics.

'Good Fortune Obligates: Albert Schweitzer's Second Ethical Principle' is an interpretation of one of his central insights, though usually not formulated by him as a special principle. It parallels the experience of the accident of birth. Schweitzer's primary applications were to the obligation of the beneficiaries of modern medicine toward the victims of ill health, particularly among the developing nations.

The new article, 'Why Compensate the Naturally Handicapped? A Case for a New Conception of Compensatory Justice', is the result of my long-standing interest in an implication of the philosophy of human equality which has been badly neglected by most moral philosophers. I consider it merely a beginning, but one which could lead to a major revision of the basic approach to social philosophy, especially to the problem of justice, whose difficulties and dilemmas we are apt to overlook in our struggle to overcome obvious injustices.

'Is There a Human Right to One's Native Soil?' is an incidental piece conceived on the occasion of the Yom Kippur War between Egypt and Israel in 1973. The tragic impasse in the conflict between Arab and Israeli claims to Palestine seemed to me also a special challenge for an international ethics based on the accident of birth and for an appeal to a conciliation on a new foundation. In an epilogue I now try to indicate how the impasse in this minor but paradigmatic and near-tragic case holds a major lesson for the much vaster and fateful problems of the have and have-not nations.

The programmatic short piece 'For an Ethics of Global Solidarity' also related to the urgent problem of an ethics for the developing Third (and Fourth) World in its relation to the 'developed' nations. This also was an incidental piece which gave me an occasion to test the significance of the ethics of the accident of birth in an attempt to strengthen the growing sense of international co-responsibility, thus far supported mostly by practical considerations and by an inarticulate sense of ethical obligations not yet fully aware of the need of challenging the provincialism of outdated patriotisms. For these will have to be overcome if the indispensable planetary world consciousness is to save the most endangered species today, man himself.

The last piece of the section on Applications ('The Nuclear Powers are Forfeiting Their Claim to Civil Obedience') grew out of an invitation of 'Concerned Philosophers' for a contribution to its newsletter. The present version omits the introductory paragraph about the general responsibilities of philosophers in a situation like the present threat of a nuclear holocaust. However, it adds a special footnote, which raises the question of the grounds and limits of political obligation in the light of the accident of being born into one's initial station.

None of the preceding essays supplied significant foundations, and particularly phenomenological foundations, for my positions. However, a new piece "Unfairness and Fairness: A Phenomenological Analysis" (Part IV) which I have been able to add recently may be considered as an installment on this remaining debt.

Except for slight stylistic improvements, the original 'steppingstones' have remained practically unchanged, even where I could and should have made some significant additions, largely in order not to spoil the historical record. I am postponing these for the fuller treatment of my subjects, of which I have been able to prepare merely drafts thus far. Only in a few cases, such as no. 3 and no. 13. I added supplements which seemed to me particularly urgent.

NOTES

* *On Einstein's Statement of 1945 on the Atom Bomb.*

I cannot suppress some doubt as to the authenticity and the meaning of Einstein's sentence, surrounded by quotes by Ralph Lapp at the end of a paragraph near the end of his article dealing mostly with Einstein's fateful letter of 1939 to President Roosevelt on the danger of nuclear weapons in the hands of Nazi Germany. No source for this supposed quotation is added. This doubt is reinforced by Lapp's later book on *Arms Beyond Doubt* (New York: Cowles Book Company, 1970), where on page 193 some unnamed journalists are quoted who had stopped Einstein at the return from a sail on Lake Saranac, but without the crucial sentence. They only mention his realization that the dropping of the two nuclear bombs on Hiroshima and Nagasaki had made the concept of national sovereignty obsolete. There is also no trace of this or any similar statement in the comprehensive biography of *Albert Einstein* (1971) by Ronald W. Clark or in the volume *Einstein on Peace* (1960) adited by Otto Nathan and Heinz Norden.

However, this book reprints an interview-article by Michael Amrine published first in the *New York Times Magazine* of June 23, 1946 under the title "The Real Problem is in the Hearts of Man," in which Einstein tried to explain his recent message to the effect that a new type of thinking is essential if mankind is to survive and move toward higher levels.

... Today the atomic bomb has altered profoundly the nature of the world as we know it, and the human race finds itself consequently in a new habitat to which it must adapt its thinking. In the light of this new knowledge a world authority and an eventual world state are not just *desirable* in the name of brotherhood; they are necessary for survival.... Today we must abandon competition and secure cooperation. This must be the central fact in all our considerations of international affairs; otherwise we face certain disaster. Modern war, the bomb and other discoveries present us with revolutionary circumstances.... Our defense is not in armaments, not in science, nor in going underground, our defense is in law and order.... Science has brought our defense is in law and order.... Science has brought forth this forth this danger, but the real problem is in the minds and hearts of men.... We must change our own hearts and speak bravely. When we are clear in heart and mind — only then shall we find the courage to surmount the fear which haunts the world.

These formulations refer indeed to the need for a drastic change in our thinking and feeling. But they do not go beyond the general admonition to cooperation and world government.

Nevertheless, I consider it legitimate to interpret Einstein's words as quoted in my motto, which in this form has become a "familiar quotation", in their widest possible sense.

Latin original of my 1937 "Creed" (translated in the main text)

A. *Facta*

Mysterium initiale: Ipse sum

1. Sum *ego-ipse*: Non sum 'persona' dramatis vitae cui sum incarnatus et consuetudine concretus, nec aliae differentiae specificae: Sunt mea, data mihi sed a me distincta, aliena. Ipse actor non est visibilis nisi revertenti e 'personis' in abyssum suae ipsitatis.

2. Ipse-ego *sum*: Non solum ago personam sed serio et inexorabiliter ad hanc existentiam condemnatus sum.

3. Homo sum in tremendis mirabilibus mundi immundi mihi oblati — minimus inter maxima.

4. Homo sum inter homines. Sunt alii ego ipsi sub eadem conditione incarnati ac ego ipse. Sed et communione sociali cum eis coniunctus ultima separatione ab eis seclusus sum.

B. *Origines*

1. Mei ipsius et incarnationis meae in mea rationem ignoro, ignorabo.

2. Sors existentiae meae est casus incomprehensibilis: casus 'metaphysicus' Quia causa mei ipsius fiendi et meae incarnationis nunquam adest, etsi talem quendam qualis sum fieri necessarium erat; casus 'ethicus' quia nec meritum nec culpa mei ipsius fiendi et meae incarnationis manifesta sunt et concipi possunt, et sic est in aliis con-sortibus meis.

C. *Moralia*

1. Suscipe casum existentiae et incarnationis tuae quatenus in via boni.

2. Bonum actu et potentia mundo immundo immixtum operando multiplica, fruendo vivifica.

3. In con-sortis locum quem casu tantum non occupas te transpone et sortem actu suam tuam potentia respice.

PART I

NEW ONTIC DIMENSIONS OF THE SELF

There is no place for pity or humanity in a society in which human beings are not regarded as individual human beings, but as impersonal classified pegs in a rigidly organized society. It is only if you feel that every he or she has an 'I' like your own 'I', only if everyone is to you an individual, that you can feel as Montaigne did about cruelty. It is the acute consciousness of my own individuality which makes me realize that I am I, and what pain, persecution, death means for this 'I'.

Leonard Woolf
The Journey; Not the Arrival Matters

1 ON THE I-AM-ME EXPERIENCE IN CHILDHOOD AND ADOLESCENCE

'Thou best Philosopher. . . , thou Eye
among the blind, that, deaf and silent,
read'st the eternal deep. . .'

William Wordsworth, ('Intimations
of Immortality') from Recollections
of Early Childhood (1806)

1.1 Purpose of the Study

The present study owes its origin to a long-standing interest in a personal experience which I have found strangely neglected by both philosophy and psychology. Its most spontaneous expression is the seemingly trivial sentence 'I am me'. I submit that especially in the context of its actual occurrence it is the outgrowth of a peculiar amazement, a vertiginous feeling which is particularly acute in childhood but by no means restricted to it. It differs significantly from the mere everyday awareness of selfhood or individuality as signified by the use of the pronoun 'I'. For the I-am-me experience involves a peculiar centripetal movement not to be found in the simple statement 'I am'. This is not the place for a phenomenological elucidation of this experience. The main purpose of the present study is to establish its existence empirically and to make it available for fuller investigation both psychologically and philosophically.

1.2 Autobiographical Material

Though academic philosophy and psychology seem to have taken

Reprinted by permission from *Review of Existential Psychology and Psychiatry* 4 (1964), 3-21.

practically no account of this experience,[6] it has not gone unnoticed by the more sensitive seismographs of the literary psychologists. The following testimonies are the most striking I have been able to collect thus far:

Jean Paul Richter, the German Romanticist, includes in an auto-biographical fragment, published posthumously, this passage:

> I shall never forget what I have never revealed to anyone, the pheno-menon which accompanied the birth of my consciousness of self *(Selbst-bewusstsein)* and of which I can specify both the place and the time. One morning, as a very young child, I was standing in our front door and was looking over to the wood pile on the left, when suddenly an inner vision 'I am me' *(ich bin ein Ich)* shot down before me like a flash of lightning from the sky, and ever since it has remained with me luminous-ly: at that moment my ego *(Ich)* had seen itself for the first time, and for ever. One can hardly conceive of deceptions of memory in this case, since no one else's reporting could mix additions with such an occurrence, which happened merely in the curtained holy of holies of man and whose novelty alone had lent permanence to such everyday concomitants.[7]

The incident must have occurred some time before Jean Paul's thirteenth year (1776), when the family moved to a new location.

I owe my acquaintance with the next two instances to a passage in Jean-Paul Sartre's essay *Baudelaire*, which asserts that 'Everyone in his childhood has been able to observe the accidental and shatter-ing *(fortuite et bouleversante)* apparition of the consciousness of self'.[8] Of Sartre's three examples, André Gide, Maria le Hardouin, and Richard Hughes, the two latter are for me the most pertinent witnesses. Hughes, from whom Sartre quotes a whole page, is the earlier one. His testimony is related to an incident in his remarkable

6. The only psychologist known to me who seems to have come close to its identifi-cation is G. Stanley Hall in his report about children's 'philosophical stirrings' in 'Some Aspects of the Early Sense of Self', *American Journal of Psychology* 1897, 9, 351-95, es-pecially 379 ff.

7. 'Selbsterlebensbeschreibung' *Werke* Munich, 1963, vol. 6 p. 106. This passage is quoted verbatim in Thomas Carlyle's review of Richter's autobiography with the reveal-ing comment: 'To some of our readers, the following circumstance may seem unparalleled, if not unintelligible: to others nowise.' *Critical and Miscallaneous Essays* (London, 1889), II, III. –There may well be some connection between Carlyle's interest in this passage and Teufelsdröckh's meditations on the unanswerable question: Who am I; the thing that can say 'I' *(das Wesen, das sich ICH nennt)* in *Sartor Resartus*, Book I, Chap. 8, which was written about the same time.

8. Jean-Paul Sartre, *Baudelaire* Gallimard, 1947, p. 21.

novel *A High Wind in Jamaica*   from which I shall quote with a few ommissions:

> . . . And then an event did occur to Emily of considerable importance. She suddenly realized who she was.
>
> There is little reason that one can see why it should not have happened to her five years earlier, or even five later; and none, why it should have come that particular afternoon.
>
> She had been playing houses in a nook right in the bows, behind the windlass . . .; and tiring or it was walking rather aimlessly aft, thinking vaguely about some bees and a fairy queen, when it suddenly flashed into her mind that she was *she*.
>
> She stopped dead, and began looking over all of her person which came within the range of her eyes. She could not see much, except a fore-shortened view of the front of her frock, and her hands when she lifted them for inspection; but it was enough for her to form a rough idea of the little body she suddenly realized to be hers.
>
> She began to laugh, rather mockingly. 'Well' she thought, in effect: 'Fancy *you,* of all people, going and getting caught like this. ——You can't get out of it now, not for a very long time: you'll have to go through with being a child, and growing up, and getting old, before you'll be quit of this mad prank.' . . . .
>
> She began examining the skin of her hands with the utmost care: for it was *hers.* She slipped a shoulder out of the top of her frock; and having peeped in to make sure she really was continuous under her clothes, shrugged it up to touch her cheek. The contact of her face and the warm bare hollow of her shoulder gave her a comfortable thrill, as if it was the caress of some kind friend. But whether the feeling came to her through her cheek or her shoulder, which was the caresser and which the caressed, that no analysis could tell her.
>
> Once fully convinced of this astonishing fact, that she was now Emily Bas-Thornton (why she inserted the 'now' she did not know, for she certainly imagined no transmigrational nonsense of having been anyone else before), she began seriously to reckon its implications.
>
> First, what agency had so ordered it out of all the people in the world who she might have been, she was this particular one, this Emily; born in such-and-such a year out of all the years in Time, and encased in this particular rather pleasant little casket of flesh? . . . .
>
> Secondly, why had all this not occurred to her before? She had been alive for over ten years, now, and it had never once entered her head. . .

9. Richard Hughes, *A High Wind in Jamaica*, New York, 1932, Chapter Six.

How could Emily have gone on being Emily for ten years, without once noticing this apparently obvious fact? It must not be supposed that she argued it all out in this ordered, but rather long-winded fashion. Each consideration came to her in a momentary flash, quite innocent of words; and in between her mind lazed along, either thinking of nothing or returning to her bees and fairy queen. If one added up the total of her periods of conscious thought, it would probably reach something between four and five seconds; nearer five, perhaps; but it spread over the best part of an hour.

I am greatly indebted to the author for a letter with the following information concerning the autobiographical element of this episode:

You have of course guessed right: the whole incident is based on the memory of my own childhood . . . I was younger than Emily, though; around six or seven years. Oddly enough, when I was writing the book I recollected it as happening to me just as casually as to Emily; but today I can't help wondering whether it wasn't triggered by another incident I now recall separately: the almost unbearable spectacle of a cat playing with a live mouse. For sympathetically I identified myself with the hopeless tortured mouse; and it could be the discovery that I really wasn't that mouse after all led on to the question 'Well, in that case who am I?' and so to the discovery that I was 'me'. Both incidents were associated with the same stretch of garden path, but I remember them separately and have no evidence they happened at the same time or even in that order. . . .

Maria le Hardouin has included a similar incident in her remarkable semi-autobiographical novel *La Voile noire* (1944), where the heroine at the age of four is suddenly overcome by the sensation 'It is strange, isn't it, I am 'me'.' *(C'est curieux! Je suis moi.)*[10] In the meantime she has published an even more authentic account of the incident, which I am translating here:

Several weeks before becoming ill (of a coxalgia at the age of 5), when I was still no more than a child full of turmoil, one morning when I was running off to play, I was invaded by a strange impression. An odor from the panelling of the staircase, a beam of sunlight heightened by a yellow

10. Maria le Hardouin, *La Voile noire* Paris, 1944, p. 17 f.

stained glass pane had immobilized me on the treads as if a hand had touched my shoulder. 'I am ME' I had murmured to my mother, who was astonished at my disturbance. The carelessness, the distractedness, the absent-mindedness which are the mark of childhood, had abruptly given way to a spirit of attention. I ceased to be merely the impersonal meeting ground of sounds, lights, and odors. A voice spoke up distinctly: 'Fancy, this somebody who feels and who looks —why, that is me (mais c'est moi).'[11]

Again I am indebted to the author for supplementary explana- actions in a most illuminating letter. Of these the following pas- sage in translation throws additional light on the account above:

> It is noteworthy that it was a certain odor of soft carpet on the stairs, combined with the light which fell through the yellow stained glass win- dow —these two sensory shocks— which provoked suddenly that intru- sion of thought in its pure state, that indescribable uneasiness of seizing oneself as a 'me'. You are right in saying that this sentiment is the oppo- site of a truism; in my opinion it is so profoundly 'upsetting' that it assumes a traumatizing character.

There would be little point in adding from my collections similar direct or indirect testimonies to the experience which I want to explore. Certainly few are as explicit, focussed, and unambiguous as the three just quoted.[12] This does not mean that they contain a phenomenologically adequate description of the actual event. But they converge sufficiently and spontaneously on the formula 'I am me' to make them a suitable basis for subsequent explorations and verifications.

11. *Recherche d'une éternité*. Paris: Buchet Chastel, 1956. p. 206.

12. I cannot resist, however, the temptation of adding here a very recent testimony from Carl Gustav Jung's *Erinnerungen, Träume, Gedanken* (Zürich, Rascher Verlag, 1962), in which he reports the following isolated episode from his eleventh year: 'At that time another important experience occurred. It happened on my long walk to school from Klein-Hüningen, where we lived, to Basel. There was a moment there in which I suddenly had the overwhelming feeling of having just come out of a dense fog with the conscious- ness: now I am *me* (jetzt bin ich *ich*). At my back there was something like a fog bank behind which I had not yet been. But at that moment I became an event to myself *(geschah ich mir)*. Before that I was also around, but everything had merely taken place. Now, however, I knew: now I am me (jetzt bin ich *ich*), now I am really here. Before things were merely done to me, but now I was the one who willed. This experience seemed to me enormously significant and novel. There was authenticity *(Autorität)* in it.' (p. 38 f.; my translation).

1.3 The 'I-am-me' Experience and the Discovery
of the Ego and the Self

At first sight it may seem that what is discovered here is nothing but what is usually described as the discovery of one's self or one's ego. The recent rehabilitation of these concepts in the psychological literature, especially since Gordon W. Allport's decisive plea,[13] preceded by the use of the concept in William James' psychology, in the social psychologies of G.H. Mead and others, and especially in Freudian and post-Freudian psychoanalysis, may well seem to afford the proper framework for accommodating this particular phenomenon. But not only is this new framework still very fragile; its main concepts, fluid as they are, seem to be quite unsuited to describe the 'me' of the 'I-am-me' experience. Without trying to cover all the current conceptions of the ego and the self, I want to show the inadequacy of this framework briefly in the case of the representative and impressive systematic attempt of Percival M. Symonds to distinguish between the ego and the self.[14] Symonds' term 'ego' refers to the self as object —the self which perceives, thinks and acts and which would be described by an outside observer' (p. vi), or later as 'that phase or personality which determines adjustments to the outside world in the interest of satisfying inner needs in those situations where choice and decision are involved. Or, to define the ego differently, it is an active process for developing and executing a plan of action for attaining satisfaction or response to inner drives'. (p. 4). Regardless of whether this ego is meant to be an object of experience or rather a theoretical construct, this is certainly not the 'me' of the 'I-am-me' experience. For this 'me' is given primarily, if not exclusively, to the inside, not the outside observer. And it is not primarily an agent of adjustment, but, at least at the start, alarmingly unadjusted to its plight. Nor is it simply a 'process'. And as to developing and executing plans of action, this is certainly not its primary function in the conditions in which it finds itself at the start, disoriented and badly in need of a new plan as it is.

By contrast, Symonds' self is wholly subjective and corresponds to the 'phenomenal self' described in the current phenomenological

13. Gordon W. Allport, 'The Ego in Contemporary Psychology' (1943); reprinted in *Personality and Social Encounter*. Boston: Beacon Press, 1960. pp. 71 ff.

14. P.M. Symonds, *The Ego and the Self*. New York: Appleton–Century-Crofts, 1951.

approach to the study of human nature (p. vi). It also 'refers to the body and mind and to bodily and mental processes as they are observed and reacted to by the individual' (p. 4). Now the 'me' of the 'I-am-me' is indeed 'subjective' in one of the many senses of this slippery term, which would need to be separated. But its primary referent is certainly not the 'body' or the 'mind', quite apart from the discredited metaphysics which these terms signify for most of us today. Perhaps one of the most poignant features of the 'I-am-me' experience is the strange dissociation of the 'me' from the body with which it used to identify. And as to the 'mind', this is much too vague a term to characterize the intensity of the personal me-experience. Also, this is a very different experience from that of ordinary bodily and mental processes (like walking or remembering).

Besides, it is usually claimed that both the ego and the self develop gradually, not abruptly (*ibid.*, p. 39, 62). But the 'I-am-me' experience, as it was remembered by our key witnesses, was certainly anything but gradual. Theoretically it may seem possible to question the realiability of their memory. But it seems beyond reasonable doubt that they remember the experience as having all the earmarks of a sudden shock.

One might think, however, that the 'I-am-me' experience coincides with what recently has been introduced by the name of the 'sense of (self-)identity'. 'Self-identity' figures, for instance, as one of the eight basic functions ('proprium') of the self in Gordon W. Allport's 'Basic Considerations for a Psychology of Personality'.[15] But as far as I can gather from his account so far, the phenomena do not coincide, although they are of course related. For what is involved in the experience of self-identity —which develops gradually, never suddenly— is the sense of identity between successive phases of a person's life ('I remember some of my thoughts of yesterday; and tomorrow I shall remember some of my thoughts of both yesterday and today') combined with the realization of being distinct from others ('the realization that he is not the other, but a being in his own right'). By contrast the 'I-am-me' experience, whether sudden or gradually developed, has to do with a very different aspect of personal identity: the sense of 'being it', of being the inescapable very me-myself right now and here. As such the experience has no primary reference to past and future phases in

15. Gordon W. Allport, *Becoming.* Yale University Press, 1955, p. 45 f.

its development nor to other comparable selves. This is, as it were, an experience of self-identity in depth rather than in temporal length and social breadth.

The I-am-me differs even more basically from Erik H. Erikson's significant and fruitful concept of self-identity.[16] For his 'sense of ego identity' is merely 'the accrued confidence that one's ability to maintain inner sameness and continuity is matched by the sameness of continuity of one's meaning for others' (p. 89). Actually 'identity' expresses here 'a mutual relation in that it connotes both a persistent sameness with oneself (self-sameness) and a persistent sharing of some kind of essential character with others' (p. 102). From Erikson's concrete development of this concept I have the impression that this 'identity' almost coincides with what is usually called a personal character or social role. But this is clearly quite remote from the 'me' of the 'I-am-me' experience, which precedes, as it were, any character or role. It is precisely the experience of one's non-coincidence with these 'identifications' which leads to the awareness of the 'I-am-me' in its most acute form.

It would seem, then, that the 'I-am-me' experience, however related to the ego and the self and to similar concepts in the literature, is fresh ground as far as psychological theory is concerned. Is it also solid ground? Or are we here confronted with some exceptional private phenomena which deserve, if at all, only the attention of students of abnormal psychology?

1.4 A Questionnaire Study Based on a Literary Stimulus

The lack of discussion of the phenomenon by psychologists and philosophers and the relative scarcity of reports in the non-technical literature have always puzzled me. How typical, exceptional, or universal could it be considered under the circumstances? My conclusion was that only an empirical investigation could answer these questions. Informal inquiries with friends and acquaintances certainly did suggest the universality of the 'I-am-me' experience. When shown the Emily story from Hughes's novel several informants could not recall anything like it among their own experiences. Others

16. Erik H. Erikson, *Identity and the Life Cycle.* New York: International Universities Press, 1959.

came up with very definite recollections of a sudden awakening. This confirmed me in my idea that only a systematic survey could throw light on the question. But I also decided that such a study would have to use special 'stimuli', not only to make sure of the proper understanding or the questions but also to serve as possible reawakeners of dormant memories. These considerations led to the development of a first questionnaire drawn up in cooperation with my colleague Chester Hill of the Department of Psychology at Lawrence College.

Using the most pertinent parts of Hughes's Emily story, this questionnaire presented it as a mere piece of fiction, without mentioning the name of the author, thus leaving the answerer completely free to discount the whole incident as unreal. He was then asked the questions listed on Table 1.

The questionnaire received a trial run in connection with a seminar on phenomenology at the University of Southern California in August 1960 with a group of ten graduate students and upperclassmen who were asked to answer it in writing over the first weekend. The quantitative results are tabulated in the first column to the right of the questions. The number of students (ten) made it unnecessary to add percentages.

At least equally important were some of the qualitative results as contained in the descriptions given in answer to the requests under A-2, A-4, B-3, and C-2. For these made it possible to evaluate and screen the answers to the preceding questions. More important, they yielded new first-hand material. However, of the answers to A-4 and B-3 only a few were pertinent to the I-am-me experience. But the following striking account by an older woman graduate student of unusual literary articulateness was at least closely related:

> The (sudden) feeling of being TRAPPED BY LIFE . . . was experienced when I was not quite three years old. I had displeased my mother and she had reprimanded me. I felt unloved, unwanted, UNBEARABLY ALONE, completely misunderstood, and unappreciated . . . I pushed my face into the pillow and thought how wonderful it would be if I could just smother myself to death. I realized at that moment that I WAS TRAPPED IN A MISERABLE LITTLE PHYSICAL BODY. I know I would continue to live in it regardless of my own desires. I knew who I was, and what I was, and I did not approve.

Table 1

Questions		Answers Univ. of So. Calif. Numbers (total 10)	Lawrence College Numbers (total 59)	%
A.1. Does this episode sound to you at all plausible?	Yes	10	54	92
	No	0	5	8
2. Comment on parts of the story which you consider implausible.	Critical	7	50	84
3. Does this text remind you of similar sudden experiences of your own childhood or adolescence?	Yes	5	29	48
	No	5	30	52
4. If so, describe them in detail and, as far as possible, date them.	Descriptions	5	29	50
	Pertinent	4	27	45
5. Have you heard from other people, especially children, about such experiences?	Yes	6	13	22
	No	4	44	74
	Undecided	0	2	4
6. Do you believe that they are (a) universal (b) frequent (c) infrequent (d) exceptional	Universal	2	12	20
	Frequent	2	22	37
	Infrequent	3	11	19
	Exceptional	2	12	20
	Undecided	0	1	4
B.1. Do you remember similar feelings and ideas about yourself which developed gradually and persisted, but were not related to such a sudden experience?	Yes	9	45	76
	No	0	14	24
	Undecided	1	0	0
2. Do you now have them at times?	Yes	9	39	68
	No	0	20	32
	Undecided	1	0	0
3. If the answer to either B-1 or B-2 or both is YES, describe them as best as you can.	Descriptions	10	45	76
	Pertinent	4	37	63
4. Have you heard from other people, especially children, about such feelings and ideas?	Yes	7	29	49
	No	3	29	49
	Undecided	0	1	2
5. Do you believe that they are (a) universal (b) frequent (c) infrequent (d) exceptional	Universal	7	22	37
	Frequent	2	20	34
	Infrequent	0	9	15
	Exceptional	0	3	5
	Undecided	1	5	9
C.1. Do you remember talking about such experiences with others before you read this questionnaire?	Yes	7	33	56
	No	3	26	44
2. What is your earliest childhood memory? About how old were you at the time?	Descriptions	10	59	100
	Pertinent	0	0	0
3. Have you found your childhood memories generally reliable?	Yes	8	50	84
	No	2	9	16

Later, the same questionnaire was given a more extensive trial in a larger and more homogeneous group: a class of 59 students in introductory philosophy at Lawrence College. No further explanation of the purpose of the questionnaire was given except that this was part of a research project by the philosophy and psychology departments.

The quantitative result can be found to the right of the first column in Table 1, both in numbers and in percentages.

Thus Emily's experience seems to have been understandable to all but 8 percent of the informants, and 45 percent could back it up by similar sudden experiences of their own, of which they gave concrete descriptions. Only about a quarter had heard about such experiences from others, which implies that there is little communication about them. Still, the largest group consider the experience frequent. The results were even more favorable with respect to the more gradual experiences, as to which there seems to be much more communication. Here, the largest group consider the experience universal.

Qualitatively, the descriptions given under A-4 and B-5 yielded an unexpected amount of first-hand material bearing directly on the I-am-me experience. There was an interesting division among students who reported only one such experience and others who mentioned repetitions; this applied equally to the informants who had more gradual experiences. There were also those who indicated a constant awareness of the I-am-me phenomenon. Of particular interest was the surprising variety of emotional reactions to the experience, from anxiety to exhilaration, and also the realization that at least in some cases this experience is of major importance in the informant's feeling about life.

I append some of the most striking of these accounts, apart from those which will be found in the second questionnaire:

1. I do remember that such discoveries (as Emily's) were mine on frequent occasions and also that they must have begun when I was quite young. They did not stop with childhood either, and I still from time to time get that strange feeling which precedes the change of perspective when I rediscover the amazing, somewhat frightening fact that I am me. These experiences usually occurred when I was alone, either at night, in bed, or when playing by myself. I remember once trying to explain all this to my

mother . . . . I find as I grow older these experiences are more frequent and in fact more upsetting. One time, about four years ago, my mother and I had a discussion about 'so I am me, so what?' It was especially disturbing at that time, in particular, and the basic question led to others equally as disturbing. (Girl, who had concluded a brief essay on her personal philosophy a week before with the sentences quoted under E in the second questionnaire)

2. Between the age of about 6 and 10, I remember wondering often what it would be like to be someone else, and being puzzled about what exactly it was that made me 'me', and not someone else. (boy)

3. As a child, about the age of 9 or so, I would quite often find myself in that state of separateness that Emily found herself in. At these times I usually asked myself such questions as: Why was I born? and why here, in America? Why were my parents the ones they were? Why was I me, instead of someone else? Needless to say, I didn't have any answers. (girl)

4. Usually (the experience) starts when I think about the infinity of space or the endlessness of time. I think of how vast space is and then slowly work back to myself. I realize how seemingly unimportant I am as an individual placed on this speck called earth, and it frightens me. I wonder why I was put on this earth, and why I am me and not someone else . . . . I think I started thinking of such ideas when I was around 11 or 12. (boy)

5. Every once in a while I am placed in a situation when I wonder what it would be like if I were not myself, but someone else. How would I react to the situation and what would be the result? Of course I realize it is impossible to tell what it would be like to be someone else, but if I could, I'd like to change myself for a while and see what would happen! I wonder just who I am and why I am like I am. (girl)

To be sure, the evaluation of the answers to the first questionnaire also revealed a number of weaknesses in its makeup. Thus the Emily episode, even in its edited form, proved to be much to complex a stimulus for eliciting definite responses focussing on the I-am-me experience. A good many positive answers had to be disregarded since they dealt with such aspects as Emily's sudden awareness of her own body, of her social isolation, and the like. While the diffuseness of the stimulus may have served to produce a greater number and variety of responses, this still left considerable doubt as to the actual sharing of the I-am-me experience. In fact, one day when one of the most intelligent informants, who had given only negative answers, got sight of some of the excerpts from the positive reports, she exclaimed: 'Is that what you wanted? Why, I have had any number of these experiences.' Hence a follow-up by way of a better focussed questionnaire ssemed to be indicated.

1.5 A Second Questionnaire Study Based on Authentic Case Material

The second questionnaire was drawn up in consultation with another member of the Lawrence Department of Psychology, John Bucklew. Now the Emily story seemed to be no longer needed. Instead we decided on a multiple choice questionnaire based on five variations of the experience taken from the actual answers to the first questionnaire, slightly edited for purposes of sharper distinction. These five types of experience were presented in this manner:

The following statements are taken from a number of reports about childhood experiences. The purpose of this questionnaire is to find out whether these are unusual cases or whether other people like you have had similar experiences.

1. *One-time* experiences of *being struck suddenly* by ideas like the following:

    When I was about 10 or 11, I was standing in front of a mirror in a bathroom and looking at myself. Suddenly I found myself saying: 'You're you'.

2. *Repeated* experiences of being struck suddenly by ideas like the following:

    From time to time I get that strange feeling when I rediscover the amazing, somewhat frightening fact that I am me. These experiences occurred usually when I was alone, either at night, in bed, or when playing by myself.

3. *One-time* experiences in which you asked yourself questions like the following:

In either the summer before or after the 4th grade I first asked myself and others, 'Why am I me?' This was the first coherent form of the question.

4. *Repeated* experiences in which you asked yourself questions like the following:

I have at times wondered why I am the person I am. I wonder why I was born into the family I was, why I was born in this country, why I look as I do, why I have the qualities I do. I also wonder about who I would be if I were not the person I am.

5. Constant awareness:

A question has haunted me from childhood. It concerns the problem of 'Why am I me? Why am I in this particular situation, why am I the one to view the world from the inside? The whys could go on forever and ever without finding a 'because'.'

The new questionnaire was administered to two sections of Introductory Psychology of 45 and 37 students respectively, taught by my colleagues Edwin H. Olson, Jr. and David Foulkes, at the end of a class early in December. However, in this case it proved impossible to collect answers from all the class members. Lack of interest is the only safe explanation for the 25 missing responses from a total of 83. It should also be mentioned that four students had answered the first questionnaire as members of my philosophy class two months earlier.

The quantitative results are found below in two columns to the right of the questions, expressed both in numbers and percentages. They show that more than three times as many informants as in the first set, in fact more than 90%, admitted to some kind of I-am-me experience, backing up their positive replies by selecting among the five types presented and in most cases also by adding individual descriptions of their own experiences. To be sure, the sudden type of experience was claimed by only 25% of the informants. In answer to the new question about the emotional character of these experiences, one-fifth admitted being upset by it, more than one-tenth were reassured, but most of the informants did not find either of these predicates applicable. For nearly one-third the experience played a great role in their feeling about life, for half of them some slight role, for only one-tenth none at all. More than half of the respondents had heard about the experience from others and talked about it, a fact which should be seen against the background of the preceding questionnaire, which seems to have been discussed a good deal among the students outside of class. Largely in agreement with the results of the earlier questionnaire most informants estimated that the experience was frequent or universal, much fewer considered it infrequent or exceptional.

Qualitatively, the new material was perhaps less original than that obtained from the first questionnaire, which may be understandable in view of the more stereotyped forms of the new questions. One interesting feature in the new accounts was the frequency with which informants associated the I-am-me experience with

Table 2

Questions	*Answers*	*Numbers*	*%*
1. Do the statements above remind you of similar experiences of your own?	Yes No	52 4	92 8
2. If so, indicate the types closest to yours by letter and describe them with as much detail as possible below or on a special sheet, adding the ages at which they occurred.	A B C D E	8 15 7 40 33	14 27 7 72 59
3. Do you still have such experiences now?	Yes No	43 13	77 23
4. Are these experiences (a) upsetting? (b) reassuring? (c) neither?	a b c No answer	12 7 34 3	21 14 60 5
5. Are they of (a) no importance (b) some importance (c) great importance in your feeling about life?	a b c No answer	5 28 18 5	9 50 32 9
6. Have you ever heard from other people, especially children, about such experiences?	Yes No	33 23	59 41
7. Do you remember talking about such experiences with others before reading this questionnaire?	Yes No	33 23	59 41
8. Do you consider these experiences (a) universal (b) frequent (c) infrequent (d) exceptional (e) undecided	a b c d e	18 24 10 1 3	32 43 18 2 5

wondering about the 'accident of birth' in their particular family and nation and even their being born as human beings. A few of the new descriptions merit quoting:

1. I think that something similar to experience B has happened to me, usually when I was alone or in bed at night. . . . Also I have experienced something similar to D.... This type of experience has occurred for many years (perhaps since I was about 11 or 12 years old), and these thoughts used to keep me awake for several hours into the night. (girl)

2. I felt this way at the age of 10 or 11 and others (sic). I have had maybe half a dozen such experiences of looking back at myself and wondering just who is in the mirror and why was she put on earth in the home she is in. Why wasn't she born a Korean and rapidly abandoned.

3. I know that some of these questions occurred before high school. I remember wondering many times what I would be like if I were born in a different family or a different country. I would imagine what I would be doing or saying. Would I be the same person within . . . would I look the same? I suppose the most recurring questions here was about my 'true me' or soul. Would I have been the same one wherever I was born, or would I be a completely different person? If I were completely different, then I would not be me and that is hard to imagine. I remember several times of looking in the mirror and seeing something different than I usually did, not just my image but myself. But I can't remember at what age that was. . . . I vaguely remember asking my mother questions of *why* I was here. (girl)

4. There are times —it can be anywhere, and it can be any time— when I wonder why I was lucky enough to be chosen to live. I always want to know why I am not my brother, and I wonder if my mother had married someone else, would I still be existing, only in the form of someone else. (girl)

1.6 Possible Developments of the Questionnaire Study

I am well aware that the number of subjects polled is not sufficient for sweeping generalizations and particularly for assigning definite percentages to each group. Nevertheless, the results obtained thus far seem to justify the assertion that the I-am-me experience is remembered by a vast majority of American adolescents of college age and intelligence of both sexes, apparently with a certain plus on the girls' side. However, the more sudden type of the experience is recalled by only about one-fourth of them.

The fact that the I-am-me experience is remembered so vivdly is significant enough in itself, and in fact it may be enough for philosophical purposes. But this still leaves the question wide open as to how far these memories are trustworthy and whether the experiences to which they refer ever occurred. This is certainly worth investigating. Thus my colleague John Bucklew and I have been thinking about tracking down the experience to its first occurrence among children. Obviously any questionnaire given at an earlier age would have to be considerably simplified, administered with extra care, and followed up clinically. With the help of my wife, Eldora Haskell Spiegelberg, a clinical psychologist, I designed a first questionnaire with this objective in mind. But on its first trial run with nine Sunday School children, aged 7 and 8, the majority of the answers proved useless. It also became clear that no written account can be expected at this stage. The proper procedure would seem to be to move down gradually from college age via high school to the grades, and to adjust the questionnaires to each level, with increasing use of clinical methods. Some such studies have been initiated at Lawrence College under the supervision of Edwin H. Olson, also of the Lawrence Psychology Department.

Thus Frances Peters administered a slightly modified version of the two earlier questionnaires to seniors at Appleton Senior High School (about 1600 students). Here, in an honors class in philosophy of 31 students, 66% asserted sudden I-am-me experiences, 28% denied them, 6% were undecided. In a sociology class of 100 seniors 53 claimed sudden experiences, 16 denied them, the rest were ruled out because of the irrelevancy of their supporting descriptions. This extension of the college study to the local high school of a Wisconsin city with a population of 45,000 confirms earlier results for a group about two years younger than our college sophomores. It would, however, be premature to consider the slight increases as sufficiently established.

One descriptive account of a girl in the philosophy class deserves to be quoted because of its specific dating:

One day when I was about five years old, I was just sitting around, doing nothing, when I realized I was me, and began to wonder why I wasn't somebody else. It bothered me for about a week afterwards and since then. The thought has come up from time to time, though less often recently.

Two more recent studies by Helen Geiler Moore used a new, much simpler, but also more wide-ranging questionnaire in an elementary school of an average suburban district of Chicago. The first study, administered to grades 4-6 (ages 9-14) contained such questions as 'Do you ever think 'Why am I me, and not somebody else?'.' In eighth grade 22 children answered with yes and 4 with no, in fifth grade 24 children with yes and 4 with no, in fourth grade 24 children with yes and 10 with no, sixth and seventh grade falling somewhere in between. In answer to the question 'If you ever have asked questions like these' —there were more of the same kind as the one just quoted— 'have you ever talked to anyone about them?', 4 in eighth grade answered with yes, 20 with no, in fifth grade 8 answered 'yes' and 26 'no'. The questions and answers in this and the following study were followed up with clinical interviews.

Helen Moore's second study in the same school included 196 children, half boys and half girls, in grades 4 to 6. Here the following sentence was used as a stimulus: 'Sometimes when I am alone, in bed, playing, or looking at myself in a mirror, I suddenly have the funny feeling that I am me and nobody else.' In answer to the subsequent question 'Did you ever feel like this?' 90% answered with yes, and 40% backed up these positive answers with concrete accounts; the percentage for fourth grade was 84%. Another stimulus was the sentence 'Since I was little, I have asked myself questions like 'Why am I me?'. Here the yes answers came from 80% of all the children polled, in fourth grade alone from 67%. Another interesting result was that 94% of the children answered positively to either one or the other question, 76% to both, in fourth grade alone 89% to either one, and 52% to both. Hence only 6% (fourth grade 11%) claimed to be totally immune to such experiences. Even these preliminary figures will need further checking. But they take us down as far as ages 8 and 9.

There would also seem to be some reason for moving systematically from the college age up to older groups. The fact that otherwise perceptive friends in the sixties and seventies told me that the whole I-am-me experience did not make sense to them may indicate that the experience, which is most intense in childhood and adolescence, gradually loses its poignancy as people get used to, and diverted from, the original phenomenon.

It hardly needs spelling out that these studies should also be extended to groups not based on age, for instance to different social groups and nationalities. Ultimately even anthropological field study may become desirable. Such explorations are clearly beyond the range of one individual investigator.

1.7 Wider Perspectives

As pointed out in the beginning, my own stake in this field is primarily and ultimately philosophical in nature. My intrusion into empirical psychology had no other goal than to ascertain the spread of an experience which otherwise may seem to be completely private and not offering enough common ground for philosophical discussion. Once this can be taken as established, the task of philosophical elucidation and interpretation begins. For the phenomenon itself is far from simple and transparent. In fact, the very formula 'I-am-me', which seemed to be most common and most characteristic for it, is more than ambiguous. At first sight it appears to be a downright tautology. Yet for anyone who has been in the throes of the original experience the formula expresses anything but a truism. A careful phenomenological investigation of the experience behind the puzzling expression is clearly the primary philosophical need; its ontological and metaphysical interpretation will have to wait.[18] However, this philosophical task does not exhaus the potential interest of this experience. Scientifically the prime need would seem to be that of causal explanation, especially in the case of the shock-experiences. Some clues for such an explanation may be found among the materials in this paper, but they are hardly adequate for a comprehensive theory. One might, for instance, suspect that the I-am-me experience is the result of some traumatic

---

18. I presented an outline of such a phenomenology and philosophy of the ego in a series of lectures at the University of Munich in 1962.

event. But this would imply that it is more widespread among the underprivileged, especially when they are aware of their 'relative deprivation'. While this hypothesis bears testing, it must be pointed out immediately that the experience also seems to occur among the more sensitive overprivileged. Further exploration would have to use clinical methods. But it may also have to probe into the sub-conscious strata.

If it should be possible to correlate the experience with certain personality types, this might have some diagnostic significance. Some responses to the questionnaires suggested connections with more or less deep-seated personality problems and disturbances. This opens up the possibility of projective tests. Using such tests may even have a certain cathartic, if not therapeutic function. Thus some respondents, especially those who declared the I-am-me experience upsetting and who up to then felt isolated in their inarticulate solitude, expressed considerable relief at being allowed to express their experience and at discovering that it was shared by a large portion of their fellow beings. For if these findings are valid, the I-am-me experience is —at least to some degree— one of the fundamental facts of human existence.

2. A PHENOMENOLOGICAL APPROACH TO THE EGO

2.1 Introductory Remarks

Of late, the question of the real difference between philosophical analysis and phenomenology has received encouraging attention. [18] There are those who think that the two are completely different ways of doing philosophy, phenomenology belonging essentially to the era before the 'revolution in philosophy'. Others believe that the difference has been vastly exaggerated and that fundamentally there is no practical difference between the two. Personally, I am not ready to side with either view. Instead, I suggest putting the matter to a concrete test which could provide the basis for a meaningful comparison.

My own analysis is based on an interpretation of phenomenology which is anything but orthodox in the Husserlian sense. Thus there will be no reference to phenomenological reductions, transcendental egos or similar concepts. Instead, I shall advocate a wider sense of phenomenology which includes the common ground of the main currents within the Phenomenological Movement. Its guiding principle is: as direct an approach to the phenomena as possible, reducing presuppositions and commitments of a merely theoretical nature to a minimum, and always reserving the right to re-examine and revise them in the light of the phenomena subsequently encountered. In the pursuit of this objective the following steps can be distinguished:

18. Symposium on 'Phenomenology and Linguistic Analysis' between Charles Taylor and A.J. Ayer. *Aristotelian Society*, Suppl 33 (1959), 93-124. See also some of the discussion at the Colloque de Royaumont of 1960 on *La Philosophie analytique* (Éditions de Minuit, 1962), thus far published only in French.

Reprinted by permission from *The Monist* 49 (1965) 1-17.

1. exploration of particular phenomena in the chosen field by way of intuiting experience *(Anschauung)*;
2. analysis of what is found by a study of its components, if any, and their connections;
3. description of the findings in terms of a conceptual framework;
4. exploration of the essential structure within the particular phenomena and of their essential relationships with other phenomena;
5. exploration of the modifications of these phenomena as they present themselves to a viewing subject (modes of appearance);
6. exploration of the way in which the phenomena take shape as they are realized by a viewing subject ('constitution' in consciousness).[19]

Not all of these steps must be taken together. The first three, however, are basic. The last (constitution) will be omitted in the present paper.

2.2 Phenomenology and Language

The phenomenological approach so conceived focusses on the study of the phenomena rather than on the language in which we talk about them. If I am not mistaken, it is characteristic of linguistic analysis to ask 'What do we mean when we say 'X' (in quotes)?' By contrast, the phenomenology I am advocating asks 'What do we see when we look at X (without quotes)?' Now this emphasis on the primacy of language may easily be misunderstood to mean that phenomenology ignores language completely. Quite apart from the fact that there is such a thing as a flourishing phenomenology of language, I should like to make it plain from the outset that phenomenology is essentially neither non-linguistic nor anti-linguistic. Since its very beginnings Husserl's phenomenology was concerned about meanings, and especially about the ambiguity of some of the key terms in philosophical and psychological language, such as 'consciousness' and 'representation' *(Vorstellung)*.[20] Phenomenology has also paid attention to the variety and shades of actual usage with a view to utilizing it as a guide to a vastly enlarged range of phenomena which previous discussions had neglected or over-

19. This conception of phenomenology is developed more fully in my *Phenomenological Movement* (The Hague: Martinus Nijhoff, 3rd ed. 1982), Part V.
20. *Logische Untersuchungen* II, I No. V, pp. 44, 45.

looked. In this respect it anticipates John L. Austin's 'linguistic phenomenology'.

Besides, there is a special form of phenomenology, developed by Alexander Pfänder, which starts every phenomenological investigation by clarifying what we really mean in our ordinary beliefs about philosophical issues as expressed in our ordinary language. Such a clarification *(Sinnklärung)* is to free us from distorting and especially from reductionist misinterpretations by going back to what we really have in mind when we use fundamental philosophical terms. Only when we have thus clarified our meanings, does it make sense to verify them by a cautious phenomenology of perception.

However, in the present context I shall pursue a different approach, which will start at once with the phenomena, going to them as directly as possible without first attending to meanings. While in principle such an approach should be possible everywhere (though it may not always be the most advisable), it is indispensable when we are faced with an entirely new and unlabelled phenomenon in uncharted territory.

In saying that such a phenomenology goes to the phenomena 'as directly as possible' I am not implying that phenomenology, any more than any other study, can do completely without language. Inasmuch as phenomenology too is a joint enterprise of several phenomenologists, it has to use language, if only for the purpose of directing fellow investigators to the same area of phenomena. The finger alone won't do as soon as we have passed beyond the reach of the pointing hand. Beyond this range only discourse can help. In this respect phenomenology, along with any other descriptive science, shares what has been called the lingua-centric predicament of man in all his socio-cultural enterprises. But the decisive difference of the phenomenon-based from the language-based approach remains that language in the former serves only as a take-off place, a stepping stone and a vehicle that takes us to the work-site, the phenomena, not as the destination of our explorations.

However, even after the phenomenologist has arrived at the phenomena and carried out his exploring and analyzing, he cannot abandon language for good. The task of description, so essential to his program, makes him once more dependent on language. It is of course no longer certain that existing language will be adequate to express and accomodate his new findings. In such cases additions to this language will be needed. Yet such expansions will have to be based on the framework of pre-existing languaga and must follow its general patterns, much as this happens in the development of scientific nomenclature and terminology. Thus the concluding task of phenomenology calls for renewed and even increased interest in a critical analysis of language. But even so, in phenomenology it will be at best a means to the understanding of the phenomena, never an end in itself.

2.3 The Choice of the Topic

As a test case for determining the actual difference between the two ways of 'doing philosophy' I suggested the topic of the ego. By using this term I myself meant nothing more technical than the subject of Descartes' 'ego cogito', without wanting to deny that this ego may do or suffer other things than to 'cogitate'. I wish we could replace the term 'ego' at once by the first person singular pronoun 'I'. In fact, I wish we could do entirely without the substantivized form of the pronoun (the 'I'), which is, to say the least, a grammatical oddity. What is more serious, it may have not only emasculated but nearly destroyed the original experience in its existential poignancy.

Are there any special reasons for making the case of the ego the test case for such an experiment, considering the fact that in the latest philosophy of mind it seems to be an almost abandoned mine? While I confess to a private fascination with this topic, I should like to plead its particular appropriateness on two less personal grounds:

1. The 'ego' has proved a particularly puzzling topic for philosophy in the past ever since David Hume challenged its right to be in the face of Descartes' claims to its indubitability.
2. The 'ego' or 'self' has lately made a remarkable comeback in psychoanalysis and more recently in psychology (Gordon W. Allport). But here it has been introduced less on grounds of direct experience than as an indispensable construct.[21]

21. See, e.g., Percival M. Symonds, *The Ego and the Self* (New York: Appleton-Century-Crofts, 1951): also Ruth Wylie, *The Self Concept* (Lincoln: University of Nebraska Press, 1961).

Besides, in psychology, concepts of the 'ego' have proliferated to such a degree that one would almost like to avoid the terms completely. All the more urgent is the need of clarification and return to the phenomena. I submit that this situation is also a challenge to philosophy.

2.4 Plan of Approach

In focussing on this ego I shall turn first to *what* appears, or what I shall call the *ontic features* of the ego-phenomenon as it presents itself in the phenomenological view, then to *how* it appears, or what I shall call the *phenomenal features* of the ego-phenomenon *through which* the ontic features present themselves, such as perspectives, aspects, and the like.

In each case I shall introduce a distinction which does not apply to phenomena generally, but which seems to me of considerable significance for the ego-phenomena. There is a difference between the ego as it presents itself on the level of *ordinary* experience and the ego as we experience it under more unusual or 'privileged' circumstances, a difference which is usually neglected in our theoretical discussions, philosophical and psychological, as well. In the first case I shall speak of ordinary, in the second of extra-ordinary ego-phenomena.

2.5 Findings

(1) Ontic Features of the Ego

Obviously the present context does not allow for a complete phenomenology of the ego. I can select only some of its facets and shall choose the ones that seem to me best suited to illustrate the phenomenological approach as here conceived. One might wonder whether it is at all possible to select such facets without first determining the nature of the ego and its ontological status. While I would agree that eventually the findings here presented will have to be integrated into a systematic ontology of the ego, I believe that some facets can be approached independently. All that needs to be pre-supposed in this case is that there is something which corresponds to the term 'ego'; that it is given in intuitive experience; and that it has a certain structure which entitles it to a place in the framework of ontology.

(a) Ordinary Ego-phenomena

In studying features of the everyday ego, I shall concentrate on what I shall call its 'volume'. In the past it has often been asserted or at least implied that the ego is something like an unextended point. Or it has been treated as if it simply coincided with the organism as studied by the biological sciences. What does an inspection of the phenomena reveal as we try to explore, analyze, and describe them?

The following typical situations, corresponding to first person singular sentences, seem to stand out:

1. Cases where the circumference of the ego is coterminous with the outskirts of the body as we experience it:
   Thus in such acts as swimming the experiencing ego seems to be reaching up to the outskirts of his skin. I identify with my swimming body, as far as I am aware of it, when I say 'I swim'. This does not mean that I am equally identified with all parts of the experienced body, e.g., the left side and the right side, the toes or the hair. There are degrees of such identifications. But there is no identification with such unexperienced parts of the anatomical organism as cells or genes.
2. Cases where the ego includes more than the body:
   a. In certain cases the ego incorporates its clothing. Notoriously, used clothes as they have adjusted to the shape and posture of our bodies and to our patterns of motion are experienced quite differently from new clothes, and especially from poorly fitting ones. Clothing has become in a sense part of ourselves. How much this is so is confirmed by phrases such as 'I am torn and tattered, mussed up, down at the heels, etc.' 'Clothes are the man' applies in this case also to the ego. I submit that the feeling of nakedness consists partly in the fact that the ordinary ego feels incomplete without the clothing which envelops the body.
   b. The ego may extend into its tools. This is particularly true of artificial limbs. Also, in writing the ego seems to incorporate the pen down to its tip. In a sense I am at its very tip when I shape

my characters, not at the tips of my fingers or in other parts of my skin which are in touch with the pen; of these I am hardly aware. There is good reason for saying 'I am writing', not 'My pen is writing' as in the case of automatic writing. The identification of the ego with the tip of the writing tool makes the claims of graphology about the expressiveness of handwriting particularly plausible and appealing.

c. Finally, there are cases where the ego incorporates a vehicle. The experienced driver, in contrast to the learner, may identify with his car to the degree of experiencing it as an extension of his own self. Thus he may well say, 'I am going 100 miles an hour', not 'my car is going 100 miles'. This may also explain some of the fascination of high-speed driving.

3. Cases where the ego does not fill its bodily frame:

a. Sometimes the ego fills merely part of its body. When Woodrow Wilson in his well-known limerick joked: 'My face I don't mind it, For I am behind it. ...' he seems to have distinguished, however facetiously, between his face and his ego. Actually, such experiences are by no means uncommon. One need not think of such pathological cases as the loss of conscious identification with parts of the body, as in local anaesthesia. Even in normal experience areas of the body may appear as merely mine, not me, as possessions, liked or disliked, which I may lose or which may be altered, e.g., by plastic surgery, without a change of myself.

b. There are even cases where the ego withdraws completely from the body. In the preceding cases the ego still kept a firm foothold in the body. But it can also happen that it stands completely apart from the body. I am not thinking so much of the reports about ecstasies, in which supposedly the ego leaves its body behind. I have in mind the way in which some Stoics such as Epictetus seem to have felt about their entire bodies, namely as possessions of the ego, as such set apart from it. A different but related situation may be observed when, awakening from a dream, our dream bodies having vanished, we find ourselves reverting to our everyday bodies, of which we have now to resume possession even before we can again identify with them. Here too we seem to have been, for a while at least, completely dissociated from our real body.

In the cases described thus far the ego seems to have definite volumes of which we can be clearly aware. However, it must not be overlooked that normally we would be hard put to determine the outskirts of our ego. Here its exact volume remains undifferentiated and indefinite. When the ego sees or hears or imagines or believes, the question of the body and its volume simply does not arise. It would therefore be highly artificial to suggest that in such situations the ego has any particular volume. In such cases it remains indifferent to the body as such.

Now what exactly is the relation of the ego to all these situations? Does a special ego correspond to each one of them, each with a different volume and perhaps even one without any volume? And if there should be many, are they completely separate or is one inside the other, as Chinese boxes are, i.e., an ego within an ego within an ego?

The best way to decide this question is to turn from the statics of these cases to a consideration of their dynamics. For the ego stands by no means in a stable relation to its body, its extensions, and its diminutions. Sometimes it expands beyond it, at other times it contracts within it, sometimes it identifies with it, and at other times it dissociates from it. There seem to be even special techniques such as relaxation, by which one can let go, as it were, of certain parts of the body and treat them as if they were extraneous objects. One may retreat from it and advance beyond it, be it only in imagination, as in putting oneself into the place of another.

Thus the ego on this level is a being capable of expanding and contracting, comparable in some ways to an amoeba, whose pseudopodia may reach out at times but are then pulled in again. Only that the kind of changes of volume of the ego are much more abrupt and extend much farther.

At this point I shall stop describing the ego at the level of everyday consciousness. Completeness was anyway not my objective; I merely wanted to show what a phenomenon-focussed phenomenology of the ego can discover in the case of ordinary phenomena. But at least I want to acknowledge the major unfinished business:

1. A fully developed phenomenology of the ego will have to deal with such additional features as its functions, active and passive, its potentialities, its dependences and independences.

2. It will also have to decide on its ontological status. Any attempt to classify the ego in terms of a more or less outmoded ontology as either substance or attribute, as an event or pattern of events, as a continuant or a disposition, would be premature. The first task is to present something like an anatomical preparation of the phenomenon, showing its structure as distinctly as possible. Then we might reflect on its place or lack of place in the framework of traditional ontology.

(b) Extra-ordinary Ego-phenomena

I shall now try to draw attention to a dimension of the ego-phenomenon which does not form an explicit part of our everyday consciousness and which seems to have escaped the attention of almost all the philosophers and psychologists. It will therefore be necessary first to improve on the access to this part of the phenomenal field. In order to do this, I shall begin by pointing out some explicit cases.

Most children and adolescents are affected by sudden seizures of an experience which they sometimes express in such seemingly tautological sentences as 'I am me'. And nearly all of them seem to be bothered by persistent questions such as 'Why am I me?'[22] Since I am now trying to illustrate a phenomenon-based phenomenological approach, I shall forbid myself to explore the real meaning of these odd sentences. Instead I want to go as directly as possible to the phenomena to which they seem to be pointing.

But first I must try to revive or evoke this experience even among hardened adults, and especially among the most hardened of them, the professional students of the ego, philosophical and psychological.

A literary stimulus may be the quickest way of including or recapturing the phenomenon. It is taken from Carson McCullers' novel *The Member of the Weddding*,[23] in which the twelve-year old heroine Frankie suddenly remarks to her older confidant, the Negro cook Berenice:

> Doesn't it strike you as strange that I am I, and you are You? I am F. Jasmine Addams. And you are Berenice Sadie Brown. And we look at each

22. I have tried to explore this fact with the assistance of members of the Lawrence Department of Psychology and have reported on our findings in an article 'On the I-am-me Experience in Childhood and Adolescence'. See no. 1 in this volume. Even Gilbert Ryle, *The Concept of Mind* (London, 1949), p. 186, mentions the fact that 'not only theorists, but also quite unsophisticated people, including young children, find perplexities in the notion of I.'

23. (Boston: Houghton Mifflin Company, 1946), p. 138.

other, and touch each other, and stay together year in and year out in the same room. Yet always I am I, and you are you. And I can't ever be anything else but me, and you can't ever be anything else but you. Have you ever thought of that? And does it seem to you strange?

Whereupon Berenice after meditating for some time in her rocking chair, finally responds: 'I have thought of it occasionally.'

I shall not try to determine why this situation strikes this adolescent as so strange. Enough if this passage can convey her sense of strangeness. I would like to use this case merely as an opening wedge. I submit that, at least in some of us, this sense of irretrievable incarnation at a specific point of time, space and history results in a feeling of a peculiar dizziness. The ego gripped by such an experience is no longer the referent of that impersonalizing noun 'the ego', but the innermost I-myself in its most personal, most poignant authenticity. Delving into this experience, and pondering on it, we are faced with a something which no longer shows the unshakable stability *fundamentum inconcussum)* of Descartes' cogitating ego, the Archimedean fulcrum of his epistemology. In becoming aware of it, one may well have the feeling of an abyss opening underneath one's normal self-assured ego, including a peculiar existential anxiety which is related to, but differs from, the more familiar anxiety-of-being of the existentialists. Besides, this ego, of which we are normally oblivious, is by no means always as conscious as Descartes' ego. In a sense it may even be normally unconscious. It is certainly not always given clearly and distinctly, as the Cartesian ego is. Yet it may be indubitable.

However, I shall not attempt to undertake the much more difficult task of analyzing and describing this ego any further, at least not in the present context. Suffice it if I can make it available for further exploration. But at least I shall make a try at determining its relation to the more ordinary phenomena of the ego, lest it be thought that I am trying to multiply egos unnecessarily.

I see no reason for maintaining that the extra-ordinary and the ordinary ego are ontologically separated. There may be a certain discontinuity in our experience of them, a jolt as we turn from the ordinary to the new sense of the ego. But this does not prove a discontinuity in the referents of our experiences. I suggest that what is involved here is the discovery of a new facet or deeper layer within the same self.

Perhaps the main significance of this new depth dimension in the ego is that it gives plastic relief to the ego as a whole. There is something strangely flat and anemic about the ego that has survived in the philosopher's writings and discussions. No wonder Occam's razor as wielded by Ernst Mach has come close to erasing it. Only if the poignancy of the original experience can be restored to it can it regain its full weight and rightful place in philosophy.

(2) Phenomenal Features of the Ego

In turning now from the ego's ontic to its phenomenal features through which the ontic ones present themselves to the viewer, I shall distinguish (1) perspectival modifications, which are essentially related to the standpoint of the viewer *(Abschattungen)*, and (2) other modifications such as degrees of clarity and intuitive content.

(a) Perspectival Modifications

One of the better-known phenomenological views about perception is that all spatial objects appear in a variety of perspectives, and that each such perspective involves characteristic perspectival deformations *(Abschattungen)* through which the object appears as the identical intentional referent of all the varying presentations. But thus far it has hardly been realized that this applies also to the ego, and that the ego too can appear only through perspectives. Husserl, after first asserting that there are no *Abschattungen* of consciousness, later came to realize that its temporal structure had implications for its appearance from different points in time. This realization has bearing also on the presentation of the ego. I shall apply it first to the ordinary, then to the extra-ordinary level of the ego.

Instantaneous presentation of the ego to itself is from the very start something of a problem. Many might consider it a priori impossible. Even such a somewhat metaphorical expression as 'reflection' is no answer. The situation may be compared to the case where the observer of a spatial object is in bodily touch with it, which means of course that there is no room for any kind of perspective, not even a frog's perspective. But even if no 'outside view' of the simultaneous ego is possible, there might be a different kind of access, a simultaneous *awareness* of one's own ego. In this way we are aware, for instance, of our present feelings. But instantaneous awareness of the ego is at best an oblique perspective which does not allow one to focus on it. The ego itself will never be in the focus of this kind of consciousness.

Our only chance to focus on the ego full-face and to obtain a 'good' perspective of it is to catch it 'in retrospect'. But this retrospect on the original experience has to catch it 'in the act' before the experience has faded out. This is the so-called retentive phase of memory as distinguished from the phase where the remembered content can only be recovered by a special act of recollection. The problem is to reach the ego during the retention as soon as it has come out of the tunnel of simultaneous awareness into the full light of retentive retrospection and before it escapes from the range of immediate experience. There is obviously no way of telling when exactly the retrospective perspective will be at its optimum.

In thus stressing the perspective of the live past I do not mean to imply that later perspectives based on reconstructive memory are worthless. However, there will be a certain shrinkage in the presentation of an ego more distant in time, quite apart from other modifications that affect the usually much depleted trace of the departed percept.

This problem is obviously intensified for the perspectives of the extra-ordinary ego-phenomenon. To be sure, in the phase of simultaneous awareness there is a gripping poignancy to the experience, making the ego-phenomenon much more vivid, though not more clear and distinct. There seems to be something strangely elusive and fleeting about it which baffles all attempts to lay firm hold on it. It seems also harder to focus on the phenomenon in retentional perspective. It certainly requires a special recapturing effort, which may well explain why it has escaped the attention of philosophers and psychologists who entered the scene too late and too cold to catch the phenomenon alive.

In addition to the temporal perspective of the ego, another perspective has to be considered, which may best be called the *social perspective*. It depends on whether or not the perceiving and the perceived ego coincide. When they do, the ego appears in the perspective of the 'I'. If they do not, it appears as 'you' or 'he'. Personal pronouns are, in fact, index words designating such social perspectives. The he-perspective is the most common and neutral one. It becomes the you-perspective only when the perceiver is drawn into direct non-cognitive social contact with the perceived ego, a contact which is apt to change the ontic relation between the two and thus the very structure and attitude of the 'he', who is now being addressed.

The I-perspective is obviously the closest, so close, in fact, that it prevents direct self-confrontation, except in retrospect. For this reason the greater distance of the he-perspective is by no means a disadvantage. It allows the simultaneous confrontation of the ego by the outside observer.[24] Besides, a certain distance may be the optimum condition for seeing oneself in proper perspective ('... to see ourselves as others see us'). There is considerable truth in Nietzsche's paradoxical saying 'everyone is the farthest one from himself: *'Jeder ist sich selbst der Fernste'.* But even if this should be true of the ordinary layers of the ego, the deeper, more 'intimate' layers of the ego may still be essentially inaccessible to any outside observer. In this respect, the you-perspective is not only a closer, but a more revealing one. In a genuine encoutner the other lays himself open to the observer. This perspective of the opened self would offer the optimum chance for approaching the deeper levels of the ego.

(b) Other Modifications

Perspective modifications, which depend on the standpoint of the perceiver, are really revealing perspectives. It used to be feared that the changes in size and shape that go with these perspectives lead to contradictions which show that all perception is merely 'subjective', and that objective perception is impossible. This fear has long given way to the realization that it is precisely these changes which allow us to see the identical size and shape of the perceived *through* its perspectives.

However, there are modifications of the ways in which an object is given that do interfere seriously with adequate access to it. To begin with, it should be realized that normally we merely *refer* to the objects of our discourse without taking the trouble of following

---

24. On this point see also Alfred Schutz, *Collected Papers I* (The Hague: Martinus Nijhoff, 1962), pp. 173 ff.

up such mere references by intuitive inspection. To do this would require a special effort, which is not only too demanding for ordinary life, but rarely required. So most of our meanings remain empty of intuitive content. This applies particularly to the ordinary use of the word 'I'. Starting with this level of intuitive emptiness our references to objects may fill up with more and more intuitive content in a continuous series. Thinking of an icosahedron we would rarely bother to visualize all its twenty triangles in their proper positions. But we can always add to such incipient intuitiveness up to the optimum of what may be called intuitive fulfillment. It stands to reason that only such fulfillment can provide adequate verification for our meanings. This is the view taken by phenomenological philosophy.

Then, there are different degrees of clearness and distinctness. Thus equally intuitive referents may be given more or less distinctly; the contrast between an impressionist and a 'realistic' painting of the same scene can illustrate this point. Also, all sorts of interferences may affect clear presentation, such as fog and insufficient illumination. So can subjective conditions such as fatigue or defective vision.

There is certainly little clarity and distinctness about the presentation of the ordinary ego as given in direct simultaneous awareness. It may be very intense, but even so it remains usually at the fuzzy fringe of our everyday consciousness. One reason is that we can watch it only surreptitiously, while paying our main attention to the absorbing business of performing our everyday acts. Thus the ego remains in the twilight zone of cognitive illumination.

When the ego moves into the zone of retrospective perception, the chances for its clear and distinct presentation improve considerably. But this does not mean that the ego is now presented clearly and distinctly. It still takes considerable reflective effort to light it up. It is a fallacy of Cartesianism to infer from the fact that the ego is indubitable that it is also clearly and distinctly given. Most of it is usually in the shadow, if not in the night of the unconscious. But this does not make the existence of the ego any less certain.

Besides, any attempt to force the ego into submission by directing the full light of attention upon it may have disastrous effects. As in the case of strong emotions or similar phenomena, they are apt to fade and disappear under such intense lighting. This too may account for the puzzling fact that empiricists such as David Hume, Ernst Mach, and even William James found nothing to report when they tried to pin down the pure ego, staring, as it were, into a void. And yet even Hume put this finding in the form: 'I never can catch myself.' Even more difficult is the problem of presentation in the case of the extra-ordinary depth phenomena of the ego. For these can be reached only in 'privileged moments' or by special effort. In spite of their poignancy they remain so elusive that they can perhaps never be adequately grasped, whether in immediate awareness or in retrospective retention. Yet even in eluding us they leave a trace deep enough to make them unmistakable to those who have experienced them.

At this point I shall stop exploring the phenomenal features of the ego. Obviously this is merely a beginning, and I shall not even attempt to outline the unfinished business. The main purpose of the present discussion was to give an idea of the amount of new features which a phenomenological approach to this area can reveal. As such it could merely break the ground and prepare it for further cultivation.

2.6 Conclusion

The main findings I wanted to exhibit could be restated in the following manner:

Ontically the ego turns out to be a being of varying volume, usually including the experienced body, often expanding beyond it, and sometimes withdrawing from parts or all of it. But this being has also a depth dimension, reaching down to the most personal level of the I-myself.

Phenomenally this ego with its different levels appears through different temporal and social perspectives, and in these perspectives it is given more or less adequately, depending on the degrees of intuitiveness, clarity, and distinctness with wich it is presented.

If there is anything to what I have presented here, phenomenology does considerably more than deal with the phenomena to which ordinary language refers. Not only does it present them with much more detail in their undescribed and ultimately indescribable richness, it also leads to phenomena which have thus far escaped the meshes of our linguistic nets. As to these nets, it should be borne in mind that ordinary language, in contrast to poetic language, is primarily a practical tool, making only such distinctions as are needed for purposes of ordinary living. Phenomenology knows of no such restrictions. It can therefore serve as a widener and deepener of experience beyond the range covered by existing language. In this respect it may be compared to the pioneer squatting in uncharted territory rather than to the homesteader settling on mapped ground. In the uncharted areas language has to *follow* experience; it is not qualified to *lead* to it.

Ordinary language fits ordinary phenomena. But not all phenomena are ordinary. If there are extra-ordinary phenomena, as I have tried to show in the case of the ego, they call for more than ordinary language. Such an 'extra-ordinary' language can be forged only in the light of an unrestricted direct study of the phenomena in their own right.

It may be true that 'whereof' the linguistic analyst 'cannot speak, thereof he must be silent.' The phenomenologist has the temerity to speak up about phenomena before which ordinary language is apt to capitulate.

3. ON THE MOTILITY OF THE EGO

A Contribution to the Phenomenology of the Ego

3.1 Erwin Straus on the Dancing Ego

Among the many instances of provocative first-hand phenomenology in Erwin Straus's article on *'Die Formen des Räumlichen. Ihre Bedeutung für die Motorik und die Wahrnehmung'* of 1930,[25] one in particular has struck such a responsive chord in my independent reflections that I hope I can offer some proof of the reproductive power of his pioneering. The following passage occurs in the context of his discussion of the changed consciousness of the body in dancing. Referring to the priority of the vital sphere over the cognitive and practical functions as the motoric system predominates, Straus (in my translation) has this to say:

> A shift of the ego in relation to the body schema corresponds to the dominance or the movement of the torso. While in the waking, active human being the ego is localized in the region of the bridge of the nose between the eyes, it descends in dancing into the torso.[26]

However, he cautions us at once:

> One must not misinterpret the expression 'localization of the ego' in relation to the body schema. It means nothing but the fact that the body is

25. Republished in *Psychologie der menschlichen Welt* (Berlin: Springer, 1960), pp. 141-178. Translated by Erling Eng as 'The Forms of Spatiality', in *Phenomenological Psychology* (Basic Books, 1966).

26. Ibid., p. 167.

Reprinted by permission from *Conditio humana*, edited by Walter von Baeyer and Richard M. Griffiths. Berlin: Springer Verlag, 1966.

experienced as a centred unity. The principle of this unitary organization
is the relative closeness of the individual parts of the organism to the ego.
Thus our feet are as a rule more distant from the ego than the eyes...[27]

Despite such qualifications, which seem to affect only the exact
spot of the localization, but not the spatial pattern of the relation
between the ego and the body, the picture of the ego presented in
these sentences remains shocking enough. For it implies at least
the following assertions:

1. the ego is distinct from its body.
2. the ego has a location within the experienced body.
3. this location is normally in the region between the eyes.
4. the ego can shift its location from between the eyes to other sites
within the body.

I suspect that to any respectable psychologist with scientific
aspirations such ideas, or at least some of them, will sound like wild
fiction with at best some analogical meaning. Doesn't the last assertion in particular convert the ego into a kind of movable kidney?
To an intrepid phenomenologist this consequence alone is no good
reason to shy away from clear evidence. I am concerned with this
evidence and its fullest and most faithful description, regardless of
whether or not it will fit into preconceived patterns. What I shall
have to present may well cause more eyebrow raising. I shall be
content if it can open some eyes and stimulate further search in
this virgin jungle. In some points I shall probably depart from
Erwin Straus's soberer views. I certainly have no right to implicate
him in some of my more risky interpretations and anticipations.

My plan is to comment first a little more in the light of the phenomenological evidence on the four implicit assertions about the
ego. I shall then suggest a pattern of the ego into which the phenomena as described would fit more smoothly. This involves the development of the outlines of a phenomenology of ego-identification.
In its light I shall then return to the question of the ego's movements
within the body. Finally, I want to present a sample of another
movement of the ego not restricted to the body, in this case its
movements in the world of music.

27. Ibid., p. 167.

3.2 Concerning the Localization of the Ego in the Body

Before taking up the subject of the ego's movements within the body, I would like to make a few phenomenological comments on the first three of the assumptions identified above:

1. *The ego is distinct from its body:* All that need be implied in this assertion is that what we experience in talking about 'me' in the first-person singular does not coincide with what we experience when talking about 'my body', and that consequently the two expressions are not always interchangeable. This is particularly true of such ego-processes as 'I think' or 'I feel', where we can not substitute the 'my body' for the 'I'. Besides, whenever we speak about the body or parts of it as something we 'have' and not 'are' there is clearly an experience of distinctness between the two. This is all that is needed at this stage.

2. *The ego has a location within the experienced body:* I likewise anticipate little if any objection to the statement that the ego is stationed within the body rather than outside in the world or perhaps on the boundary between the two. Only, what exactly does it mean to say that the ego has a station at all? Does it mean that it has a seat, after the manner of Descartes' pineal gland, that it occupies it and displaces all other possible occupants? Clearly the ego as we experience it can make no such claims. Even if it cannot be described as completely unextended, it certainly has no definite dimensions, let alone space-filling properties, making it possible to put it in exclusive possession of a certain area in space. Phenomenologically all we can say is that it is *in* space but not that it *has* space.

3. *The location of the ego is normally between the eyes:* In what sense can we ascribe to the ego a 'normal position' somewhere in the body, e.g., between the eyes (which, incidentally, as may be pointed out for the benefit of brain-phrenologists, is a location that would put the ego in front of the brain)? We may well admit that we experience the ego as being vaguely associated with a certain region in the head. But can we assign it any definite locality? Suppose someone would put it at the distance of one inch behind the bridge of the nose with a spherical volume of two square inches. How much sense would this make, quite apart from the question of possible verification? Is our experienced ego

the sort of thing which can be pinned down unequivocally in a coordinate system? Or isn't it rather the kind of phenomenon which essentially refuses any such definite assignment to a metric framework? I submit that this refusal is indeed essential to the ego. In this sense the ego is an alien in space, essentially unassimilated and unassimilable. But this circumstance does not preclude the fact that the ego remains essentially related to space, though not to any specific place in space. Phenomenally, it 'sojourns' in a certain region of the organism, although it does not reside in any definite spot. Also, I see no good reason for denying that when the ego is in its customary observant frame of mind, this region will be associated roughly with the region near the observation spots in our heads, i.e., in the vicinity of the eyes as we experience them.[28]

4. *The ego can shift its location from the eyes to other sites within the body:* In asserting this migratory power of the ego we have to be particularly careful about sticking to the phenomenological evidence. I would not deny that we experience a local shift of the ego, as we switch from a merely contemplative attitude to one of such physical action as dancing. Not only is there a transformation in our experience of the body as we stand up, sit down, or lie down,[29] but the ego itself appears in an entirely different profile. The region between the eyes is no longer in the foreground of our attention. Instead the ego seems to be at the starting point for our bodily action and movement.

But does this mean that the ego in its entirety has moved from its home base into new bases, comparable to a baseball batter after making a hit? Asking the question in such an analogical manner may seem like loading the dice. At least it may make us pause and consider whether the shift of the ego really implies its total transfer into its new position to the extent of a complete abandonment of its original place, pulling up its roots, as it were. This would seem

28. The indefiniteness in the usual localization of the self within the body, especially among children, is shown strikingly in the questionnaire study of Eugene L. Horowitz: Spatial Localization of the Self, *Journal of Social Psychology* VI (1935) pp. 379-389.

29. See also the hints in Viktor von Gebsattel: *Prolegomena einer medizinischen Anthropologie* (Berlin: Springer, 1954), especially as to the differences between the working, marching, fighting, athletic, and dancing body *(Leib)*, and in particular about the sex-body.

to me an overstatement. Not only does the abandoned base remain 'home' to the ego, to which it will return after the 'run'; also, the ego never leaves it completely, however much it may forget about this 'home' temporarily.

If this should be a better phenomenological account of the local shifts of the ego in the body, it certainly has strange implications for the ego itself. For this would mean that the ego can be in two different places at one and the same time, even though its main attention may be merely at one, e.g., its new base in the torso. Can the ego really be 'multi-present'? If this should be the case, then the ego can certainly no longer be conceived of as an unstructured entity. Instead, it would have to be pictured as a complex being with different sectors.

I consider this picture not only inevitable but phenomenologically demonstrable. The ego stands in a unique, ambivalent or, better, multivalent relation to space and spatial entities. Clearly, this new conception of the ego has to be developed much more fully before it is possible to show what the motion of the ego can mean in such a framework.

3.3 An Outline of the Structure of the Ego

What I am presenting here will probably appear unconventional to the extent of extravagance. As far as I can see, this is fresh ground and it calls for a fresh approach. Nothing but the courage of saying what one sees can advance the discussion. Readiness to reconsider and revise is of course just as important as descriptive boldness.

In what follows I shall try to condense the main findings of my search into a few descriptive theses with a minimum of illustrations, first about the framework (topology) and then about the functioning of the ego (dynamics).[30]

30. The use of the terms 'topology' and 'dynamics' suggests a connection with the topological psychology of Kurt Lewin. I frankly admit that at a fairly advanced stage of my explorations the example of Kurt Lewin was highly encouraging and stimulating to me. But neither my use of his terms nor any of my specific views about the ego can be blamed on him. As far as I can see, in his picture of personality the ego makes only a brief incidental appearance on page 77 of his *Principles of Topological Psychology* as part of the personality, and again in the diagram on p. 177, figure 41, as 'I' or 'innerpersonal region'. In any case I shall refrain from a graphic symbolization of my conception as probably unnecessary and potentially misleading.

(1) Topology

1. The ego is not a point without extention, but has volume. It extends, for instance, over parts of the body, especially when it uses them in moving or touching, reaching out to its fingertips and even beyond into its tools.[31]

2. The ego has a center and a periphery, where it maintains outposts, as it were. Thus, in performing certain learned but automatized functions, as in playing an instrument or typing, we no longer have to be fully present in the outposts, as we had to be during the learning phase. Now the ego no longer has to 'man' these posts, though it clearly still keeps in touch with them.

3. Between the center and the periphery are connections which keep the ego center in touch with its outposts. By such connections I mean here merely the experienced power of immediate access to the outposts.

4. The ego has such 'organs' as its glance or its attention by which it can reach out beyond its boundaries. One might compare them with antennae, which can be moved, extended, expanded, and contracted.[32]

(2) Dynamics

1. The ego is never at complete rest, but always 'on the go'. Its condition can best be described in terms of Williams James's characterization of the entire stream of consciousness, i.e., 'as an alternation of flights and perchings'.[33]

2. The ego can expand and contract in such a way that for instance

---

31. I have developed this point more fully in 'A Phenomenological Approach to the Ego', *The Monist* 49, pp. 6-9 (1965); see above no. 2. The 'complexity of the ego' has been claimed before by Kurt Lewin and Kurt Koffka (see *Principles* 1935).

32. To my relief I discover that no less an authority than Pierre Janet in his *L'État mental des hystériques* (2nd ed. 1911, p. 35) expresses a similar idea as follows: 'If I dared say it —and this is not completely absurd— I would say that the 'I' is a living animal, extremely voracious, a kind of amoeba which sends out a process (for seizing and absorbing a very little being, the little sensation which has just been born next to it).' — A similar idea seems to have been expressed by Heraclitus, who compared the psyche to a spider which rushes to any part of its web which is damaged (Diels-Kranz, *Die Fragmente der Vorsokratiker*, 12.Herakleitos, fragment 67a).

33. *Principles of Psychology*, I, 243.

at one time it includes the whole experienced body and at another time merely part of it. A good indication of these changes in volume is whether we refer to part of our body as 'I' or as 'my leg' (possession).

3. The ego may move its center of gravity from its normal base to any outpost on the periphery. This does not mean that it abandons its 'seat' at the original center completely. It is always aware of this center as its home base, and the ego will return to it, once it is no longer needed at the periphery.

4. The ego can move with the antennae of its glance over the whole phenomenal field far beyond its outposts.

5. The ego can direct its attention beam at any point or area in this field. In this case the ego actually moves its center of gravity not only to its periphery but also to the tip of the attention antenna.

6. In addition to moving its center of gravity (to the tip of the attention antenna) it can move into the object touched by it and 'identify' with it. This happens particularly when we get 'involved' in what we pay attention to.[34] This is certainly an amazing phenomenon. To understand it, we need a phenomenology of the process of ego-identification.

3.4 On Ego-Identification

'Identification' is a term of many meanings, particularly in psychological and philosophical contexts. It would be as impossible as useless to explore them here in detail. I shall indicate only some of its puzzles: In what sense can we possibly think of identifying something not yet identical? Is it really meaningful to speak of making two separate objects identical? Even blending two liquids does not make them identical. As the term is commonly used, it can at most mean the attachment of some identifying characteristics, e.g., of tags allowing us to recognize a thing or a person as identical with one previously observed. But otherwise identification means merely the theoretical recognition of something as being already identical. But identity of what? Obviously two terms are required, two

---

34. The use of the term 'involvement' suggests a link with the *Psychology of Ego-involvement* by Muzafer Sherif and Hadley Cantrill (1947). While there is clearly a connection, and while their book contains rich material for my present enterprise, no phenomenological clarification of the structure of involvement is undertaken, and 'ego-identification' is not even mentioned.

conceptions or expressions. Identification implies that the referents of these terms either coincide, e.g., the referents of 'thing' and 'res,' or hang together, e.g., the criminal on the FBI poster and its original in life, the person I saw yesterday in the street and today in the store.

But such meanings, intriguing as they are, have very little to do with the use of the term 'identification' in psychology. For what is involved here is no mere tagging or recognition of identity, but a process in which the actual balance of things is changed. In identifying with something, e.g., a cause, or someone, e.g., the victim of injustice, we establish a connection between our identifying self and the being with what it identifies, a connection which did not exist before. But it is not an identity in the strict logical sense which results, but a new relationship, which we shall have to explore.

Apparently this concept of 'identification' has been developed chiefly in psychoanalysis, especially in Sigmund Freud's *The Ego and the I,* and since then, for instance, in Erik H. Erikson's studies. In Freud it stood primarily for 'the process by which some other person, preferably the father, is chosen as an ideal model'. However, as the plot unfolds it becomes clear that much more may be involved than the choice of an ideal. When a boy identifies with his mother in the typical oedipal situation, he does not choose her as an ideal so that he becomes changed over into her to the extent that he almost loses his own 'identity'. It would seem therefore that the term 'identification' as used in psychoanalysis covers a variety of different though related phenomena, which phenomenology would have to separate. There is also need for a much more detailed description of what actually goes on in the formation of such identifications.

Much more significant in the present context is the fact that identification as conceived by psychoanalysis has primarily an interpersonal or social character: one always identifies with someone else or with some social role. But one does not identify with non-personal things, beginning with one's body or possibly with phenomena in one's wider environment.[35] In order to understand such non-social identification, a much more comprehensive study is required.

35. This is also true of the meaning of 'identification' in a very stimulating article by Erwin Singer on 'Identity vs. Identification: A Thorny Psychological Issue', *Review of Existential Psychology and Psychiatry* V, 160-175 (1965).

A concept which at first sight promises such a wider and deeper understanding is that of empathy (*Einfühlung*), first studied in detail by Theodor Lipps. Indeed empathy implies a way of identification not restricted to persons. Thus Lipps, especially in his aesthetics, speaks of identification of the ego with lines, with columns, and with sounds. But as the very term *Einfühlung* suggests, feeling is the main ingredient of this identification, and actually it is merely an imaginative transfer of feeling into the object of our empathy which is involved. However, the emotional ingredient is at best an element, and not even an essential one, in the ego's identification with other beings with which we are here concerned.

It is therefore of considerable interest that one of Lipps's foremost students, Alexander Pfänder, who later joined Husserl's phenomenological movement, abandoned the term and the idea of empathy in favor of an act which he simply called 'union' (*Einigung*) and contrasted with the act of opposition (*Entgegensetzung*).[36] Such union and opposition were exemplified especially by the ego's relation to its body but also to other parts of his world. However, beyond his very concrete descriptions of instances of this act, Pfänder made no systematic attempt to clarify its nature. He simply introduced it as an act of taking a stand (*Stellungnahme*) for or against something. But this is hardly enough for an understanding of what is involved in identification. After all, even approving or disapproving from a distance are acts of taking a stand. But in 'identification' we are not only taking a stand, but we are changing it, moving over from our original stand to a new one and 'uniting' with its occupant.

What more could be done than simply to point to this unique performance? I shall try to bring out at least a few more of its characteristics by relating it to our picture of the ego and particularly its dynamics.

Two situations should be distinguished here from the start: (1) identification with an object which has no ego of its own; and (2) identification with another ego-endowed being (social identification). The first one is clearly the basic phenomenon.

Suppose we identify with a certain piece of material, say a piece

36. *Die Seele des Menschen* (Halle, 1933), especially, pp. 33 ff.

of clothing. What happens? At first we may merely observe it with our glance or touch it with our hand, scanning its texture. In this case our ego is still uninvolved, its 'center of gravity' remains at the home base. But we may want to examine it more thoroughly. Now our attention becomes involved. This also means that the ego is 'with it', as an American slang expression tellingly puts it. (The German 'bei der Sache sein', being *at* the thing, is an even more explicit and established phrase.) This also means that the ego's center of gravity has moved up to the object. In 'following it' the ego really is at the tip of its glance, in touching the object the ego is really in the touching, stroking hand. But it still remains outside the object, keeps apart from it.

The next and decisive step is that the ego crosses this almost artificial boundary and enters into the object, e.g., some clothes, which thus far it had approached only from the outside. Now the ego 'annexes', assimilates the previously foreign body, makes the clothes part of itself, moves its center of gravity right into them. All these obviously figurative expressions mean to convey the idea that the usual boundary line between ego and the world vanishes as the ego no longer sets itself apart from the object of its external attention but takes it into itself to the extent that it will apply the first person singular to the areas thus annexed. Now the ego permetates even the piece of clothing with which it feels at one. One might think of it as a matter of fictional make-believe. But the plain fact is that, at least phenomenally, the ego is present in the experienced object. In this sense and to this extent there is now identity between the ego and the permeated object.

The situation is somewhat different when we identify with another person. Such social identification embraces a number of rather diverse circumstances. There is the identification of solidarity, where the other is fully acknowledged as an independent entity, and all that happens is that the ego 'makes joint cause' with the other, at least as far as his own aspect of their mutual relationship is concerned (his approach may not be reciprocated). Identifying with him means in such a case not much more than putting oneself at the disposal of a 'we', still to be adopted by the other.

Much more is involved when we identify with someone else to the extent of actually taking his place and merging with him. This may best be exemplified by the actor of a role created by the playwright and not yet occupied by a real person. Here are two possibilities: one where the ego becomes so absorbed into the other person, or rather his image of him, that he no longer feels like himself but merges with the other. He pretends that his ego has ceased to be itself and has become identical with that of the other. Thus I am no longer me but the hero whom I have emulated. The other possibility is just the opposite. It is prepared by the attitude of 'if I were you'. The next step is to pretend that I *am* you to the extent of displacing you, the other, substituting my *identity* for yours. This is the way of all irreverent dabbling with the lives of others. Thus it differs fundamentally from putting ourselves into the other's place without violating his personal identity; in this way lies true understanding. Social identification then does imply an element of make-belief or rather of fictional disbelief. But this does not affect its actual occurrence as a phenomenon.

However, at this stage I am not interested in social ego-identification. My major interest is in the kind of identification which allows us to expand the ego into a world not yet occupied by other ego's, beginning with one's own body.

The account, then, which we can now give of the 'migration' of the ego into the spatial world is not that of a complete transfer. What is involved is

1. the extension of the antennae of the ego's glance and attention toward the outside object;
2. the shift of its 'center of (conscious) gravity' toward this object; and
3. the identification with it by way of 'annexation'.

Applying this pattern to the shift of the ego into the dancing torso, I would now suggest the following interpretation of this experience: As the ego prepares to dance it is not only intensely aware of all the parts of its body which will enter into the dancing movement; it also moves into it with its full concentrating attention, particularly into those areas where the main movements are to take place, i.e., into the torso, from which the wave-like movements of the dance are to radiate through the legs and arms to the 'extremities', the feet and hands. As soon as the actual movement is initiated, the ego shifts the center not only of its attention but also of its identification into the actual movement focussing on the central areas of these movements in the torso.

What then is the nature of the ego shift? The most pronounced change is clearly one in the profile of givenness, in the phenomenal aspect of the ego. The main light of consciousness now is focussed on the torso, the usual location of the ego is in the shade. But there is also an ontic shift which I would not like to minimize. The weight of the ego has shifted from its usual center to the periphery. It now 'lives' at the normal outpost of its attention and identification. But this transfer is not a total transfer. Even in shifting, the ego remains present in two places, its home base and its varying places in the outside world.

3.5 Identification with the Body

Before attempting a more detailed application of the new interpretation of the ego-shift into the body, I would like to enrich the picture of the phenomenology of the body in its relation to the ego by introducing some evidence which has been buried too long in Pfänder's largest work, *Die Seele des Menschen*, published in 1933, his supreme attempt to develop an interpretive synthesis on the basis of a phenomenologically enriched description. His initial phenomenological conspectus includes among other things a detailed account of the relations between the ego and its body. I shall insert in translation one of the most pertinent passages from this section, replacing, however, Pfänder's usual term 'subject' uniformly by 'ego', which is justifiable in the light of several sentences in the text:

> The ego is not only aware of its own body; it is also related to it cognitively, and knows that the body is its own. It adopts involuntarily a certain inner attitude toward it and what it finds in and upon it. To begin with, the ego in being aware of its body can expand into it in a steady stream, as it were, fill it to its very limits, and fuse with it in a firm union. Then its own organism is for the ego no longer anything like a foreign body, it is inwardly united with it, all its stirrings appear to it automatically as acts of the ego, and everything that happens in the body appears as happening in the ego. In contrast to this total union with one's body, which normally happens involuntarily, there are the rare cases in which the ego keeps its own body totally separate while being aware of it, or opposes it in its entirety, pushes it away from itself, secretes it like a foreign body. In this case,

the acts of the ego's own body do not appear to its automatically as its own acts but as acts of a foreign body which merely affect the ego more or less. Thus the bodily drives of hunger or thirst and the sex drive confront the ego from a certain distance. In the case of such a separation from or opposition to the body the fortunes of one's own body no longer appear automatically as fortunes of the ego, but primarily as fortunes which happen to a living being different from the ego. Of course in establishing and maintaining such a separate or opposed position, the ego can also exert its will.[37]

In further describing various types of such unions and oppositions Pfänder shows how they affect not only the body as a whole but special parts, states, and processes within it; that they can have various degrees, can be more or less intimate, be permanent or merely temporary. However, in full accord with his much vaster plan, he is not interested in developing a systematic phenomenology of the ego-body relation. He makes no attempt either to show in detail what is involved in the unions and oppositions between the two, or how they come about. This is where we still need a good deal more light. The following section is an attempt to go beyond Pfänder in a preliminary fashion.

Suppose we simply observe our own body as we may do in a state of complete relaxation while sitting in a comfortable chair or reclining horizontally. Let us for instance look attentively at some such details of our hand as the lines, whose puzzling patterns have given rise to palmistry. Under such circumstances the hands may seem strangely alienated, even if they are not numb with frost or anaesthetized. Certainly our ego does not extend into them. It touches them at best from the outside by the antenna of its glance. But this touch hardly differs from the one by which we touch objects outside our body.

But what if the body loses this external object-character? This can happen in at least two ways. In the first case it is the body itself which attracts attention by a special signal, most commonly in the form of a pain or a twinge. Its immediate effect is to pin down our free-floating attention upon a certain spot or area of our lived body. It requires an unusual effort or a powerful diversion to liberate the attention from such entrapment. But when it is in pain, it certainly does not identify with the pain, but actually struggles

37. Ibid.

against it and tries to escape from it.

The case of such captive attention and ego-involvement is obviously not the normal situation. Usually in full health the ego can roam freely over its body, as it can turn its attention from one area to another. Actually it may switch such attention almost instantaneously, e.g., from the tip of a finger to the tip of a toe (allowing for the fact that, except for the big toes, our inner body image does not register any individual toes). It can even turn to such completely neglected areas as the back of one's skull. One thing worth pointing out is that the lived body is much too large for us to pay simultaneous attention to all of its parts at once. There is always a certain profile of attention, with some areas standing out, others being only in a kind of penumbra, and some so far in the dark that we have to remind ourselves of them.[38] (But the fact that even normal body-consciousness seems unable to maintain full and constant contact with the entire body may well be a partial explanation of the puzzle why after a catastrophic event in the sense of Kurt Goldstein (see especially *Der Aufbau des Organismus*, pp. 25 ff.) the ego cuts off its connection with that part of its domain which it can no longer control. There is a title of a French play (by Sarment, mentioned in passing by Sartre), 'I am too great for myself'. (It deals with the 'bad faith' of characters living beyond their resources.) Thinking of our relations with our body I would consider as much more appropriate a formula such as 'I am too small for myself', i.e., to fill my body with ego-consciousness in equal density. Seen in this light it is also understandable why a one-centered ego cannot maintain equal and constant relations with all parts of a two-sided symmetrical body.)

Now in ordinary health the ego rarely pays much explicit attention to its body and is thus rarely 'with it', thematically occupied by it. It passes through it in order to roam beyond in space and time, in the social and even in the intellectual and cultural world. Later we shall try to accompany it at least on one of these journeys. In fact it seems that even sportsmen with all their 'body culture'

---

38. This over-size of the body in relation to our possible body-consciousness may actually hold part of the answer to one of Erwin Straus's favorite unanswered questions to phenomenologists: Why is it that in hemoplegia the victim dissociates completely from half of his body? I have no answer to the question why it should be the left side rather than the right side, at least not if the contingent facts of right-handedness or left-handedness should have no connection with it.

are oblivious of their body when they perform.[39] However, the memoirs of as perceptive a champion of the cinder track as Roger Bannister in *The Four Minute Mile*[40] reveal a much more complex and variable relation of the 'I' to his body and his body's energies.

But even if the body is usually not in the forefront of the ego's attention, and so the ego is not always present at and with the body, this does not mean that the ego does not identify with the body in close union, and incorporate it as a part of its own volume.

Now, as Pfänder had pointed out, this is clearly a field for considerable individual variation. The most intimate and intense identification with the body will occur in the case of obstructed bodily movement, particularly where the body requires our full attention. In trying to reach for an object, in pushing and pulling, the ego not only supervises the body and its movements, but it is right within them, permeates them, is 'all there'. Note however that it does not pay attention to the contraction and swelling of the muscles. The greater the physical effort required, the greater the identification of the ego with the active body and with the outposts of the ego in the body. Nevertheless, this does not always mean total and uniform identification with the active body. Even in such total body behavior as swimming and racing we are not equally 'in' all of its parts. We have to man the initiating and controlling posts for the body's actions, wherever they are located, and our identification with the body is strongest at the points where these are.

Identification with the body is not restricted to cases of active movement. For one thing, we may identify even with the passive movement which a vehicle imparts to the body, e.g., the movements of a car or an elevator. But what about the more static features of our body? There are, for instance, transitory parts of our body. From some of these parts we seem to dissociate by a kind of alienation, even before they are eliminated. But even the relatively more permanent parts are more or less accepted or rejected, cherished or resented. Usually, though not necessarily, this will also be a sign of how far we identify with them, though in self-hatred we might

39. See, e.g., Nicolas Beets, 'The Experience of the Body in Sport' (Jokl, E., and E. Simon, ed., *International Research in Sport and Physical Education.* Springfield, Ill., 1964), p. 75.
40. Bannister, Roger: *The Four Minute Mile.* New York: Dodd, Mead, and Co. 1954.

identify with the very features which we detest. For men and women alike, the face, ever since they encountered it in the first mirror, is the main target of such acceptances and rejections, as expressed by our constant 'self-editing'[41] from shaving or beard-trimming to hair and skin treatments. Even before removing parts of our body, such as scabs, we have clearly ceased to identify with them as we do with the fingers which do the removing.

Thus the parts of the experienced body with which we seem to identify most are those which function smoothly, require little attention, and respond instantaneously to any beck and call. In such cases the attitude of a Saint Francis, looking upon his body as his little brother donkey (*fratello asino*), would seem artificial. For in our case it is not only our loyal supporter, interpreter, and representative, it is an extension of our ego which we hardly notice as such as we pass through it on our way to the world beyond. Taking it for granted, we identify with it without even being aware of it. The more we notice it, the less is it a part of ourselves, until it becomes a burden, an obstacle, and even an enemy. We know of our body as a separate being chiefly when it rebels. But the philosophical and pre-historical amazement at the 'mystery' of the body does not depend on such rebellions.

Recent existential phenomenology talks a lot about man's essential incarnation in the body, often rather sweepingly and dogmatically. One of the, to me, most stimulating recent ideas of Erwin Straus is his suggestion that incarnation or embodiment is matched by an opposite phenomenon, which he calls 'excarnation'. While looking forward to his own development of this idea I would offer my own observations in the hope that they may be pertinent to his concern.

'Incarnation' is clearly a 'secularized' term, whose theological origins are still obvious. What sense does it make now to speak about human beings as incarnated? Who is it that is being incarnated? And into what?

Apparently the 'who' of incarnation in this new sense is the conscious subject or ego, not any substantial soul, let alone a divine principle. But what is the *'caro'*, the flesh into which it is supposed

41. See Ducasse's chapter on 'The Art of Personal Beauty' in *Art, the Critics and You*. (New York 1944).

to be inserted? Clearly not the anatomical flesh, nor the bone, connective tissue, or skin. Of course the ego enters into indirect connection with the physical organism too. But its direct connection is with the living body as immediately experienced. However, even with regard to this body, incarnation does not mean the transformation of the conscious subject into bodily shape. Nor does it mean that it becomes embedded in the body so that the flesh now surrounds it solidly. What it does mean is that now the ego has an intimate relation with its body, is to some extent dependent on it, but also to some extent its master. It seems to me highly dubious that the use of the old term has more than analogical value. It certainly involves metaphysical dangers. And its descriptive value is mostly negative, insofar as it prevents a fresh look at the phenomenon in its richness and fluidity.

From this point of view a term such as 'embodiment' deserves preference. Here the idea is that of a body giving expressive shape to the embodied subject without implication of a pre-existing *caro* surrounding the incarnated entity. This relation seems to be less miraculous and less extraneous. However, it is not the terms that matter. What does matter is the phenomenon directly experienced and described of the symbiosis of the ego and its lived body in their intimate yet variable relationship, with the ego not completely enslaved to the *caro* but able to stand at various distances from it and being in this sense both in and above the body.

3.6 The Ego in Music

We 'live' mostly outside our body. The ego on its way into the world usually passes through it without paying much attention to it. (*'Passer sur silence'* is a characteristic existentialist phrase for the process). To this extent we are never completely incarnated. We are incarnated not only in the body but in the world. This potentiality for reaching out into the world and identifying with it may well be the true measure of man's greatness, insignificant though he is in his power to fill physical space. He may not be able to displace any of it, but he can reach out into and permeate unlimited ranges of this world in his experience.

In thinking about such opportunities we are apt to consider

mostly tactual and visual space. It may therefore be fitting to turn instead to the one of the more neglected but equally amazing realms for ego-expansion, the world of sound. The few remarks I can devote to this enormous field are meant merely as an attempt to open up an area in the experience of music which seems to me virgin territory for phenomenology.

A phenomenology of the place of the ego in music presupposes a considerable development of the general phenomenology and ontology of music. I am not familiar with enough research in this field to support my present raid. But Erwin Straus's aesthesiology, with its plea for the uniqueness of each sense quality and with his special emphasis on the spatial peculiarities of sound as separating from its source, is an example of what is badly needed before a real phenomenology of music can emerge.[42]

All I would like to try in this context is to indicate the kind of opportunities for ego-movements and ego-identifications which are open in the world of music. Apparently very little has been tried in this direction even by psychologically minded aestheticians of music. Theodor Lipps, whose views on empathy should have pre-disposed him to this kind of study, refers to the empathic transfer of the ego into music only at the very end of his discussion of empathy in music. For in talking about passion and quiet, longing and peace, etc., in sounds, he also mentions that they contain an *'ideelles Ich'*. But he merely adds 'This ego is —myself, i.e., the ego empathized into the sounds, not a merely imagined but a real, i.e., actually experienced ego, an ego which experiences an inner history reaching a conclusion in the successively arising and structuring tonal whole.'[43] Suggestive though this sentence may be, its puzzling formulations, which can be understood only in the light of Lipps' total scheme, raise more questions than they answer.

---

42. See especially 'Psychologie der menschlichen Welt', p. 142. For the beginnings of a more systematic phenomenological ontology of music, consult Roman Ingarden, *Untersuchungen zur Ontologie der Kunst*. Tübingen: Max Niemeyer, 1962. Perhaps the most stimulating, though psychologistically unclarified, ideas leading to a phenomenology of music can be found in Ernst Kurth, *Musikpsychologie* (2nd ed., Bern, 1947).

43. *Ästhetik*, I, 481. There is, however, a much more explicit account of such experiences in Heinz Werner: 'Das Problem des Empfindens und die Methoden seiner experimentellen Prüfung', in *Zeitschrift für Psychologie* 114 (1930).

All I shall attempt in the following pages is to give a first idea of the relations between the ego and the world of sound which have to be considered. In attempting this, I shall distinguish two levels of musical phenomena, that of the single static tone, and that of the musical patterns where change and movement enter in.

Consider first a simple tone, sounding for a limited period against the background of preceding and subsequent silence. In simply hearing it the ego may be merely in perceptual contact with it, regardless of its spatial characteristics, whether it is given at a (safe) distance or attacks us to the extent of reverberations in our ears. All this does not imply ego-involvement. But now we may pay special attention to the tone, as in trying to determine and describe its pitch and its timbre or to distinguish its overtones. In paying such attention the ego is at least close to the sound. But it still remains outside it, merely touches it with its listening antennae, its hearing 'look', as it were.

But there is a possibility for a different attitude even with regard to a single tone. We can absorb it, so to speak, in such a way that we actually identify with it. This can happen particularly as we 'perform' it by humming or singing it, if only imaginatively. Such 'introception' or introjection of the tone can lead to a situation where the tone becomes a modification of the ego in the sense that the ego itself begins to sound inwardly and moves along with the sound. Thus it assumes a special musical state or 'mode of being'. I submit that such a musical mode of existence deserves the serious attention of existential philosophers and psychologists.[44]

Isolated tones are not yet music. Music begins only where several tones combine, where they follow each other and where we hear patterns of movement on a scale, rhythms, and pauses. Here, by way of example, I shall introduce the melody, that sequence of tones which is more than a sequence since it is permeated by something that persists, rises, and falls in powerful or relaxed fashion. How can the ego relate to this amazing phenomenon?

It may perceive the melodic event merely in a detached manner and watch it unfolding, which does not require much effort in the case of a simple melody and even less in that of a catchy tune.

---

44. See Heinz Werner's subject (*op. cit.*, p. 156). 'I am filled by that resplendent resonant tone material as if I had become a violin or a bell which is being played.'

(The latter may develop into a real threat to the inner peace of the ego.) But the situation changes when the melody demands careful listening. In hearing a fugue it is not enough to let it pass by and run off. We have to follow it, voice by voice. Such listening attention requires that the ego reach out toward the melody or the theme (and sometimes several themes at the same time). It also requires that the ego be with the moving melody and move along with it actively.

But even then the ego may still stay outside as an attentive listener. This may well remain the attitude, and even be the proper attitude, for the student and critic of music. But what about the music lover and even the creator of music himself? Take the case of such powerful ascending melodies as the second theme of Beethoven's violin concerto, with its simple scale and its thrilling acceleration at the fourth and fifth step, or the breathtaking soar of the beginning of Bruckner's Seventh Symphony, the majestic downward sweep in the second movement of Brahms' Second Symphony, or the vigorous descent of the supporting double basses in the Credo of Bach's B-minor mass. Personally I shall leave it here with the confession that I cannot help being carried away by them, and that I become identified with the tonal movement of these sweeping manifestations of tonal power. Equally important is the ability to identify with these melodic events on our own initiative. Such identification may occur in two forms: either by our introjecting the music, sucking it into ourselves, as it were; or by protecting ourselves into it in a form of 'ek-stasy' in which we leave our home base. Again this experience can be intensified and even joined with our bodies, as we hum along not just silently but loudly or finally sing it 'with all our might' or perform it on an instrument. In any case we now move into music or music moves into us in inextricable fusion. Now not only the static sound but also the sounding movement becomes part of ourselves, a moving state or mode of existence, in which our whole being is lifted up to a new level.

In the present context I shall not attempt to explore these ego-identifications with music any further. The ground is much too new for any further adventures, the risk of discrediting phenomenology too great to let myself be lured into this vast continent before I am ready for more than an exploratory raid. I shall be satisfied at this stage if I can open up what may well be one of the most exciting dimensions and opportunities of human existence.

3.7 Coda

Pythagoras and Plato introduced us to the view that the body is a mere prison for the soul. Perhaps the very fact that we can experience the body as a prison is a testimony to the inner freedom of a being whose aspirations transcend the limits of his physical existence, so much so that they are experienced as prison walls. This is no reason to think of them as impenetrable. There is no point in minimizing them, whether we are paralyzed' or merely experience the inevitable narrowing of our range of physical or even mental freedom within those limits. But this liability does not prevent the fact that this body, properly handled, is also the wedge for entering the larger world and the Archimedean point for moving it. In this light the body too is a field for freedom, limited, but all the more real. In fact, the body can be our liberator from isolation, a link with a world where there may be the echo of other egos, of friendship, and of music answering the cry in the wilderness.

3.8 Postscript 1978

Since writing this article in 1966 I have become aware of several anticipations of some of its ideas by way of incidental references without explicit descriptions. Without reporting on them in detail I would like to mention them here as partial confirmations for my preceding accounts in the hope that such support will make them less implausible, shortening the limb, as it were, on which I may seem to have been sitting.

Thus I find hints to the double presence of the ego in Martin Buber's introduction to his dialogue 'Daniel' (1913), especially in his story of the cane, both at the place where he held it and where it hit a tree. (*Werke*. Munich: Kösel, 1961, vol. I, p. 11). Husserl in refering to kineaesthetic experiences speaks about the ego's motility *(ichliche Beweglichkeit)* in *Die Krisis der europäischen Wissenschaften und die transzendentale Phänomenologie* (section 28). And Sartre in his *Transcendance de l'ego* transfers the ego comple tely into the world to the extent that in his article on 'une idée fondamentale de Husserl; Intentionalité' he states '. . . everything is outside in the world, among the others.' *(Situations* I, p. 34). However, I have not yet come across any explicit acknowledgement of the characteristic motility of the ego as flitting back and forth between an inner and an outer pole, as I have tried to describe it in this article.

4. INITIATING: A PHENOMENOLOGICAL ANALYSIS

4.1 The Theme

Human beings are initiators. Thus far this dimension of their existence seems to have been neglected. The source of this initiating power is each one's I-myself.

4.2 On the Language of Initiating

The verb 'to initiate', for which parallels occur also in German, Italian and Spanish, is not entirely without ambiguities. In fact, the noun 'initiation' stands for a specific group ceremony by which an individual is introduced into organizations with its special rites and, originally, mysteries, to which the initiate is given entry *(initium)*. 'Initiating' in the sense of beginning is a later, 'secularized' use of the word. So is the noun 'initiative', which has also assumed a specific legislative meaning.

This semantic situation suggests that it is better to avoid this label for the phenomenon which I want to explore. Why not simply talk of the act of beginning or starting in English, and similar equivalents in other languages? My main reason for preferring 'initiating' is that the relative unusualness of the term can help to bring out some of the features of the phenomenon which the plainer words do not sufficiently spell out. The beginning or the start of a new year is primarily a mere temporal occasion whose 'newness' is a matter of social convention. Even as transitive verbs, 'to begin' or 'to start' do not indicate a special personal activity yielding a novel result. By contrast 'initiating' indicates a deliberate personal act

aimed at bringing about an extraordinary, 'historical' new development, an *initium*, inaugurating a break in the continuity of ordinary
life. An *in-itium* makes something enter the scene that was not
there before.

4.3 The Novelty of the Phenomenon

To my knowledge the act of initiating has not yet been made the
subject of a separate study.[45] Thus far psychologists and philosophers thought of it not as a separate phenomenon, but as an inte-
gral part of voluntary acts such as decisions or choices at their very
start without giving it special attention. Nevertheless, I maintain
that initiating is a very distinctive phenomenon in need of special
investigation and description, both for its own sake and for its wider
significance. Specifically, initiating does not coincide with the act
of willing, neither with its phase of deliberating, decision-making,
choosing or projecting, nor with the executive phase of such acts
through doing. Initiating such acts differs not only in time but in
its structure from the acts that are initiated by it and follow it. In
what way it differs remains to be shown. Initiating occurs not only
in connection with willing but with other voluntary acts: I can initiate thinking about a problem by analyzing it, classifying, calcula-
ting and similar operations. I can initiate giving attention to a situation, recalling, imagining, guessing, etc. without the intervention
of a previous phase of decision-making. In these cases initiating
opens up directly upon action.

At first sight it may seem that initiating as an acts that makes a
fresh start (de novo) would be a complete anomaly among personal
acts. But there may be a precedent for it since Arthur C. Danto introduced the concept of a 'Basic Action' (1963)[46] which he defined
as action performed by an individual which he cannot be said to
have caused to happen, in contrast to others caused by him. A
prime example of such a basic action is raising one's arm, although

45. I am aware only of a passing reference to the act of *Inangriffnahme* (attacking,
undertaking) in Dietrich von Hildebrand's *Die Idee der sittlichen Handlung, Jahrbuch
für Philosophie und phänomenologische Forschung* III (1916) pp. 61-62.

46. See *American Philosophic Quaterly* II (1963), reprinted in Care, Norman S. and
Landesman, Charles, eds., *Readings on the Theory of Action*, Indiana University Press,
(1968), pp. 93-112.

Danto admits that this example is ambiguous: sometimes we do not move our arm directly but cause it to move, presumably by an intermediate cause.

Is initiating a basic act in this sense? Certainly it is not insofar as initiating is not a complete act as is arm-lifting. But it may well be considered as the initial phase of a basic act performed directly. To this extent the model of the basic act does apply to initiating acts. Only that there is more to be said about it than the rather sketchy treatment of the concept of a basic act as offered by Danto.

4.4 The Place of Initiating in Everyday Life

I shall begin by showing the role of initiating processes in ordinary life by focussing on and examining typical sequences of our ordinary experience. In describing these episodes I shall depart slightly from our usual way of talking about them by inserting the intensifying word 'initiating' where generally we would speak only of 'beginning to do' or even by merely designating the actions initiated. I shall do so in order to focus attention on the crucial phases in this sequence.

1. After a period of wavering or paralyzed indecision I break the deadlock by initiating a review of possible courses of action such as reading, writing, doing manual work, going for a walk, etc.
2. I initiate the selection of one of these courses and pick, without or with a conscious motive, e.g. going for a walk.
3. In doing so I may also initiate the choice of a seemingly adequate motive or ground for this choice, e.g., for exercise or for running an errand, as a support for my action.
4. I initiate the readying of my body for walking action, especially my legs or feet.
5. I initiate rising to my feet and, perhaps as yet without a clear plan, getting them to move in alternating sequence, leaning over forward, especially in speeding up.
6. I initiate looking at the ground ahead and at the scene around in a global survey.
7. I initiate the closer inspection of single features of the surrounding scene such as bushes, trees, flowering plants, sometimes because they attract my attention, at other times 'arbitrarily',

without being aware of such a special 'pull'.

8. I initiate a new phase by turning away from them, picking other features across the street or elsewhere, again without a plan or a special decision.

9. While going on with such observations I often initiate parallel chains of 'thought', recalling a previous event, wondering about future possibilities and finally 'thinking through' an old or a new problem picked at random or emerging from the reservoir of my constant or intermittent wonderings, worryings or hopings.

This may suffice as a casual sample from the more trivial range of our solitary life without the usual stresses and interruptions. Obviously the situation will become much more complex as all the distractions of social life will crowd in. My point was merely to show in a simplified fashion how even a very brief slice of seemingly unexciting daily life is shot through with initiating acts on a minor scale. The real significance of these findings has to be tested in the case of the major initiatings in individual and joint human undertakings.

I want to make it clear that the above selection of nine episodes of initiating is a very incomplete record of all that goes on in the continuity of daily life. This would have to include a description of the initiated acts and of all the perceivings, feelings and states that accompany them. Obviously this would be a much bigger assignment and in fact an impossible one. By singling out the initiating episodes within this total flux I wanted to restore, or rather to instate initiating to the place which it should have had long ago, especially in an existential perspective.

4.5 The Essential Structure of Initiating

1. There is no separate independent act of initiating, comparable to the acts of perceiving and thinking. All initiating is an act of initiating an act other than itself. It is in this sense an intentional act directed toward another intentional act such as thinking or willing. These acts are themselves intentional but in a different sense, namely as directed toward something thought or willed. Initiating is thus an intentional act of the second order, as it were.

It is an act dealing with and actually directing another act.

2. If acts, but not objects, are thus the targets of initiating acts, what is it that can (and cannot) be initiated? Primarily only acts and actions that are under our voluntary control like imagining, thinking or willing. However, we also speak of initiating other events. Thus we talk about initiating a new way of doing something or a new approach to a problem. But we cannot initiate a new road, a new building or a new art work. More technically, in legislative practice we can initiate a 'bill', but not an 'act'. Its achievement does not depend on the initiating legislators alone. Initiating is merely the first phase of a voluntary act. Initiating can send the rocket on its course, but it cannot direct it to its target.

By pleading for a separate status of initiating I do not imply that it deserves a special chapter in (phenomenological) psychology comparable to those on perception, feeling, or willing. Rather it intersects with such chapters inasmuch as initiating occurs in thinking as well as in imagining and willing. Nevertheless initiating in all these cases has enough in common to deserve special treatment, which I would like to 'initiate'.

3. The initiated event in the case of successful initiating is no longer in need of initiating support. It proceeds under its own momentum, as it were. This does not preclude the need of occasional maintaining or sustaining 'infusions' by secondary initiating, once the original momentum is slowed down or lost.

4. The original initiating act is an instantaneous occurrence or episode, starting abruptly from one moment to another and ending just as suddenly by melting into the initiated act. This episodic character sets it in contrast to such continuous processes as attending to, or states such as elation.

5. What happens at the 'point' of initiating is an 'impulse' or 'push', an experience which activates the initiated process. Other more metaphorical words like 'blow', 'stroke', or 'flash' suggest themselves. Using them as synonyms may neutralize the misleading literal connotations of any particular metaphor. William James used the striking and influential Latin word *fiat*, meaning literally 'let it be done', adding the expression 'element of consent' or resolve.[47] The danger in this case is that the passive mood of

47. *Principles of Psychology* II, Ch. XXVI, p. 501.

the verb *facere*, i.e., *fieri*, stresses too much the result of the initiating act rather than the active aspect of the event (which calls for the imperative 'fac' or the interjection 'now'). But regardless of the proper accompanying linguistic expression, the main phenomenon is the shock-like transformation of the initiating agent into a new state or condition.

6. No initiating without an initiand (initiator) who pulls the trigger, as it were. In this sense an initiating agent or self is an essential part of initiating.

T

There is incidentally a corresponding act to initiating: terminating. I can terminate an action deliberately, killing it, as it were. Thus we terminate a walk by stopping, sitting down, etc. This may require an effort if the action has been proceeding by some kind of ongoing momentum or inertia. But terminating is clearly a secondary act based on the previous initiating phase and the main act that follows it. Consequently the significance of this act does not require separate treatment in this place. Actually it may be a mirror image of the initiating act.

4.6 Ways in which Initiating Appears

Initiating acts do not appear to the initiating subject all at once and completely. In fact his absorption in the decisive phase of the act makes it particularly difficult for him to achieve an adequate grasp of the phenomenon. Contrary to what Husserl originally asserted, not only contents of our experience but acts themselves appear in different perspectives *(Abschattungen),* though they usually dovetail. In the case of initiating the following three stages can be distinguished.

(i) Preparatory stage: Before the actual initiation there is a dynamic vacuum. But the subject is already in a state of alert and his energies are in a state of growing mobilization. At this stage the actual initiation is at least anticipated, sometimes in the form of a more or less definite project.

(ii) At the onset of the initiating act there is a kind of convulsive contraction of the agent absorbing him almost completely, to the extent that he cannot attend to what he is doing or describe what is going on in him at the moment. A striking example may be the actual initiating involved in getting up or giving one's signature.

(iii) As the initiated action gets under way, the initiating agent is still aware (in a fading retention) of what has happened just before and is now receding rapidly from direct awareness into memory, from which it can be recalled by a special effort with more or less confidence.

4.7 The Role of the Initiator

In describing the essential structure of initiating I went so far as to say that there can be no initiating without an initiator. But this brief assertion does not yet describe adequately what the relation between initiating and the initiating subject is. In fact, in the every-day occurrence of an initiating process, especially at the crucial phase, the attention is diverted from the subject to the initiated act, and it is only at the subsequent retentive phase that part of the original experience can be salvaged. However, on this basis a reflective retrospection on the act of initiating can reveal the way in which it issues from the conscious self and how this self actually injects its impulse into the act. In the case of everyday initiating such as the turn of the look, the 'I' involved is a relatively superficial one, sending out its impulses in a somewhat casual way. This is different where a major new enterprise is initiated or an 'existential' decision or new step is taken. Here the sense that it is I myself who is sending out the decisive impulse permeates the experience of initiating. It is this type of initiating which gives the existing self a new dimension and a special dignity.

4.8 The Validity of the Evidence for Initiating

How far can the appearance of the abrupt introduction of new acts into the tissue of a causal world be considered proof positive of breaks in the network of strictly causal chains. Such a first impression must not be accepted as conclusive before a careful appraisal of actual and possible counter-evidence, phenomenological as well as epistemological and metaphysical.

(a) Phenomenological Quandaries

While our first impression of initiating acts may be that they start abruptly *de novo*, more thorough examination in retrospect may reveal that they were preceded by events that not only prepared the ground for such acts, but had at least an input into its formation. Thus in initiating a walk we may realize in retrospect that a growing restlessness and need for exercise played an important role in our initiating a walk.

This realization raises the question of how far even initiation is determined by such psychological factors as motivation, desires, drives and similar factors. A full answer to such questions would require a much more comprehensive treatment than I can offer in the present context. Among other things it would have to weigh the evidence of the empirical psychology of motivation and of psychoanalysis. I shall confine myself here to a consideration of the phenomenological evidence.

Here the prime case is that of motivation. Now the phenomenology of motivations as undertaken particularly by Alexander Pfänder but also by the philosophical analysis of R.S. Peters' *The Concept of Motivation* has shown that at least in one sense what ordinary language understands by motive is a ground of willing and action that owes its effectiveness to the adoption by the motivated subject. In this sense it is not the motive that controls our conduct, but it is we who control the choice of motives by which we support our decisions and actions. In this sense, then, even if initiating can be traced to motives, it remains 'autonomous' in the sense that motives do not dominate it. Initiating while not starting *de novo* is still 'its own master'.

But what cannot be ignored is that in general literature and in psychological research motivation is understood in a wider sense as a term for all the factors that determine human behavior, including desires, drives, wants and needs, which do not depend on our more or less conscious adoption. Here the question arises whether and how far they control our eventual action. While a final decision would certainly have to take account of empirical and even experimental evidence, I submit that the phenomenological evidence is far from conclusive. While desires and similar factors are clearly important in preparing our initiatings, rarely if ever are we aware of them as compelling factors. Whatever it may mean that we find desires irrepressible or even irresistable, such language is often a hyperbole. The case certainly differs from that of physical enforcement. This would be the end of all genuine initiating.

(b) Epistemological Aspects

There are also more general reasons for questioning the validity of the phenomenological evidence for initiating. Can there be no illusion, no self-deception or error with regard tot he phenomenon of initiating just as there can be with regard to the perception of physical object? The idea that 'inner perception' is essentially certain and error-proof had to be abandoned anyhow, not only because of the possibility of 'idols of self-knowledge' (Scheler) but because even consciousness can appear in different perspectives and with varying perspective shadings (Abschattungen). In principle we may be mistaken in the belief that we initiated a certain action because of our superficial self-observation and because of errors of memory. Pride may be a special reason for affirming our free initiative even when we have serious reasons for suspecting self-deception.

But even if this possibility cannot be ruled out, this is no sufficient reason for denying the possibility of its truth. Dubitability does not prove dubiousness and even less actual error. This would require concrete proof of such a deception by the demonstration of its opposite. Even such concrete counter-evidence is mostly second-hand, based on inference and hypotheses which are not conclusively verifiable and rarely falsifiable. In any case the impression, and especially the first impression, of initiatings cannot be gainsaid. As far as it goes the phenomenon as such is ultimate and must not be ignored without good reason.

(c) Metaphysical Quandaries

The possibility of real initiating could be questioned on the basis of a metaphysics of a universe without beginnings and endings. Strict determinism would be a prime example of such a system in which there would be no room for breaks and fresh starts. At least such a metaphysics no longer seems to be demanded by the scientific evidence. Even for Kant's Critique of Pure Reason the denial of beginnings was only the antithesis to an equally self-evident thesis asserting such beginnings. Since then the metaphysics of C.S. Peirce with its tychism has reopened the possibility not only for metaphysical chance but for first beginnings. Hence, at least today any attempt to outlaw on metaphysical grounds genuine beginnings, and with them genuine initiating acts, appears to be gratuitous, especially insofar as it conflicts with the phenomenological evidence of the consciousness of initiatings.

4.9 The Significance of Initiating for Self-Existence

Initiating and especially initiating by the I-myself means a turning point in human existence. Without it self-existence, beginning with the I-am-me-myself, presents us as beings who are the passive, if not helpless victims of a universe that has 'condemned' us to being none other than ourselves and to irrevocable existence. But this is clearly not the whole story. With the power to initiate, the self can turn the tide. Now he can pull the lever for re-forming, in fact revolutionizing, his existence. The I-myself is no longer a focus for the world of experience, it also becomes a new nucleus of energy, of world-reorganization.

Does the phenomenon of initiating also provide evidence for 'free will' or rather for genuine alternatives for the I-myself to choose and shape his life and world? All I would claim in this context is that the phenomenon of initiating is not less but rather more than the consciousness of freedom which has been one of the favorite arguments of indeterminism or self-determinism. But ultimately it cannot be considered any more conclusive, especially in isolation. Nevertheless even the phenomena are a part of ultimate reality and the phenomenon of initiating is certainly a part of the evidence that strengthens the case of existential metaphysical freedom.

By making man's initiatorship the decisive feature of his significance, I may seem to be denying or at least playing down what has been frequently proclaimed as his most distinctive glory: his creatorship. My primary reason for deemphasizing creativity in this context is the ambiguity of this concept. Certainly, if creation should involve 'creation out of nothing' in the theological sense of God's creation, no such power can be claimed for a finite being like man with his finite capacities, which require at least preexisting materials out of which man creates. However, if creativity means no more than the power to arrange and rearrange preexisting materials into new and original patterns as in the 'creative' arts or even in our everyday speech, then there is no good reason for denying creativity to man too. Considering that etymologically the stem for the word 'create' is to (make) grow, man the grower and breeder of natural plants is a creator even for more than merely artificial objects. However, creation as an achievement of man is something which is never fully under his power. In Gilbert Ryle's terms 'to create' is an achievement or get-it word, not a try-it word as is starting or initiating. In any case, initiating is at the root of all creation. Even non-creative or ineffective people can initiate. This is the reason why initiativeness seems to me a more fundamental potential of man than creativity, even if the latter is the source of greater values.

5. PUTTING OURSELVES INTO THE PLACE OF OTHERS: TOWARD A PHENOMENOLOGY OF IMAGINARY SELF–TRANSPOSAL[48]

1. To dwell in general terms upon the imperative need and duty of maximum understanding of others in a world as shrunken in space and as divided in spirit as ours would be trivial in theory and ineffectual in practice. I shall therefore concentrate on the concrete task of exploring means for raising curtains, iron and otherwise, that separate the mental and moral isolationists of our time, especially in those almost desperate cases where the normal appeals to mutual understanding are no longer able to penetrate the walls of accumulated misunderstandings. Among the operations increasingly involved in this context is the act of putting ourselves into the place of others. Social psychology, group dynamics, the study of communication and education are becoming aware of its significance. But we still lack a phenomenological clarification of the basic phenomena. The purpose of this sketch is to outline some of the contributions which a descriptive phenomenology can make to the solution of this task. It is meant as a first account of the essential nature of the phenomenon, regardless of whether it actually occurs among human beings, such as we know them.

2. The act of putting ourselves into the place of others belongs to the larger group of imaginative acts. Hence, it shares the general structure of these acts. In this context I shall presup-

48. Revised version of 'Toward a Phenomenology of Imaginative Understanding of Others', Proceedings of the XIIth International Congress of Philosophy at Brussels VII (1953), pp. 235-39.
Reprinted by permission from Human Studies 3 (1980) 169-173.

pose that the structure of these acts has been sufficiently explored by phenomenologists such as Jean-Paul Sartre, Eugen Fink, and others.

3. However, in the case of imaginative understanding of others, the following modifications of this general structure must be considered:

a. In putting ourselves into the place of others we deal with a very special kind of object of our imagination. For it is the real imagining subject who transposes himself imaginatively from his usual vantage point into the world outside. In self-transposal, as I shall call the putting of ourselves into the place of others, we leave the origin of the coordinate axes for our world, as it were.

b. The ingredients used in imaginary self-transposal are all supposedly real, not imaginative. All that is imaginary about the product of this imagination is the relationship of these elements, inasmuch as the real self transmigrates imaginatively into the other's real place; in other words, self-transposal is merely an imaginary rearrangement of reality.

c. This imaginatively transformed relationship is not merely imagined without any thought of whether or not the imagined object is real or not, as when we imagine ourselves to be healthy or sincere, which we may in fact happen to be. Here we are fully aware that the imaginary transposal is not only contrary to fact but also contrary to all normal possibilities: Not only are we riveted to our own place in reality, but it is downright preposterous to think that any such transposal can ever happen to us in the normal and even in the abnormal course of events. The type of imagination involved in self-transposal is thus of the nature of a fiction deliberately flying into the face of the facts.

4. Among the distinguishing characteristics of self-transposal, the following call for special investigation: (a) the 'place' into which we transpose ourselves; (b) the 'self' which is being transposed; (c) the position occupied by this self after the performance of the transposal.

a. Little reflection is needed to realize that the place into which we are to transpose ourself is more than the geographical spot, describable in terms of longitude and latitude, at which the other happens to be located. More is involved if we imagine ourselves to be in another's 'shoes', 'skin', or however elso colloquial language expresses the fiction 'if I were in your place'. It is rather the whole perspective as seen from this place, the 'viewpoint' and the view which opens up, into which we have to enter or slide, as it were. Nor is it only the point in space we have to take over, but just as well the point in time and its perspectives toward past and future as seen from the other's place. In other words, what we have to consider is the whole 'frame' of existence which the other occupies.

In order to understand what self-transposal implies, we ought to remember the structure of man as a conscious existence, i.e., as a being incarnated in a body and characterized by a mental structure whose chief features have been indicated by Husserl's familiar pattern '*ego cogito cogitata mea*' (I am referring to referents). We shall, therefore, first consider what is involved in taking over the *cogitata* or intended referents of another person's life. Under this heading we have to consider not only isolated *cogitata,* even if this might be enough for certain limited cases of self-transposal; rather we have to consider these *cogitata* with their 'horizons', and ultimately in the context of the 'life-world' (*Lebenswelt*) to which they belong. This life-world is obviously not the 'objective world', as we can determine the world by the methods of science. What matters is the world as an individual sees it, with an individual's selection, accents, limited information, as well as with his misinformation. This world includes, for instance, the peculiar perspective or scheme of the body in which one happens to be incarnated, rather than the scientific picture of the organism. It comprises his environment as one conceives of it: the natural world as one sees it, the social world in which one lives, the religious world to which one relates oneself, etc.

As to one's '*cogitationes*', or acts of reference toward the world, we have to picture the network of thinkings and feelings by which the other is in contact with the life-world and which also has sedimented strata; an individual's more or less careful flighty perceptions, preferences and idioscyncracies, aspirations and resignations.

Finally, we have to consider the *cogitator,* the self of the other at the source of individual acts of reference to one's world. It is of paramount importance that we learn to put ourselves into the frame of personality and mind at the root of this world and of one's responses toward it. What this means is that we try to assume imaginatively not only an individual's own self-experience. Even more important is that we take on in imagination the individual's 'personality', one's intellectual and moral equipment, temperament, and all that goes customarily by the name of character. An actor impersonating different roles knows best what this implies. Personality in this sense also includes the social role which a person is expected to fill in the framework of society. Otherwise we cannot hope to 'see the world through another person's eyes', as self-transposal should enable us to do.

A current idiom has it that we also imagine ourselves as becoming the other's own self. I submit that the common phrase 'if I were you' interpreted literally involves a contradiction in terms: an 'I' that becomes a 'you' is no longer an 'I'. In any case, such a complete absorption of the other would no longer be a self-transposal. What this phrase seems to suggest is the highest degree of taking over the part of the other, slipping, as it were, into another's shell, as it might occur when we experience the feeling of existence peculiar to the other, and lived under his assumed name.

b. Next, I shall consider who the self is that thus transposes itself into the place of the other. Most attempts at self-transposal suffer from the fact that the transposing self carries with itself its own equipment, physique, ideas, experiences, frame of mind, etc. It is obvious that such self-transposals have the character rather of invasions and occupations than of attempts to enter into the world and personality of the other; hence they do not stand a chance of giving us real understanding. Before any meaningful transposal can take place the transposing self has to strip itself of those peculiarities which are not essential to selfhood as such. Such radical and conscientious abstraction from one's own empirical personality is not an easy assignment. It requires negative imagination. This does not mean that we first convert ourselves into disembodied colorless pure selves. But it does involve our learning to detach ourselves from our regular existential involvements. One might well call this a type of phenomenological reduction in which all our empirical determinations are suspended, relativized, or neutralized. Thus, self-knowledge and self-discipline are prerequisites of any meaningful self-transposal. There is enough evidence, even of a psychological nature, to back up this conception of man.

c. Putting oneself into the place of the other is obviously a transitory operation. If successful, it results in the self's occupying the other's place. Thus the question arises whether and to what extent we are to 'stay put' in the station into which we put ourselves.

It is obviously out of the question to live the life of the other from the inside at the same rate and pace as would the other, thus abandoning one's own station completely, if only in imagination, to the extent of cutting off one's retreat to one's own place. At best, we can expect to stay there for an exploratory period to become oriented in another's existence and to experience the reactions of our remodeled and transposed ego to it. In fact, any understanding of the other by the self requires that we maintain our position outside the other, while moving back and forth between another individual's and our places. To *become* the other is no longer to *understand* the other. The exact determination of the optimum of sojourn in the other.s place presupposes a much fuller phenomenology of the types and degrees of self-transposal than I can offer here, and specifically of the various stage of intuitive fulfillment that can be given to our imagining the lives of others.

5. Self-transposal is to be distinguished from such related acts as sympathy, empathy, identification, role-taking, and similar acts, but their exploration can help in bringing out the unique nature of the act of self-transposal.

6. Likewise, the question of the *varieties* of the act has to be postponed. Only one phenomenon shall be mentioned by way of contrast: There is such an act as putting the other into the place of oneself. It occurs particularly where we choose another person as a model, asking ourselves what that person would do if in our place. Obviously, this reverse transposal makes sense only where we believe we know the other at least as well as ourselves.

7. What is the epistemological validity of the method of self-transposal? Offhand it would seem to be preposterous to claim knowledge of others by a type of imagination as extravagant in scope as the act of self-transposal has turned out to be. Yet we would do well to remember that scientific imagination has been recognized more and more as perhaps the most important step in the

methodology of the sciences, much as it has to be buttressed by subsequent verification. Besides, Husserl pointed out that free variation in the imagination is the most effective method of phenomenology. Anyway, this method represents our only chance of penetrating minds different from our own. Realizing the precariousness and pretensiousness of such a method can provide one of the most necessary lessons in social humility and respect for others that a critical social philosophy can teach us.

8. Finally, the ethical question must be raised: Why should we be under any obligation to perform an operation as fantastic as pretending to be in another's place, which is contrary to fact and reasonable possibility? It would be relatively easy to summon up prudential reasons why putting ourselves into the place of others is our best chance for getting along with them. But this is neither always necessary nor enough for a genuine ethical imperative. While a final answer has to be postponed, I submit that man's contingency and specifically the 'accident' of his actual situation (birth and environment)[49] makes it a matter of 'fairness', of an existential moral exigency, to realize that what has happened to others might, as far as ethical claims are concerned, just as well have happened to us; in the words of John Bradford: 'There but for the grace of God go I.'

49. On this concept and its ethical significance see my "Accident of Birth': A Non-utilitarian Motif in Mill's Philosophy', *Journal of History of Ideas,* 22 (1961), 479-492 and number 6 of this volume.

PART II

NEW ETHICAL DIMENSIONS

Man is wholly chance.

Solon

Fellowship is life, and lack of fellowship is death.

William Morris

6. 'ACCIDENT OF BIRTH': A NON-UTILITARIAN MOTIF IN MILL'S PHILOSOPHY

> I remember the very place in Hyde Park where, in my fourteenth year, on the eve of leaving my father's house for a long absence, he told me that . . . whatever I knew more than others could not be ascribed to any merit in me, but to the very unusual advantage which had fallen to my lot of having a father who was able to teach me, and willing to give the necessary trouble and time . . . I felt no disposition to glorify myself upon the circumstances that there were other persons who did not know what I knew; nor had I ever flattered myself that my acquirements, whatever they might be, were any merit of mine; but now when my attention was called to the subject, I felt that what my father had said respecting my peculiar advantages was exactly the truth and common sense of the matter, and it fixed my opinion and feeling from that time forward.[50]

6.1 Introductory

The primary objective of the following study is not to indulge in the familiar passtime of ferreting out inconsistencies and fallacies in the thought of one of the keenest, noblest, and least expendable thinkers and doers of the nineteenth century. I want to bring out a certain motif in his philosophy of justice which comes to the surface only intermittently. The phrase which is most closely asso-

Reprinted by permission from the *Journal of the History of Ideas* 22 (1961), 475-492.

ciated with this motif is that of the 'accident of birth'. It stands for the sum of those natural and social circumstances which are basically unfair and which our social reforms are called upon to remove or at least to relieve. The very fact that Mill appeals to this idea more often than any comparable philosopher seems to me sufficient reason for attention and acknowledgment.

Perhaps it is in order to give an explanation for my inordinate interest in what may at first seem a minor motif in Mill's thought. For it was definitely not the result of a concern about the adequacy of utiliarianism, which in Mill's case had anyhow become widened so far that it could include not only most of ideal utilitarianism but even the ethics of self-realization. What first aroused my curiosity was an antecedent interest in the concept of accident of birth, a concept whose absence from philosophy has puzzled me, since I consider it to be of major importance for an understanding of our idea of social justice. It was therefore a happy surprise to me to find it a pervading theme in Mill's thinking. The fact that he did not develop it is all the more reason to make it explicit and to explore it further.

However, my objective here will be more limited. First, I shall present the textual evidence from Mill's writings. Second, I shall show that this concept is fundamentally a moral, not an ontological one. Third, I wish to show its place in the framework of Mill's thought. And finally, I propose to discuss the relation between it and Mill's utilitarianism.

6.2 The Textual Evidence

In lining up the key passages from Mill's writings in which he refers to the accident of birth one need not restrict oneself to this stereotyped phrase. In fact, the characteristically personal and concrete modifications which he chooses for the idea are particularly good indications of its live significance for him. So instead of 'birth' he will speak of 'sex' or 'skin', and instead of 'accident' of 'fatality', a term which, as the context will show, he uses synonymously with 'accident'. Here, then, are some of the most striking passages which I have come across:

1. The ideas and institutions by which the *accident of sex* is made the groundwork of an inequality of legal rights, and a forced dissimilarity of social functions, must ere long be recognized as the greatest hindrance to moral, social, and even intellectual improvement.[51]

2. If it be said that . . . virtue itself is the greatest good and vice the greatest evil, then these at least ought to be distributed to all according to what they have done to deserve them, instead of which every kind of moral depravity is entailed upon multitudes by the *fatality of birth*; through the fault of their parents, of society, or of uncontrollable circumstances, certainly through no fault of their own.[52]

3. Let us hope that . . . before the lapse of another generation the *accident of sex* no more than the *accident of skin* will be deemed a sufficient justification for depriving its possessor of the equal protection and just privileges of a citizen.[53]

4. The disabilities to which women are subject from the mere fact of their birth are the solitary examples of the kind in modern legislation. In no instance except this, which comprehends half the human race, are the higher social functions closed against anyone by a *fatality of birth* which no exertions and no change of circumstances can overcome.[54]

5. . . . We looked forward to a time when . . . the division of the produce of labour, instead of depending, as in so great a degree it now does, on the *accident of birth*, will be made by concert on an acknowledged principle of justice.[55]

Apart from these explicit passages, there are many others which express similar ideas. Thus, wherever Mill speaks about the way certain people are 'born to riches or poverty, to natural differences of strength or capacity', the underlying idea seems to be the same. In

51. *Principles of Political Economy* (1838), ed. W.J. Ashley (London, 1923), 259 f.

52. *Three Essays on Religion* (New York, 1874), 38. According to the editor, Helen Taylor, the posthumously published essay 'Nature' was written between 1850 and 1858.

53. *Considerations on Representative Government* (1861) in *Utilitarianism*, Everyman ed., 292.

54. *The subjection of Women* (1869) in Mary Wollstonecraft, *The Rights of Women*, and J.S. Mill, *The Subjection of Women*, Everyman ed., 236 f.

55. *Autobiography*, Ch. VII, 162.

fact, the idea of the 'accident' or 'fatality' of man's initial situation pervades nearly all his writings on political, economic, and religious philosophy. It will be my next task to clarify its meaning. As preparation for this it might be well to make a brief survey of earlier occurrences of the conception.

6.3 Antecedents of Mill's 'Accident of Birth'

Mill was not the first to use this phrase. He certainly never implied that he had coined it. Indications are that it sprang up in ordinary language without any traceable ancestry. Nevertheless, some of the early occurrences of the phrase and its equivalents and of their context are interesting enough to be recorded here.

The first instance of the idea with which I am familiar, and almost the phrase itself, can be found in Shakespeare's *Hamlet*, where the hero, meditating on the sources of human corruption, remarks:

> So oft it chances in particular men
> That for some vicious mole of nature in them,
> As in their birth, —wherein they are not guilty,
> Since nature cannot choose its origin— . . .
> (Act I, Scene IV, lines 23-26)

(The remainder of this rather involved chain of thoughts is irrelevant to the point in question.) True, these lines do not permit us to pin down Shakespeare beyond saying that he seems to have toyed with the idea of 'chance', illustrated particularly by birth, as accounting for a vice like drunkenness. But this passage is not unrelated to Shakespeare's conception of the tragic flaw, which is not always man's fault. Hamlet's lines suggest that Shakespeare even thought of blaming some flaws on the 'chance of birth'.

The place where the idea of the chance of birth seems to have crystallized first in modern times is in the discussion of the privileges of noble birth. Actually the first to make use of it seems to have been as religious and non-revolutionary a thinker as Blaise Pascal. The main context for introducing this conception is his *Three Discourses on the Position of the Privileged ('le grands')*, given apparently around 1660 to young noblemen, but not written down until seven or eight years later by Pascal's student Nicole, who does not claim to give a verbatim report. Yet the argument he reports deserves quotation:

> Do not think that you possess the wealth which you happen to own by a lesser accident than that which made that man find himself a king. You have no right to it by yourself and by your nature, any more than he had. And not only do you not find yourself the son of a duke, but you do not even exist in the world except through an infinity of chance happenings. Your birth depends on a marriage, or rather on the marriages of all those from whom you are descended. But on what did those marriages depend? On a chance visit, on some idle talk, on a thousand unforeseen things ... Another turn of fancy in those who made the laws would have made you poor; and it is only that concurrence of the chance which gave you birth with the whim of laws favourable to you that put you in possession of all these benefits.[56]

Pascal's *Thoughts* contain parallel ideas about the precarious justification of social privilege and about the unreasonableness of differences in laws based on frontiers made by mountains and rivers (*Pensées*, 292 ff.).

In Pascal's case it was thus no longer, as in Shakespeare, man's character but his place in society which dominated his interest. This was clearly social dynamite. It exploded in the attack of the 'third estate' on the aristocracy of birth during the period of Enlightenment, but also in the attack on religious intolerance.

What is also remarkable in the case of a thinker as Providence-minded as Pascal is that he begins to think of areas within the order of nature as no longer part of a divine plan. This is a significant indication of a secularization of modern thought in which natural privilege is no longer interpreted as a sign of natural or supernatural grace. Apparently the sense of the social injustice of such an order had gradually undermined the theological defenses of social discrimination.

Voltaire, the spearhead of the attack against social privilege, uses the new weapon implicitly in his attack on religious bigotry when the heroine of his *Zaïre* (1732), a crusader's orphan brought up as a Mohammedan, exclaims:

56. Pascal, *Oeuvres*, ed. L. Brunschvicg, IX, 365 f.

> I see only too well that the care one takes of us in infancy shapes our feelings, our customs, and our faith. Near the Ganges I would have been the slave of false gods, at Paris a Christian, in these regions a Mohamme-dan. (Act I, Scene 1)

However, the most aggressive use of the idea of the chance of birth occurs in Figaro's famous monologue in Beaumarchais' *Mar-riage de Figaro* (1778) in passages like the following:

> Because you are a nobleman you think you are a genius . . . Nobility, fortune, rank, position, this makes you so proud! What have you done for so many goods? You have given yourself the trouble to be born and nothing else. (Act V, Scene III)

Without using the exact phrase, this ironic answer clearly implies that Beaumarchais thinks of the privileges of the nobility as mere 'accidents of birth'. Incidentally, this passage appealed to Mill so much that he referred to it in his *Subjection of Women.*[57]

A similar idea is expressed in the well-known defense Lord Thur-low (1731-1806) made of his self-earned peerage against the snub of the hereditary Duke of Grafton by calling the latter's title an 'accident of accidents'.

Not only the idea but the exact phrase 'accident of birth' *(Zufall der Geburt)* occurs in Gotthold Ephraim Lessing's famous plea for religious as well as racial and national tolerance, *Nathan der Weise* (1779). It is actually the Sultan Saladin, a Muslim, who uses it in the following lines:

> A man like you does not remain where chance
> of birth has cast him: if he so remains
> It's out of insight, reasons, better choices.[58]

Perhaps even more important is the fact that earlier in the same play Lessing, through the mouth of his Nathan, had expressed the idea that

> . . . Neither one has chosen
> his folk. Are we our folk? What is a folk?
> Are Jew and Christian sooner Jew and Christian

57. Everyman edition, 297.
58. Act III, Scene V, lines 44-45. Transl. B.Q. Morgan (New York, 1955).

than man?
(Act II, Scene V, lines 106-108)

Thus even the membership in a 'folk' is for Lessing a matter of 'chance of birth'. These passages should be read in the light of Lessing's general adherence to an almost Spinoza-like belief in universal necessity, if not in Providence, which prompts one of his main characters in another play from the same period, *Emilia Galotti*, to declare: 'Accident is blasphemy. Nothing under the sun is accident' (Act IV, Scene III). Thus Lessing's accident of birth has clearly nothing to do with causal chance or indeterminism.

As far as English usage is concerned, the *Oxford English Dictionary* (s.v. Accident 7.) gives as its first instance a passage from Benjamin Disraeli's novel *Venetia* (1837), which speaks about 'all the brilliant accidents of birth, and beauty, and fortune' (I, i, 2). Here too the writer refers primarily to 'high birth' and the advantages of nobility rather than jointly to all our congenital circumstances. The quotations from Mill prior to the one from his *Autobiography* suggest that the phrase had not yet jelled into a stereotyped combination. But there seems to be little doubt that in the second half of the nineteenth century the idea had established itself. But what did it stand for at the time? All we can conclude thus far is that prior to Mill the idea of the accident of birth was one of the levers of religious and social criticism in the cause of a more rational, less prejudiced approach and of a fairer order of society based on non-accidental reason.

6.4 What Mill Meant by the 'Accident of Birth'

In the case of a thinker like Mill any attempt to explain his ideas from influences upon him would seem to be of limited value. 'Influences' are for him at best stimulants for his thought. They could not have flowed into him had there not been a channel waiting for them. Whatever ideas he finds in his environment are incorporated into his thought only in so far as he finds them congenial to his basic pattern. Only with this reservation does it make sense to look for influence on Mill's adoption of the idea of the accident of birth. Yet it may help in the understanding of his very meaning to examine briefly the climate which according to his own account surrounded his early development and which contained some of the first stimuli for his thought.

There is good reason to think that one of these supporting influences was that of the St. Simonian school in France. Mill himself, in discussing in his *Autobiography* the 'important transformation' which took place in his 'opinions and character' after the period of 'youthful propagandism' in the line of Benthamite radicalism and his 'mental crisis', credits the writers of this school 'more than any others' with having introduced him to 'a new model of political thinking'. Specifically he mentions their calling into question the institution of hereditary property and their principle of remunerating everybody according to his work:

> Their aim seemed to me desirable and rational, however their means might be inefficacious . . . I honoured them most of all for what they have been most cried down for —the boldness and freedom from prejudice with which they treated the subject of family, the most important of any . . . In proclaiming the perfect equality of men and women, and an entirely new order of things in regard to their relations with one another, the St. Simonians . . . have entitled themselves to the grateful remembrance of future generations.[59]

It is therefore of particular interest to consider those ideas of the Saint-Simonians that are related to the idea of accident of birth. Even though I have not come across this phrase in their more accessible writings, their basic principle of opposition to privilege based on birth shows the importance of such considerations for their entire scheme. Mill, who 'read nearly everything they wrote', must certainly have been aware of the fact that they 'demand the abolition of all privileges of birth without a single exception, together with the complete extinction of the right of inheritance, which is today the greatest of all privileges and includes every other.'[60]

According to F.A. Hayek, Mill even read the daily Saint-Simonian newspaper, the *Globe*,[61] whose masthead carried such aphorisms as 'All privileges of birth are abolished without exception'. Mill himself expressed this principle in his articles on *The Spirit of the*

59. *Autobiography*, Ch. V, 117 f.; *Works* I, 174.
60. Program of the Saint-Simonians addressed to the President of the Chamber of Deputies, published as Appendix to the second edition of the *Doctrine de Saint-Simon, Exposition* (1829-30).
61. J.S. Mill, *The Spirit of the Age* (Chicago, 1942), p. xxi-ii of Hayek's Introduction.

Age:

> There must be a moral and social revolution, which shall indeed take
> away no men's lives or property, but which shall leave to no man one
> fraction of unearned distinction or unearned importance. (p. 33)

In particular he called 'the predominance of the aristocratic classes,
the noble and the rich, in the English constitution . . . the great de-
moralizing agency in the country.'

While all this throws light on Mill's increasing emphasis on the
conception and even the meaning which he attached to the phrase
'accident of birth', it does not dispense us from a closer study of
its full import and its implications. This involves first of all a clarification of the sense of the two component parts of the central
phrase 'accident of birth'.

I shall begin with the relatively less problematic term 'birth'.
Actually, in his writings, Mill referred even more frequently to such
concrete circumstances as sex, race, skin, health, etc., to designate
such 'accidents'. But it is fairly obvious that all these are meant as
examples of congenital conditions, and that the term 'birth' covers
all those more or less specific hereditary circumstances in which
we find ourselves born.

To be sure, the emphasis on 'birth' in this context may seem a
little incongruous at our stage of scientific information. When birth
was considered something like a cosmic event synchronized with
the constellation of the zodiac, the event of the separation of the
mature foetus from its mother organism may have seemed a much
more cataclysmic event.[62] It would certainly make much more
sense in our day to focus on the accident of conception, or more
specifically, on the fertilization of the one ovum involved in each
ovulation by the several hundred million spermatozoa which it en-
counters, a circumstance which reduces the probability of any one
particular combination to less than one hundredth of a million.

But even this embryological accident is clearly not the beginning
of the origin of an individual organism in the gamble of bisexual
selection. Hence there would be little point in replacing the word
'birth' by a more scientific expression like 'accident of fertilization',

---

62. One might wonder whether the use of the term 'accident' in connection with the
word 'birth' did not imply an intentional challenge to astrological beliefs about the cosmic fatedness of the minutest details in our lives.

a substitution which might very well endanger the whole conception, since it would divert attention to a scientific area where accident has a much more questionable meaning. 'Birth' as used in the combination 'accident of birth' is simply the symbol for all sorts of circumstances in which a new organism finds itself at its start prior to any possibility of doing anything about them. There is no reason to doubt that this is the meaning which Mill had in mind.

We are on much more treacherous ground when we want to clarify the meaning of the term accident in this context. We certainly do not mean to imply that birth is accidental in one of those senses in which we say that accidents will happen or that it is always the unexpected that happens, i.e., accidents against which we may try to protect ourselves by accident insurance. Thus far, with the exception of some of our pessimistic humorists,[63] hardly anyone would classify birth as one of those hazards against which Lloyd's, let alone a social insurance scheme, would write out a policy, either for the innocent *nasciturus* or, more meaningfully, for the not so innocent parents.

(a) Accident as 'Accidens'

Even some of Mill's more careful though not uncritical interpreters seem to have been misled by the term accident. Thus Leslie Stephen,[64] perhaps the only one who gave any thought to Mill's meaning, assumed at once that in speaking about the 'accident of colour' and the 'accident of sex' Mill thought that these are 'accidental or superficial differences', 'mere accidents', and that he implies that 'the difference between men and women, Whites and Negroes, is 'accidental', that is, apparently removable by some change of outward circumstances.'

But this is hardly in line with Mill's expressed or implied opinions. For in the most pertinent (and most attacked) text on the issue, *The Subjection of Women,* Mill never goes so far as to deny all congenital differences between the sexes or to assert that these

---

63. See, e.g., the doleful reflection of the German poet Wilhelm Busch on the accidental unhappy ending of our alleged pre-natal bliss: 'But you forgot to keep good track. And –plop– you're born and can't go back.' *(Die Haarbeutel.* Introduction. Translation by Bayard Quincy Morgan.)

64. *The English Utilitarians* (London, 1900). III, 282 f.

are merely superficial. He merely maintains that we are still ignorant of their extent in the absence of sufficient empirical and experimental evidence. Moreover, he accepts the verdict of the 'medical practitioners' about the differences in bodily constitution (Ch. I). And there is no reason to believe that he considers physical differences in health and strength between different individuals as removable by a change in the environment. It is true that Mill discusses the possibility that 'at some future, and, it may be hoped, not distant period, equal freedom and an equally independent social position [may] come to be possessed by both [sexes] and their differences of character are either removed or totally altered.'[65] But this possibility would not yet entitle him to prejudge the issue by calling these differences 'accidents'. Besides, Mill's proposal of a plural vote for the intellectually superior suggests that the considers some of the congenital differences as more than 'superficial'. Also, it would be strange if a believer in individuality and variety like Mill should consider congenital differences as removable and, what is more, worth removing. Finally, if we turn from sex to other congenital differences like race ('skin'), or health, it becomes clear that Mill cannot be thinking of them as accidental in the sense of superficial and removable. Clearly, then, the 'accident of birth' does not mean that congenital circumstances are all 'accidentia', unessential modifications in contrast to essential properties.

(b) Accident as Causal Chance

How far do Mill's own writings throw light on his use of the phrase? One obvious possibility would be to look into Mill's discussion of chance in his *Logic*[65] all the more since the phrase 'chance of birth' occurs quite frequently as a synonym for 'accident of birth'.

In considering Mill's logical doctrine of chance one has to be aware of his firm conviction that 'whatever happens is the result of some law; is an effect of causes, and could have been predicted from a knowledge of the existence of those causes and their laws'.[66] Consequently for Mill a chance that conflicts with causal law is inconceivable. No wonder that his logical discussion of the subject

---

65. *System of Logic*, Book III, Ch. V, paragraph 3.
66. *Ibid.*, Book III, Ch. XVII, paragraph 2.

goes under the title 'Of Chance and its Elimination'. The outcome
of this elimination is that the only defensible conception of chance
is that of a 'coincidence of a phenomenon, from which we have no
ground to infer a uniformity; the occurrence of a phenomenon in
certain circumstances, without our having reason on that account
to infer that it will happen again in these circumstances'. Of such
pure coincidences, however, we can never be quite sure. There may
always be some still unknown causal connection between them.
Whatever remains of chance after our eliminating efforts is clearly
only a relative matter: relative to causal, i.e., invariable and unconditional circumstances that have no connection with the event under
consideration, and relative to our ignorance of any other connection. In other words, chance is nothing but a sign of our causal
ignorance *pro tem.*

If we tried to apply this conception of chance to instances of
the accident of birth, it would make some sense to consider congenital conditions as coincidental with certain other conditions of
our environment such as the weather or celestial constellations. In
this sense, being female may be coincidental in relation to being
American, but not to having an even number of chromosomes. Even
here, according to Mill, we would have to make a reservation in view
of causal connections of which in our ignorance we are not yet
aware. In any case, the accident of birth interpreted in the light of
this conception would be a relative matter, whose relativity has
been reduced considerably in the light of our new knowledge of
genetics and embryology since Mill's days.

However, close consideration of the examples of the accidents of
birth in Mill's pertinent writings would make it plain that he was
not concerned with mere coincidences, with the not yet eliminated
vanishing penumbra of our causal knowledge, in short, with a merely
relative concept, based on our ignorance. When he speaks of skin
or sex as accidents of birth, he certainly does not think that any
amount of causal knowledge will divest them of their 'accidental'
character. Even if we should be able to predict the sex of a baby,
his sex would still be an accident of birth in Mill's and even, I submit, in anybody else's sense. Mill's scientific concept of chance as
coincidence is irrelevant to the problem.

There is, to be sure, one passage in *On Liberty* which might at
first sight suggest that Mill's concept of accident of birth is related

to his idea of scientific cause. For in speaking about the 'mere accident' which has decided for man which authority he will trust among many on this globe that compete for his allegiance he states: 'The same causes which make him a Churchman in London would have made him a Buddhist or a Confucian in Pekin'.[67] Are we to understand 'the same causes' here in the sense of the same 'invariable and unconditional antecedents', i.e., Mill's definition of cause? To begin with, this would give rise to a conflict with the law of uniformity according to which the same cause is always followed by the same effects. Besides, it seems hard to conceive even of ways in which such a causal hypothesis could ever be tested in accordance with Mill's canons of experimental inquiry. For such reasons it seems to me clear that Mill was really not concerned here with a causal problem, but with undermining the naive self-righteousness of the orthodox believer. I submit that here 'same causes' is to be understood in the sense of 'the same type of causes'. It is not so easy to interpret Mill's meaning of the phrase 'mere accident'. But it seems to me more than likely that what Mill had in mind was again the 'accident of birth'.

(c) Accident as a Moral Category

If then 'accident of birth' means neither inessential nor causal chance, what else can we say in the absence of any fully explanation of the phrase by Mill himself? At this point our one and only chance of clarification would reside in a study of the main contexts in which Mill speaks about the accident of birth. These contexts, as I shall try to show, are invariably discussions of justice in the distribution of advantages and benefits on a social or cosmic scale.

Thus the very first example of the 'accident of sex' in the *Principles of Political Economy,* quoted above, is preceded by the sentence:[68]

> That there should be no option (for women), no other career possible for the great majority of women (than as wife and mother) except in the humbler departments of life is a flagrant social injustice.

67. *On Liberty*, Ch. II (Everyman edition, 80).
68. See above, 1 on page 109.

But what does he mean here by 'social injustice'? It is well known that Mill's treatise, beginning with Book II on 'Distribution', is shot through with considerations of moral and social desirability, which throw considerable light on his conceptions of social justice and injustice. Thus, in discussing the problem of a fair distribution of property he refers to the possibility that

> in the original apportionment (of property) compensation might be made for the injuries of nature, and the balance redressed by assigning to the less robust members of the community advantages in the distribution sufficient to put them on a par with the rest. (*Ibid.*, 202)

Likewise in the discussion of the problem of fair remuneration he criticizes distribution according to work done as

> really just only in so far as the more or less of the work is a matter of choice: when it depends on natural difference of strength or capacity, this prinicple of remuneration is in itself an injustice: it is giving to those who have; assigning most to those who are already most favoured by nature. (*Ibid.*, 211 f.)

The social justice, then, which Mill contrasts with 'accidents of birth such as sex' is a principle which is to make up for undeserved handicaps in our natural start.

What throws even more light on Mill's conception of social justice and indirectly on that of the accident of birth is his perhaps most original and influential economic doctrine: the 'unearned increment'. While David Ricardo was the first to identify the factor of economic rent as an economic phenomenon, it was Mill who attached to it the censuring label 'unearned' and suggested the moral need and justification for doing something about it.[69] Mill's objection to the rent is that it constitutes

> a kind of income which constantly tends to increase, without any exertion or sacrifice on the part of the owners: those owners constituting a class in the community whom the natural course of things progressively enriches, consistently with complete passiveness on their own part . . . . (If the state should appropriate this increase of wealth, or part of it, as

69. See, e.g., Lewis E. Haney, *History of Economic Thought.* Fourth edition. (New York, 1940), 467. See also Mill's 'Papers on Land Tenure' in *Dissertations and Discussions* (New York, 1875), V, 225 and 280.

it arises), this would merely be applying an accession of wealth created by circumstances to the benefit of society, instead of allowing it to become unearned appendage to the riches of a particular class. Now this is actually the case with rent . . . . (The landlords) grow richer, as it were in their sleep, without working, risking, or economizing. What claim have they, on the general principle of social justice, to this accession of riches? [70]

In fact, Mill is even aware that the same considerations apply in principle to all congenital equipment of the individual:

The extra gains which any producer or dealer obtains through superior talents for business . . . are very much of a similar kind. (*Ibid.*, 476)

It also accounts for his proposal for a drastic reform in the law of inheritance

If it be said, as it may with truth, that those who have inherited the savings of others have an advantage which they may have in no way deserved over the industrious whose predecessors have not left them anything; I not only admit, but strenuously contend that this unearned advantage should be curtailed, as much as is consistent with justice to those who thought fit to dispose of their savings by giving them to their descendants. (*Ibid.*, 219)

Thus Mill considers as unjust any advantage that is not based on individual desert. Such an advantage is morally accidental, be it based on natural facts or on social developments which are none of the individual's own doing.

Of later writings that confirm this interpretation of Mill's conception of the accident of birth I refer to the text of the *Subjection of Women*, and specifically to the fourth passage quoted above (n.4), which contrasts the 'fatality of birth' with conditions which can be overcome by exertions or change of circumstances. That justice is the real opposite to the accident of birth is also expressed in such sentences as the following:

Think what is is to a boy to grow up to manhood in the belief that, without any merit or any exertion of his own, though he may be the most

---

70. *Principles of Political Economy*, 817 f.

> frivolous and empty or the most ignorant and stolid of mankind, by the mere fact of being born a male he is by right the superior of all and every one of an entire half of the human race . . . (Everyman, 296)

> Human beings do not grow up from childhood in the possession of un-earned distinctions without pluming themselves upon them. Those whom privileges not acquired by their merit, and which they feel to be dispro-portioned to it, inspire with additional humility are always the few, and the best few. The rest are only inspired with pride, and the worst sort of pride, that which values itself upon accidental advantages, not of its own achieving. (297)

The contrast between accident and the justice of desert is equally plain in Mill's posthumous essay on *Nature*, not only from the second passages quoted above but also by such as the following:

> If the law of creation were justice and the Creator omnipotent . . . no human being would have a worse lot than another without worse deserts; accident or favouritism would have no part in such a world.[71]

There is the equally impressive passage from the *Autobiography* where distribution of the produce of labour according to the accident of birth is contrasted to 'an acknowledged principle of justice based on industriousness and work.' ((5) on page 109).

To Mill, then, accident in the context of the accident of birth is something which is determined by its relation to the non-accidental standard of justice. The congenital conditions of human existence are in this sense mere accidents, devoid of moral justification. They demand the kind of rectification which Mill may have expressed best in a letter in which he refers to one of these conditions, which is, incidentally, beyond all possible elimination by modification of the environment:

> I do not think it indisputable that the physically strongest must neces-sarily be dominant over the physically weaker in civilised society, since I look upon it as the fundamental purpose of civilisation to redress as much as possible all such natural inequalities, and I think the degree of which they have been redressed one of the best tests of civilisation.[72]

71. *Three Essays on Religion*, 37 f.
72. Letter to R. Russell (written 'By Helen Taylor'), 2nd April 1867, in *The Letters of John Stuart Mill*, edited by Hugh S.R. Eliot (London, 1919), II, 81.

I conclude that what Mill means by the accident of birth and of specific conditions of birth has nothing to do with causal considerations; this conclusion is corroborated by the fact that Mill uses the term 'accident' interchangeably with 'fatality', a term which makes it plain that it is subject to the strictest of causal laws. Instead, 'accident' as used by Mill in his practical philosophy constitutes a moral category related to the fact that there is no moral connection of desert between condition at birth and moral worth. Accident of birth might thus be defined as any circumstance in a person's congenital condition not based upon principles of just distribution such as desert or guilt. It is accidental in the sense that there is no 'necessary', morally justifiable connection between our actual condition at birth and our moral claims. Whatever causal factors like heredity may have led to this condition, they are morally without weight.

The accident of birth is thus fundamentally a moral category. But it is not so in the sense of utilitarian ethics. For no other human being is directly responsible for its observance. Its addressee is not man but the cosmos. Its primary requirements are the balance between man's basic physical equipment and his moral claims. It is only in so far as the claims of this justice are not met by the cosmos that society has to make an effort to redress them. To this extent this balance becomes the burden of our reforming efforts, social, political, and economic, and in particular of that type of individualistic socialism which contains Mill's final word on economic reform.

It appears, then, that the conception of the accident of birth is ultimately related to Mill's ardent concern for justice, a concern which reaches even deeper than his concern for happiness and charitable philanthropy. The following passage from his early essay on 'The Claims of Labor' (1845) is a particularly vivid expression of this passionate concern:

> Let it be remembered . . . that we live in a political age in which the desire of political rights, or the abuse of political privileges by the possessors of them, are the foremost ideas in the minds of most reading men: an age, too, the whole spirit of which instigates everyone to demand fair play for helping himself, rather than to seek or expect help from others. In such an age and in the treatment of minds so predisposed, justice is the one needful thing rather than kindness. We may at least say that kindness will be little appreciated, will have very little of the effect

of kindness upon objects of it, so long as injustice, or what they cannot but deem to be injustice, is persevered in.[73]

6.5 The Accident of Birth and Utilitarianism

How does this conception of the accident of birth and the implied conception of cosmic justice fit into Mill's general philosophy of justice? More important, how does it comport with his utilitarian moral philosophy?

It is certainly a significant part of Mill's intellectual biography that, according to Helen Taylor's 'Introductory Notice' to the *Three Essays on Religion*, Mill wrote a separate essay on 'Justice' in the years between 1850 and 1858; in fact she mentions this title ahead of those of 'Utility' and 'Liberty'. According to F.A. Hayek[74] he had conceived of such an essay during a Channel crossing in 1854. Yet he reports to Harriet on June 30:

> I do not find the essay on Justice goes on well. I wrote a good long piece of it at Quimper, but it is too metaphysical, and not what is most wanted — but I must finish it now in that vein and then strike into another.

It would seem that the topic was one of major importance for Mill at that time, considering the fact that he took it up during the period of his active tuberculosis, when he and Harriet had laid out an emergency plan for the works which he wanted to write before his expected early death. However, the refractory essay does not seem to have been completed but survives only in the version of the final chapter of *Utilitarianism*. Here its function is to meet one of the major objections to utilitarianism based on its supposed inability to account for and support demands for justice.

Indications of Mill's own difficulties may be found in a passage from the *Principles of Political Economy* where he had declared that remuneration according to work done is 'in itself an injustice', but nevertheless 'highly expedient'.[75] Around the same time Mill had pleaded the justice of socialism 'against the unjust distribution of social advantages' based on the accident of birth. But he had not

73. *Dissertations and Discussions* (Boston, 1863-68), II, 290.
74. *John Stuart Mill and Harriet Taylor* (Chicago, 1951), 207 f.
75. *Ibid.*, 212.

claimed its expediency, as can be gathered from this passage on 'the existing order of society':

> No rational person will maintain it to be abstractedly just that a small minority of mankind should be born to the enjoyment of all the external advantages which life can give, without earning them by any merit or acquiring them by any exertion of their own, while the immense majority are condemned from their birth to a life of never-ending, never-inter-mitting toil, requited by a bare and, in general, a precarious subsistence. It is impossible to contend that this is in itself just. It is possible to contend that it is expedient . . . [76]

However, it would seem that after rethinking the matter in the essay on *Utilitarianism* (1863), Mill decided he could integrate the valid parts of justice into his philosophy of 'utility'. Thus when he finally took up the case for women's suffrage before Parliament (Session of May 20, 1867) he based it 'entirely on expediency', and specifically on 'that important branch of expediency called justice'.[77]

How far is this attempt to reduce justice to 'expediency', and the demands of social justice to the principle of Utility, convincing? The answer to this question requires a discussion of Ch. V of *Utilitarianism*, 'On the Connection between Justice and Utility', the survivor of the 'Essay on Justice' of 1854.

Here Mill begins his analysis of justice in true empirical fashion with an analysis and description of the concrete situations in which we talk about justice and, even more frequently, complain about injustice. Five types of injustice are distinguished in this way:

1. depriving a person of his personal liberty, his property or any other thing which belongs to him by law (legal right);
2. taking or withholding from a person that to which he has a moral right (which concept, however, Mill leaves undefined and unexplained, much as one might desire elaboration, both on general and practical grounds);
3. withholding from a person 'that (whether good or evil) which he deserves' and letting him 'obtain a good, or be made to undergo evil which he does not deserve . . . the clearest and most em-

---

76. 'Vindication of the French Revolution of February 1848' (April 1849); *Dissertations and Discussions*, III, 59.
77. Hansard, *Parliamentary Records*. Third Series. Vol. 187, p. 817.

phatic form in which the idea of justice is conceived by the general mind. Speaking in a general way, a person is understood to deserve good if he does right, evil, if he does wrong';
4. breaking faith with anyone;
5. being partial toward one of several parties.

Justice emerges from this investigation as 'a name for certain moral requirements which, regarded collectively, stand higher in the scale of social utility, and are therefore of more paramount obligation than any others'. But in the process it became necessary to discredit and discount some of the most insistent demands for justice, notably those for fair punishment and for fair remuneration. Mill justifies this retrenchment by the ambiguity and even the self-contradictoriness of these demands. 'Social utility alone can decide the preference'.

My major concern in the present context is how compatible this utilitarian trimming down of justice is with Mill's conception of the accident of birth and with its underlying concept of cosmic justice.

Obviously neither case 1 (legal rights) nor case 4 (promise keeping) has anything to do with this situation. At best the injustice of the accident of birth can be argued in terms of case 2 (denial of moral rights), case 3 (neglect of desert), or case 5 (partiality). The 'accident of sex', for instance, might seem to interfere with a woman's moral right to free opportunity, with her claim to everything that she deserves on the basis of honest effort, and with her claim to impartial consideration of her case regardless of her mere physical characteristics where these are irrelevant to the issue at hand.

How far can these three bases for our considerations of cosmic justice and the accident of birth be derived from the general principle of utility? A good deal would depend on whether we interpret the principle of utility in the strict sense of the greatest pleasure of the greatest number or in the wider sense which would give preference to the 'better' dissatisfaction of a Socrates compared with the more intense dissatisfaction of the happy fool, in which case happiness would be nearly identical with perfect development of the personality.

Can we then derive a moral right, such as the one to equal opportunity, from its utility for society? Specifically, would there be more pleasure all round if the accident of birth did not discriminate among humans? It would, as usual with the hedonic calculus, seem hard if not impossible to make any definite predictions on this point. We would certainly have to take into consideration the minus of pleasure among the now overprivileged, sometimes a majority, as well as the frequent lack of displeasure among the underprivileged who have become used to their loss of freedom and may even enjoy the lack of responsibility and need for choices under a benevolent paternalism. At least it would seem highly dubious that equal opportunity for people of unequal susceptibility for pleasure, for Polyannas and Scrooges, would result in the maximum total of pleasure. Only the fiction of 'everyone to count for one' in regard to pleasure could protect us from such doubts. For instance, in the interest of maximum pleasure it might be advisable to give a headstart to all those who are most likely to add more to the sum total of pleasure. But such headstarts could hardly be reconciled with the moral rights of each individual. Even if, with Mill, we should include with happiness such values as individuality *(On Liberty)*, progressive development *(Considerations on Representative Government)*, and dignity *(Utilitarianism)*, it would seem far from obvious that giving an equal opportunity to everybody would be a more effective device than giving a headstart to those having a better chance to achieve these goals.

This would seem to hold even more in the case of justice and injustice based on desert (case 3), the hinge of Mill's conception of the accident of birth. For one thing, the ideas of 'earned' and 'unearned' can hardly be reduced to those of expediency and productiveness of pleasure and happiness. But it would seem even doubtful that desert is a necessary consequent of such productiveness, a fact of which Mill was aware when he stated that

> proportioning of remuneration on work done . . . when it depends on natural differences of strength or capacity . . . is itself an injustice: it is giving to those who are already most favoured by nature. Considered, however, as a compromise with the selfish type of character formed by the present standard of morality and fostered by the existing social institutions, it is highly expedient; and until education shall have been entirely regenerated, it is far more likely to prove immediately success-

ful than any attempt at a higher ideal. (*Principles of Political Economy*, 212)

Whether or not a person deserves reward in the form of remuneration, or recognition ('honors'), can hardly be made dependent on whether the consequence of his efforts is conducive to happiness. This outcome is obviously only partly under his control. At best it would therefore make sense to make desert dependent on the effort to bring about such happiness. However, this factor of effort as the independent variable for desert would introduce a new and even more elusive unit into the utilitarian calculus, for which Mill has not made any provision. Yet this is clearly the crucial point for the conception of accident of birth which is essentially related to considerations of merit and guilt. What sense would it make to judge the question of moral accident in terms of utility? Isn't the cosmic justice to which the concept of accident of birth is related liable to the same type of contradictions which make Mill abandon justice in the cases of punishment and remuneration in favor of utility? But in that case, what would become of Mill's battle against social injustice regardless of utility?

Finally, there is the justice of impartiality (case 5). Can impartiality be reduced to expediency? Can it be said that impartiality is always linked up with expediency? That the first question would have to be denied, as long as the ordinary meanings of these terms are left intact, would seem to need little proof. As to the possible connection between the two, we would of course have to take full account of the wider implications of expediency in the utilitarian sense, such as consequences in the long run and the number of people benefited. It would be rash to assert that impartiality is always either expedient or inexpedient. Our narrow personal interest would certainly often favor partiality. But the larger the group to be considered, the less expedient would it seem to be. Besides, the question 'partial to whom?' would enter. Partiality in favor of the high and mighty might very well increase our personal chances. The partiality of the weathervane might be better policy than honest impartiality. In short, the expediency of impartiality is certainly far from self-evident.

I conclude that Mill's utilitarian theory of justice does not fit the conception of justice which permeates his own social reform program. In particular, it does not fit the conception of cosmis justice which underlies his conception of the accident of birth. Mill himself saw that in order to make our everyday notion of justice coincide with that of expediency, we would have to abandon part of the former as an irrational leftover based on our thirst for vengeance. But the question arises whether this same sacrifice would not have to be made in the case of the idea of cosmis justice. In that case, what would become of the idea of the accident of birth?

If, then, the quesion arises as to which deserves preference, Mill's theory of justice or his operative conception of justice expressed in his idea of the accident of birth, my own preference is frankly for the latter. It is true that Mill never clarified it sufficiently and that much more will have to be done to state its full meaning and its metaphysical and moral implications.[78] But Mill more than any other philosopher before and after him gave vivid expression to the fundamental moral idea involved. What is more, he put it to work in his social philosophy and his political action. At a time when the problem of the relation between the overprivileged and the underprivileged has reached new and frightening proportions on a world scale, this part of his work must not be forgotten.

78. For a first attempt see my article 'A Defense of human Equality', *Philosophical Review*, LIII (1944), 115 ff. and this volume no. 7.

7. A DEFENSE OF HUMAN EQUALITY[79]

> In society all are equal. No society can be founded upon anything but the concept of equality, never upon that of freedom. It is equality that I want to find in society, freedom, that is the moral freedom to subordinate myself, I bring along anyway. The society which I enter is therefore bound to tell me: You shall be equal with all the rest of us. All it can add is: We wish you would also be free; that is, we wish you to renounce your privileges with full conviction, by free and intelligent assent. (Translated from J.W. Goethe, Maximen und Reflexionen, *Werke*, Weimar 1887 ff., vol. 42, 2. Abteilung, p. 234)

7.1 The Challenge

'Equality of all men is the biggest lie ever told'. Thus Nietzsche summed up his great indictment of the 'self-evident truth that all men are created equal'.[80] To him the idea of human equality was nothing but the expression of the 'slave's revolt in morals'. Its first manifestation was the 'Christian dynamite'[81] of the idea of human equality before God. Its final outcome is modern secular democracy.

Nietzsche and his immediate followers inside and outside philosophy were by no means the only challengers of human equality. Today his denunciation is echoed by a worldwide campaign against

79. This paper was read in part at the Meeting of the Western Division of the American Philosophical Association at Madison in 1942. I wish to acknowledge the many helpful criticisms which I have received in the formulation of this article from Professors Brand Blanshard, Richard B. Brandt, and Maurice Mandelbaum, of Swarthmore College, and from Dr. Arnold Brecht of the New School of Social Research, as well as the practical help of several unnamed friends.
80. *Gesammelte Schriften* (Musarion edition) XV 488; XVI 200.
81. *Ibid.* VIII 313.

Reprinted by permission from the *Philosophical Review* 53 (1944) 101-124.

what is considered to be the foremost buttress of democratic philosophy. In fact, human equality represents the favorite target of antidemocratic propaganda and argumentation. And human inequality is one of the basic articles of faith which the fascist rulers try to hammer into the minds of totalitarian youth.[82] Thus Italian fascism in its fulminations against the 'absurd conventional lie of political equalitarianism . . . asserts the irremediable and fertile and beneficient inequality of men, who cannot be levelled by any such mechanical and extrinsic device as universal suffrage'.[83] And National Socialism holds the 'Jewish theory of the equality of all men' responsible for the 'criminal absurdity of training a born half-ape (i.e., a Negro) until one believes a lawyer has been made of him, while millions of members of the highest culture race have to remain in entirely unworthy positions'.[84] It is not our task to decide whether it was not precisely the steamroller of authoritarian centralization and coordination *(Gleichschaltung)* which has led to an equalization much more sweeping than any democracy would have dreamed of. But, however that may be, this does not affect the seriousness of the challenge to the idea of human equality. How, if at all, can it be met?

One may perhaps think that the whole anti-equalitarian campaign is based upon a grotesque misrepresentation of the idea of equality. Yet it cannot be denied that the champions of human equality are partly responsible for such misinterpretations. Some of their formulations read indeed as if all individuals were born with exactly the same physical and mental equipment and as if all individual differences were only products of different environments. The situation is in fact so serious that some of the advocates of democracy are on the point of abandoning the whole doctrine of equality.[85]

82. See, e.g., *The Nazi Primer, Official Handbook of the Hitler Youth*. Chapter I: The Unlikeliness of Man, pp. 5-12, Harper Brothers, 1938.

83. Benito Mussolini, Article on 'Fascism' in the *Enciclopaedia Italiana;* translated in *The Corporate State.*

84. Adolf Hitler, *Mein Kampf;* translation (Reynal Hitchcock, New York, 1939) 639; also Alfred Rosenberg, *Der Mythos des 20. Jahrhunderts* (1934) 202, 669.

85. Thus George Morgan Jr. in a significant recent article on 'Human Equality' (*Ethics* LIII 115-120) infers first —as a result of a trenchant analysis of seven 'axiological' and four 'pragmatic' theories of equality, all of which he finds wanting— that 'relevance, equality of consideration, and the sacredness of life are the only universally valid forms of equality'. His final conclusion, however, is that 'the whole notion of equality is, after

7.2 Unravelling the Problem

Our first task will be a clear statement of the real issue. For rhetorical pathos and stereotyped slogans have blurred the discussion to such an extent that the opponents mostly talk at cross purposes.

There is first the difference between *equality as a fact* and *equality as an ideal.* This distinction may appear so obvious that it should have occurred to anyone who considers the question at all seriously. Yet most anti-equalitarians seem to think at once that the principle of equality was meant as a statement about factual equality. That may have been true of the celebrated French triad of 'Liberty, Equality and Fraternity'.[86] The nineteenth century brought at any rate a decided shift from equality as an asserted fact to equality as a postulated[87] ideal. This ideal in itself may be questioned, but it certainly does not conflict with the fact of existing inequalities. For facts are neither sufficient proof nor sufficient disproof of ideals.

A second distinction is perhaps less obvious, that between *actual* and *potential* equalities. Beings that are actually unequal may still be potentially equal. It may often be a rather elusive puzzle to determine whether such an unactualized potentiality exists. But there are clearly cases, chiefly in biology, where experimental methods, by eliminating the inequalities of environments, show conclusively that, e.g., certain organisms are potentially equal and actually different only as a result of different climatic conditions.

---

all, a somewhat cold and external thing which tends to drop out of focal consciousness as human relationships deepen in intimacy . . .' What is to take its place is the 'reality of comradeship in the trenches or in the cellars of London or in any of the deeper crises of man's existence; it is the sense of solidarity and communion ...' I confess I fail to see how such a solution offers any better prospects than the doctrine of equality. For, unfortunately, the totalitarians deny just as violently any solidarity and communion among all the members of the human race as they oppose human equality.

86. The same holds for such staunch defenders of the idea of equality as the American John Taylor in his noteworthy controversy with John Addams, the advocate of natural inequality, in which he stated quite definitely and explicitly that the doctrine of human equality does not assert 'equality of duties'. (P.R. Anderson and M. Fisch, ed. *Philosophy in America,* 224).

87. Cf. the illuminating account by T.V. Smith, *The American Philosophy of Equality* (Chicago 1927) Chapter iv; also R.H. Tawney, *Equality* (London 1931) 52 f.

Even more important is the distinction between equalities and inequalities according to how *essential* or *unessential* the strata of human existence are to which they refer. Equality and inequality are both relations. According to a well established theory, relations always exist with reference to specific 'respects'. Thus things may be equal with respect to weights but not with respect to shape; and persons may be equal in fortune but unequal in character. Equality before God, in one of its possible meanings, seems to refer to such an equality in a special respect. Some of these respects are obviously quite superficial, peripheral, unessential, such as color of hair or eyes or height of body as such; others, such as physical and mental constitution, character, intelligence, energy, sociability, concern much more fundamental strata of human nature. The decisive question, therefore, will be whether the obvious inequalities between men reach the fundamental strata of the human personality; and, if they do reach these strata, how wide is the range of variations within them?

One type of this distinction between equalities according to their different respects is of particular significance for our specific problem. Human equality may refer primarily to the descriptive characteristics of human nature like height, weight, etc. The question of this *descriptive* equality has to be distinguished from the question whether men are equal or unequal in their *values,* as expressed, e.g., in their contributions to civilization and, ultimately, to the universe as a whole, and again from a third question, that of their equality with respect to *rights (or freedoms) and duties.* Finally, there is a kind of equality which can be designated best by the term *equality in dignity;* this equality would mean that humans, regardless of their contributions to a larger whole, have a certain common rank by virtue of which they possess a claim to equal respect and consideration.[88]

These four issues are largely independent of each other. Although equals in descriptive characteristics would generally be equals in values as well, it is by no means certain that unequals in descriptive characteristics would have unequal values: men and women, though

---

88. For the concept of equality in dignity see Leonard Nelson (*Kritik der praktischen Vernunft.* Göttingen, 1916, pp. 132, 520), where dignity itself is defined as the 'claim of a person to consideration of his interests'.

descriptively unequal, might still have the same human value. Similarly, persons of unequal value might possess the same rights and duties, not only before the law but before the court of ethics as well: the equal 'rights' of persons standing in line at a counter may illustrate this. Again, people might even have unequal claims to public benefits, for instance, to a higher education, and still be equal in dignity, i.e., in their ultimate ranking and in their claims to full and impartial consideration.

The distinction between equality as a fact and equality as an ideal postulate is certainly far from new.[89] But the more specific issues of equality in value, of equality in moral right and duty, and of equality in dignity, have not yet been sufficiently heeded and kept apart. Nor have all of these distinctions been fully utilized.

7.3 Human Inequalities and Human Equalities

It is not the purpose of this discussion to give a full answer to all these questions. That would presuppose a complete study of the human structure, of human values, of human rights and duties, of human dignity and of human destination, and, moreover, a determination of their relative significance within the framework of human nature. This would seem to be one of the major tasks of a philosophical anthropology. Here I shall merely indicate some of the more obvious results which the utilization of our distinctions can yield. I claim that, once these distinctions have been properly observed, these results can be fully established, either by direct insight or by deductive reasoning.

There is no total or partial *equality in descriptive characteristics* among human beings, neither an actual nor a potential one. It is not only in the subhuman sphere that biology gives conclusive evidence of congenital inequality. Human genetics confirms that, except for the case of identical twins, men fail to be potentially equal, that inequalities exist in the very germ plasm of human beings, inequalities which cannot be accounted for by different environment or by different personal choices. As far as the mental equip-

---

89. Cf., *e.g.*, T.V. Smith, *loc. cit.* and the literature quoted by him. Also Leonard Nelson, *System der philosophischen Rechtslehre und Politik* (Leipzig, 1924) 331 and Arnold Brecht, 'The Search for Absolutes' in *Social Research* VII (1940) 215 ff.

ment is concerned, intelligence tests are hardly needed to prove the fact of inequality. It is true that men still have enough in common to preserve the unity of the human species; and, generally, what they have in common belongs to a more fundamental stratum of human nature than their perhaps more striking inequalities. But even in these common characteristics of man we find differences in degree which sometimes amount to differences in quality, and that, to be sure, even among normal persons.[90]

But is there is not, at least for every religious person, some kind of descriptive equality in what has often been called the equality before God, before whom, it is said, all our differences become insignificant? Unfortunately, this idea of equality before God, apart from its other presuppositions, is far from clear in its meaning. In spite of its present popularity it has been very little analyzed, either by historians or by systematic theologians. Thus there seems to be little hope that such a theological concept could restore human equality to its former dignity of a self-evident truth extending to the whole of human nature.

This leaves descriptive equality among human beings in a rather precarious position. One might hope for a better line of defense in human *equality-in-value*. However, even this hope is on the whole mistaken. Assuming that there is such a thing as objective value independent of the value-perceiving subject,[91] can we seriously doubt that men possess higher or lower values depending upon

90. The difficulty of appraising the relative importance of the common features of humans as compared with their distinguishing characteristics is the crucial difficulty for Paul Weiss' courageous attempt to buttress the 'principle of human equality', as expressed in the right 'to exercise the functions characteristic of beings of the human kind, equally deserving of human shelter and food, of an opportunity to grow, feel, think and know, and to protection against injury, disease, and unnecessary pain,' by the argument that all men belong to one natural group. ('Democracy and the Rights of Man' in *Science, Philosophy, and Religion, Second Symposium.* New York. 1942; see also Morris R. Cohen's critical remarks p. 288). This attempt leaves it, furthermore, unexplained how the fact of such membership in the group entails the *obligation* of treating them as equals. The additional premises needed for such a deduction require at least explicit formulation.

91. Recently, Hans Kelsen (*Vom Wesen der Demokratie*, Tübingen, 2nd ed., 1929) and especially Gustav Radbruch ('Le relativisme dans la philosophie de droit' in *Archives de philosophie du droit et de sociologie juridique* IV, 1934) have argued that a relativism of values can supply an adequate basis for the absolute postulates of equality, democracy, and related ideals. But that can hardly be achieved without additional absolute standards, which are introduced here surreptitiously. The more obvious consequence of an axiolo-

whether they are, for instance, more or less integrated and forceful personalities, more or less efficient in their work and thought, ugly or fair in their appearance, graceful or clumsy in their manners? Is there really no ultimate difference between the person who, in his unique value, is practically irreplaceable, and those who, in Schopenhauer's terms, are only mass products (*Fabrikware*) of nature? Of course, it might be extremely difficult to evaluate these differences impartially. And that in itself may be an important argument for treating men as equals in spite of the fact that we believe them to be unequal in value. But some of these differences are certainly pronounced enough to allow of general assessment and recognition.

However, it must not be overlooked that among the moral values there are *some* which involve a potential equality in one important respect. If we exert ourselves for a certain cause with all the energy at our disposal, however weak it may be, the outcome of such exertion will certainly vary. But the intrinsic ethical value of our effort, as distinguished from the value of the *result,* will not depend upon the latter. Nor will this value be dependent upon the actual goodness of our cause. If the agent was in good faith and was, without undue negligence, mistaken about the goodness of his goal, such error will certainly affect the value of the *act* which proceeds from his effort. Intrinsically this effort will have the same value as if it were spent on a truly good cause. The moral value of our effort, then, depends exclusively upon the question how much of our momentary intellectual and moral energies was spent in the attempt to ascertain and to realize the right goal. The absolute amount of our energies and of our effort is immaterial. It is only the relation between them which counts. Now these effort-values reflect also upon the agent. It is this fact which gives every agent equal access to the moral values consequent on moral effort. In the court of this particular value he faces no handicaps. Everybody who is able to run at all is given an equal chance. The tasks assigned to different

gical relativism is the reckless self-assertion of one's own subjectivity in claiming one's superiority over anybody else, as Fascist activistic subjectivism practices it so blatantly. To admit that other subjectivisms would have just as much right as oneself already presupposes the acknowledgement of an objective standard above the parties, i.e., of some kind of justice which demands the consideration of the subjectivistic claims on an equal level.

individuals may be very different. In fact, the higher the abilities, the more exacting will be the demands; the smaller the means the more lenient will be the expectations. All that matters is: how great were our efforts in proportion to our unequal and varying momentary endowment?

However, these values are by no means the only human values. It may even be questioned whether they are man's *supreme* values. Nor is it certain that they are the only *moral* values. Besides, the potentiality of equality in moral values can never guarantee that men's moral scores are actually equal.

Suppose, then, that men are equal neither in descriptive characteristics nor in value. Would it follow that they ought not to have the same rights and duties? First of all, facts in themselves can never sufficiently justify either rights or duties; not even values can, at least not immediately. Thus the fact of inequality in descriptive characteristics as well as in values does not yet entail inequality of rights and duties. Actually, the situation does not allow of sweeping answers. It is true that equals generally ought to have equal rights and duties. But if it comes to unequals we have to consider that certain rights and duties depend upon *specific* qualifications which, as a matter of fact, are not equally distributed, for instance those of studying and teaching; it is a fatal misunderstanding of the postulates of equality if, for the sake of equal justice, a gifted pupil is not offered the opportunity for a more rapid and individual advance than his less gifted companion. On the other hand there are a good many differences, and even rather fundamental ones, which are unessential with regard to educational and other rights and duties, for instance sex differences; relevant in this case is only the intellectual aptitude, and this does not appear to depend upon sex. In other words, inequality in rights and duties among unequals presupposes that their inequality is relevant to the particular rights and duties in question. In this connection is should also be remembered that greater gifts do by no means always entail greater rights, as is often so glibly assumed, as a rule they mean decreased privileges as a consequence of increased duties: 'And to whomsoever much is given, of him shall much be required.'[92]

92. Luke XII 48.

On this basis, then, I maintain that with regard to a number of fundamental moral rights and duties there exists full equality and that such equality can be clearly demonstrated. At this place I shall undertake this only for a few representative cases.

Most universally acknowledged and perhaps best accredited among all equal rights that are independent of factual equalities is today the right to equality of opportunities. To be sure, the full meaning of this right and the problems which it involves are rarely fully realized.[93] Nevertheless, it seems safe to assert that, at least before we know anything definite about native inequalities, each individual, however unequal, should have an equal chance of demonstrating and developing his gifts independently of the advantages or handicaps to which, for instance, economic differences expose him. The greatest possible equalization of educational facilities at the start of our careers is one of the most obvious expressions of this right. But it should be added at the same time that this equality of initial opportunities does by no means imply that the one who on the basis of equal opportunities turns out to be a 'stepchild of nature' should simply be abandoned to his fate. As soon as a congenital inability is discovered, there may be reason for any number of compensatory measures. The need for providing initial equality of opportunities may be comparatively obvious even for the denier of other equalities. For without equality of opportunities it would be impossible to determine and evaluate in an objective and impartial way even those natural inequalities which, according to him, should be the basis for differential treatment.

Some equal rights may be deduced from other equal rights of a more fundamental character. Such rights would include, for instance, the right of equal suffrage regardless of factual inequalities among the citizens, both in their descriptive characteristics and in their values, and, in particular, regardless of the undeniable differences in their potential judgment and efficiency. For a demonstration of this right I shall simply have to make the assumption, which in itself would, of course, require much more thorough substantiation, that every person capable of determining his own acts and to that degree of shaping his own fate has a right to make use

93. See, e.g., Hastings Rashdall, *Theory of Good and Evil* I, p. 230, who argues that equality of opportunity would bear too heavily on the weak.

of this capacity to the widest possible extent; and that this right to selfdetermination, which equally belongs to all but the demonstrably insane or feebleminded, includes even the right to make one's own mistakes. Such a right would entail that any determination of one's fate by others, i.e., any political compulsion by social action, be avoided as far as possible or at least be kept at a minimum. Now every political decision of the community involves a restriction of our freedom of individual selfdetermination and means to that degree political compulsion. Political compulsion can be minimized only if everybody is given the same consideration in the formation of the political decisions which direct social action. To be sure, the majority will always determine the fate of the dissenters. But in the case of a majority vote it will at least be only a minority which has to suffer determination of its will by others. It is thus, I submit, the interest in maximization of selfdetermination and in minimization of social compulsion which forms the real and primary basis for equal suffrage. This would imply that the current criticism of the democratic process as being less efficient than totalitarian practice could be dismissed as immaterial, quite apart from the factual question whether it is true that even in the long run totalitarianism can guarantee greater efficiency.

In this context the preceding examples may suffice. Needless to say a comprehensive philosophy of moral rights and duties will have to examine these and other equalities in much greater detail, each with regard to the special issues involved.

7.4 The Basis for the Postulate of Human Equality

The chief positive result of applying my distinctions to the issue of human equality has been: There is an ethical equality with respect to a number of define moral rights and duties. It includes such fundamental rights as those to equal opportunity, to equal self-determination, to equal social protection against undeserved hardship, to equal treatment by the public courts and authorities, and to similar benefits. There is, however, no equality with regard to the *descriptive* features of human nature nor with regard to the actual *values* of human beings. Ethical equality in rights and duties can therefore not be based upon equality in descriptive characteristics nor upon equality in value.

But this result makes the postulate of human equality a complete paradox. It deprives equality of all connection with the world of facts. What is it, then, that requires and justifies a distribution so contrary to all existing order? Why equality?:

(1) Earlier Arguments

(I) The answers to this question are none too numerous. Among them there is, for instance, one which tries to defend ethical equality by considerations of *social utility*. 'But such a defense would hardly work except under strictly limited conditions. Very often it might be much more advantageous to fulfill the demands of the stronger, the more powerful, and the more efficient, especially as long as the weaker group is unable to revolt successfully against discrimination.[94] No wonder, then, that J.S. Mill stated quite frankly that social expediency may support inequality as well as equality.[95]

(II) An original *pragmatic justification* of the postulate of human equality has been advanced by T.V. Smith. As a consequence of his functional interpretation of the ideal of equality he suggests that even if, as a matter of fact, men are not equal, they should be treated as equals in order to encourage community cooperation. 'It will hardly be thought to demand argument that men work together better, when they regard themselves as substantially equal.'[96]

Unfortunately, this argument is no longer as impressive as it was before the surge of totalitarianism. One might even argue that cooperation is most efficient in a 'cooperative' organization after the totalitarian model in which the members of the social body, like the members of the physical body, are assigned unequal parts. This seems all the more suggestive since what T.V. Smith calls the 'utter centrality of oneness with the group' is nowhere stressed to such an extent as in a totalitarian state. Granting for the moment the supreme value of cooperation, one might argue that it would be best secured when everybody takes the place for which he is best fitted by his

94. Cf. the typical difficulties of a modern biologist pleading for democracy in J.B.S. Haldane, *The Inequality of Man* (London, Chatto Windus, 1932) 24 ff.

95. S.J.S. Mill, *Utilitarianism,* Chapter V.

96. *The American Philosophy of Equality* (Chicago, 1927) 276 ff.

special (unequal) qualification, and when all collaborate for the sake of the whole, the less significant member in his subordinate post working in the spirit of spontaneous subordination, the superior one in his commanding position providing care for his subordinates. Such a system is definitely workalbe in the case of a well functioning ecclesiastical group or an army. To that extent, at least, it seems to promise a more successful cooperation than an equalitarian society, where the inferior members would be apt to be bungling and unduly conceited, while the more gifted ones would lack the incentives for greater efforts and for a sustained interest in responsible work.

(III) Probably the most obvious argument for the ideal of equality is based upon the postulates of *justice*. In fact, since Plato and Aristotle, justice and equality, if not actually identified, have always been thought to be intimately related.[97] Yet, according to the traditional conception, justice demands only that an equal share be assigned to equals, and not to unequals.[98] So this kind of justice can never justify equal treatment of unequal human beings, once inequality-in-fact has been admitted.

(IV) *The Argument from the 'Moral Chance' of Inequality*
There is, however, a deeper sense of justice in which it does require equality not only of equals but of unequals as well.

The argument for the demand of universal equality based on the conception which I am going to suggest rests on the following two premises:

1. Undeserved discriminations call for redress.

2. All inequalities of birth constitute undeserved discriminations.

   I shall conclude that

3. All inequalities of birth call for redress. Such redress implies, at

97. Cf. the recent discussion of this topic by Dorothy M. Emmet, 'Justice and Equality', *Philosophy* XIV (1939) 46 ff; Gerhart Husserl (*Ethics* XLVII (1937)) simply declares that 'an act is to be just, if it bears the stamp of equality' (274). Cf. also Arnold Brecht, 'The Search for Absolutes' *Social Research* VII (1940) 215 ff.

98. This would also apply to Leonard Nelson's attempt (*Kritik der praktischen Vernunft* 180) to derive the postulate of equality from the moral law. Inasmuch as there is qualitative inequality between persons, unequal treatment seems to him perfectly legitimate.

least in principle, the cancellation of all inequalities of birth by equalization. In this sense, then, it follows that

4. Equality is a fundamental ethical demand.

(1) In the first premise the term 'discrimination' means any kind of unequal lot by way of privilege or handicap, 'undeserved' indicates the lack of legitimating support by a normal title such as moral desert; 'redress' stands for any measure which restores the upset balance.

The premise that undeserved discriminations call for redress thus implies that only morally deserved inequalities justify unequal lots: without such special justification all persons, whether equal or unequal, ought to have equal shares.

I submit that the first premise thus interpreted contains a truth which is at least as self-evident as any other ethical insight. In order to make this truth fully apparent one might refer in addition to the severe moral disequilibrium which the violation of the demand for redress entails. This disequilibrium is, moreover, apt to rouse in a person with a clearly developed sense of justice and fairness a feeling of outrage. A further confirmation may be found in the legal sphere. Here the lack of a title for a particular benefit serves, under specified conditions, as the basis of an action for restitution because of 'unjust enrichment'. A legal institution of this type is, as a rule, not unconnected with ethical truths. In the case under discussion it may well be claimed that the ethical demand for redress of undeserved discriminations forms the ultimate basis for the legal regulation.

(2) It will require much more to establish my second premise to the effect that all inequalities of birth constitute undeserved discriminations. All I can do here is to point out certain aspects of the fundamental status of man which may help to make this assertion more evident.

Among our inequalities some are initial inequalities or inequalities of birth. Others arise only during the course of our lives. It is next to impossible to determine how many of the second type of inequality are morally deserved. Most of them are certainly on a level very different from that of the inequalities of birth. But even they are based on the conditions, equal or unequal, accompanying our birth. The first step toward determining the ethical significance of our inequalities is therefore to appraise the inequalities of birth.

There is a sense in which none of our unequal characteristics, whether actual or potential, is part and parcel of our innermost selves. We find ourselves 'born into' very different stations of life, into extremely varied social environments and groups, into most diverse families, nations, states, denominations, classes, majorities or minorities. Moreover, we awake to the consciousness of our selfhood to discover ourselves already irrevocably assigned to 'roles' of being male or female, white or colored, native or foreign, strong or weak in physical and mental constitution. We are in these respects from the very beginning equipped with very unequal 'gifts', both in body and mind. We thus distinguish clearly between ourselves, who are born into such different stations, and the physical and mental lots into which we are born, which is, as it were, 'alotted' to us.

But it is not only this natal lot which we thus distinguish from ourselves, who are 'born into' it. The inequality of these lots is likewise an initial fate into which we find ourselves born. Inequality, too, is therefore something extraneous to our innermost selves.

It is this fundamental human plight of being born into our initial stations and their inequalities which is sometimes rather vaguely referred to by the phrases 'chance of birth' or 'accident of birth'. To be sure, these expressions are nowadays used very loosely and thoughtlessly. Generally they are applied only to the more peripheral circumstances of a man's life. [99] I maintain that these phrases can be the expression of a fundamental aspect of human existence.

For it is chance in a specific and very definite sense which is ultimately responsible for all we initially are and have. Prior to any conscious action or choice of our own we find ourselves already born into our stations and into their inequalities. They are, as it were, thrust upon us, certainly without any consciousness of our having deserved them. Nor is there any objective evidence that they depend upon any moral desert. This lack of moral title and primarily of any moral desert for our initial shares I am going to call here 'moral chance'. I maintain that in this moral sense it is merely

---

99. Thus James Bryce (*Modern Democracies* New York, (1929) I, p. 62) uses this phrase only with regard to the 'external conditions of well-being'.

chance which discriminates between us, which grants or denies one individual a set of brilliant 'gifts', mental and physical health and vigor, or the heritage of a great family tradition,[100] and which makes him a member of this or that vaunted community and withholds this privilege from other 'less fortunate' fellow beings.

Ethics offers no brief for any such discriminations of moral chance. It allows for no inherited desert. In its court everyone is given an equal start. And for each one the initial score is zero. This equality of our initial score is the basic ethical equality among all human beings. It follows that all initial inequalities in the form of privileges and handicaps are ethically unwarranted.

The fact that all our inequalities of birth are thus without a moral title establishes at the same time a secondary ethical equality: In the fate of being blindly subject to the unequal chances of our unequal births we are all equals.

The ethical equality of our initial scores and the ensuing equality in the moral chance of our factual inequality do not, however, imply that our innermost selves are completely equal. To be sure, there may be good reasons for believing in such an ultimate equality. But even if these reasons should be inconclusive and if, consequently, our innermost selves should be unequal, we should remain equal in the fate of being equally born into the same ethical start and to the position of equally lacking a moral title to whatever inequalities of birth there may be among us. The only essential similarity between these selves refers to the fact that they are all *human* selves, equipped with the fundamental characteristics of human nature, and primarily with reflective self-consciousness.[101]

100. With regard to the prerogatives of nobility, this point was made very impressively in the first of Pascal's 'Trois discours sur la condition des grands', as recorded by Arnauld (*Oeuvres complètes*, ed. Brunschvicg, IX, 365 ff). He even pointed out that, because of this chance of birth, we should consider ourselves equals 'in a true and ultimate sense'.

101. In a correspondence about this point, Arnold Brecht raised the objection that the argument above proved too much. For it would not only apply to human beings but would have to be extended to animals as well, from the anthropoids down to the smallest microbes, since ostensibly they too are what they are without any previous desert, merit, or demerit. This objection overlooks the question of what it involves 'to be born into' any kind of existential station. Obviously there must be a being of its own which, in such a case, would have to be *born into* whatever station or plight. Unless one should plead for some kind of speculative panpsychism, it does not make any sense to say that something is born into being, for instance, a particular plant or stone.

Now this situation may be somewhat different in the case of higher animals. To be

Such reflections are by no means unfamiliar to the man in the street. Whenever he tries to do full justice to others, he finds, for instance, that 'After all, it is not the poor devil's fault that he 'happens to be' illegitimate. You cannot hold him responsible for having a poor constitution. You cannot blame him for having been born stupid.' Or, in evaluating the merits of a man, the average person is likely to argue that 'After all, he just 'happened to have' a fine 'start', a marvelous physique and a brilliant mind, and you can not credit him for that personally. But look at what he made of that start.' It seems, then, that in daily life we distinguish very well between the accidental endowment of a person and his personal merits or demerits, and that we discount the former when we try to judge him fairly.

(3) The next step follows directly from the preceding premises: If it is the mere chance in the moral sense here defined which underlies our initial factual inequalities, these are in an ultimate sense

sure, it seems highly improbable that they are capable of any behavior involving ethical merit or demerit. And that in itself would make the correlative term 'moral chance' inapplicable. I should, however, not hesitate to admit that, if the selves of animals were really as human as children's stories and animal fables would have it, our attitude toward them would have to change fundamentally. Meanwhile it seems noteworthy to me that even our actual behavior toward them does vary, apparently according to the closeness of their mental structure to our own. We do not treat anthropoids, horses, dogs, and cats, whether domestic or not, on the same level with insects or even with cattle. Does the greater similarity of their expressions and other behavior to our own suggest to us subconsciously that, after all, we might have been in their places?

It appears, then, that as far as the moral chance of birth is concerned, we have to consider the basic difference between human and animal selves (if any). Human selves simply would not fit into the mould of an animal and vice versa. By this I do not mean to say that a human self requires exactly the kind of endowment which we empirically find in humans, i.e., the actual human body and its peculiar mental outfit, with its special type of sensation, perception, memory, speech, and the like. But this human self must be one with at least the possibility of reflective consciousness of his selfhood. Under such circumstances, then, it seems reasonable that we do not grant animals an equal status with ourselves, even if they should have selves who are born into their existential station by the mere 'chance of birth'.

It may be added that basically the same consideration would apply to the problem of our attitude toward mentally retarded and psychotic individuals. What is it that forbids us to dispose of these 'unfortunate' fellow beings in the way in which totalitarian eugenics actually did? Is it not again the consciousness that it is through no merit of our own that we have been spared their fate and that it is through no fault of theirs that they do not share our better lot?

void of moral legitimacy. Our unequal shares constitute an 'unjust enrichment' (or an unjustified deprivation), i.e., undeserved discriminations. 'Corrective justice' demands redress for inequalities which are supported by nothing but the 'chance of birth' in accordance with the equality of our initial ethical score of zero.

(4) But does such redress necessarily call for the establishment of absolute equality? Certainly not in *all* cases of unjustified discrimination. Such discrimination may require nothing beyond the restoration of the status quo. Or it may demand some kind of compensation for irreparable damage or disadvantage.

Furthermore, it should be clear that inequalities which do not represent initial advantages or disadvantages but merely varieties on an equal level are in no way subject to cancellation. The postulate of equality does not require dull uniformity. Only inequalities that involve privileges or handicaps call for anything like redress.

In the case of most of our congenital inequalities, however, the principle of redress does require, if not a total redistribution, at least some kind of equalization of fates, much according to the same principles which in the case of a public calamity demand an equalization and compensation for abnormal individual losses. High inheritance taxes and far-reaching social security measures, are some of the more obvious means to promote such equalization. And, even more important, the postulate of equality calls for the greatest possible prevention of initial inequalities by equal social and medical hygiene and protection. Moreover, in as far as the science of genetics provides us with reliable knowledge about human heredity, it suggests a eugenic policy which prevents the birth of hopelessly handicapped individuals.

On the other hand, the demand for equality does not require that, regardless of the consequences, every privilege or handicap be discarded and equality be made retroactive, as fanatical levellers would have it. That this is not the case can best be seen by considering that equalization constitutes by no means an unambiguous program. It can be achieved by a variety of procedures none of which, judged alone by the standards of the desired equality, would seem preferable. Thus one way of establishing equality would be by achieving *equality in kind,* another by securing *equivalent* shares. Equality in kind may in turn be realized by three different methods:

1. by the transfer of an excessive share from the overprivileged to the underprivileged party. Such a procedure would be feasible only in the case of material goods; it would be out of the question in the case of mental advantages.

2. by an increase in the assets of the underprivileged party up to the level of the overprivileged without depriving the latter of his present benefits. In the case of the mentally handicapped this would amount to providing him with special educational services.

3. by the destruction of the excessive share of the overprivileged party in the way suggested by the proverbial Solomonic justice. An equalization of mental differences would in this case have to consist in withholding from the overprivileged party a normal education or in other appropriate measures of stultification, certainly again of very problematic effectiveness, quite apart from more serious objections.

Mechanical equalization is, then, in a good many cases a physical impossibility. There remains, however, even in such cases the possibility of achieving at least an equivalence of benefits. And such an equalization of benefits in goods of equal significance may again be obtained by two different procedures:

1. by giving the underprivileged party benefits which would make his status equivalent to that of the overprivileged. It is by no means certain that this is always possible. Thus, in what sense physical enjoyments could make up for inaccessible intellectual benefits is quite problematic, not to say a moot question.

2. by taking equivalent benefits away from the overprivileged. Even here we should have to consider that certain mental advantages simply cannot be stripped from their owner without destroying his entire personality. And how are we to determine such equivalences?

Which one of these five possible methods of equalization are we to choose, supposing that all or several of them are applicable to the case in question? The principle of equalization or redress in itself cannot help us to decide this. For such a decision we need an additional standard. The one which would best recommend itself appears to be that of the common well-being of all fellow beings involved in the fate of inequality.

This principle would rule out from the very start any kind of Solomonic justice. For any destruction of values would impoverish the community as a whole and thus reduce the common well-being. The only exception to this rule would be the case where the existence of inequalities promotes a spirit of caste snobbery and segregation destructive of the solidarity of the fellows-in-fate. In such situations the destruction of individuality may be preferable to the preservation of inequality, however valuable for other reasons. Also it should be considered that the destruction of congenital advantages may easily constitute a cruel injustice against the better equipped individual. To keep him down and prevent him from developing his special gifts would penalize him for a fate which was, after all, his too through no fault of his own. To choose this destructive way of equalization would simply mean to give way to the forces of envy and blind resentment.

For the same reason it will be as a rule undesirable to choose the method of equalization by transfer, unless the implied deprivation of the overprivileged works at the same time for the general, including his own, good. What seems most important is that the underprivileged receive an improvement of his lot. Here it has to be carefully considered whether such a compensation is likely to work out for his own good. It is very doubtful whether this can be achieved by an equalization in kind, considering how different the meaning of equal goods may be for unequal persons. All that can safely be stated is that the underprivileged should be granted such equivalents for his handicaps as will provide him with the means for the type of well-being most suitable for him. It would by no means be a suitable compensation to given the mentally handicapped more means for physical pleasures if these would only endanger his well-being and would be used in a way injurious to the community. All that he can expect is more facilities for his physical development, for healthful recreation and enjoyment, and similar compensations for the handicap of not being able to share the more refined enjoyments accessible to the mentally privileged. It would be definitely against the common interest to waste a huge amount of goods and education on the handicapped. It may well be that such limitations make it permanently impossible for us ever to achieve a full and satisfactory compensation. Regrettable though this may be, it does not constitute a good reason for resorting to destructive equalization against the overprivileged. It is in the equal interest of every individual that their gifts be not wasted. Equality thus does not, for instance, stand in the way of a qualitative democracy which would offer an individualizing education adjusted to the individual needs, inclinations, and capacities, of its members. If such treatment should involve special privileges for the superior members of society, it only demands that they be accepted in the spirit of favors which entail special obligations.

It appears, then, that equal consideration of their cases,[102] regardless of the chance inequalities of birth, is the only absolutely equal claim shared by all. This consideration implies that, with respect to the fundamental benefits of human existence, everyone should have equal opportunities, or, if unable to utilize them, access to equivalent resources of a life worth living, *i.e.*, to those sources of 'happiness' which are suited to his individual nature. In considering individual cases we should, therefore, not disregard the relevant inequalities for the persons involved. What we *should* disregard is that the person we have to deal with is either our friend Tom or Mr. Jones, whose nose we happen to dislike.

It is this claim to equal respect for human selfhood, based on each one's equal existential plight, which seems to me to be at the root of what we mean by the phrase 'equal human dignity'. Certainly, with regard to their actual achievements and conditions in life, men seem to have very different degrees of dignity and may, for that reason, be worthy of more or less respect. Still, no one who is born into this world can claim any special birthright over anyone else; for in a moral sense all start equally, without initial merit or demerit. To this extent no one ever has more and never less than an equal claim to impartial consideration of his case in all of its relevant aspects. This basic claim to equal respect of his selfhood gives man a certain ultimate dignity. Such dignity does by no means attribute to man anything like absolute perfection worthy of veneration or worship, as an exaggerated humanism *à la* Comte seems to imply. Dignity in the sense here upheld means nothing but a fundamental claim implied by human nature. In this sense,

102. For the conception of equal consideration, cf. Hastings Rashdall, *The Theory of Good and Evil* I 224 ff.

but only in this sense, is it true that 'each one is to count for one and no one for more than one', as Bentham postulated so appropriately but, in view of his predominant interest in sheer maximization of happiness, so inconsistently.

How far can the use of a category like moral chance be reconciled with a religious interpretation of human existence? Is it not a flat denial of 'Divine Providence' to speak about the human situation as a matter of chance?

Such an objection would be a serious misunderstanding of what I am advocating. 'Moral chance' denies divine providence as little as it denies strict mechanistic determination. In fact, the Christian interpretation of human existence supplies most valuable confirmation of the consideration developed here. Thus the Christian idea of grace implicitly acknowledges the ethical unaccountability of the inequalities of our initial fates.[103] Because of this unaccountability it stresses the special obligations implied in our privileges, which are not, and even cannot be, morally deserved.[104] It is only the speculation about a migration of the souls, as represented in ancient mysticism or in Indian thought, which, by explaining our earthly fates from merit or guilt incurred in a previous existence, flatly contradicts the idea of such moral chance of birth. But not only is the hypothesis of preexistence gratuitous; it is certainly not without significance that Plato, in order to clear the Deity of any suspicion of unjustice, felt the need of justifying the inequalities of our births and fates by a prenatal choice of our lots, a choice in

---

103. Take, *e.g.*, Jeremy Taylor: 'If a man be exalted by reason of any excellence in his soul, he may please to remember that all souls are equal; and their differing operations are because their instrument is in better tune, their body is more healthful, or better tempered; which is no more praise than it is that he was born in Italy.' (*The Rules and Exercises of Holy Living*. Chapter II Section IV: On Humility 6) and Hastings Rashdall: 'In most men at least this feeling (of humility) will be strengthened by the recognition that the differences between themselves and their fellows are largely due ... not to any efforts which begin exclusively with themselves. To use theological language, the good man will ascribe his goodness to 'grace', recognizing that his good qualities are due in the first instance to parentage, influence, example, social tradition, education, community, Church and ultimately, if he is a religious man, to God.' (*The Theory of Good and Evil* (2nd ed., Oxford 1924) I, p. 206).

104. Cf. Jeremy Taylor: 'Whatsoever other difference there is between thee and thy neighbour ... if it be good, thou hast received it from God; and then thou art more obliged to pay duty and tribute, use and principal to him: and it were a strange folly for a man to be proud of being more in debt than another.' (*ibid.* 8).

which, as he is anxious to show, the odds were even for every participant.[105]

7.5 Related Arguments

It may be worth pointing out that it is not only justice which in the form of the demand for the redress of undeserved discriminations supports the equalitarian demand. It is, for instance, but the minimum of *charity* to fulfill the demands of justice. Already justice expects that we should give equal consideration to all those who are initially unequal. How much more does charity enjoin that we should not let others remain at the undeserved disadvantage to which the 'accident of birth' exposes them.

Moreover, on quite a different level, it is precisely Nietzsche's ideal of *noblemindedness* which, if thought through in its implications, would lead to the demand of equal treatment as a duty of the privileged, if not as a right of the underprivileged. Nietzsche himself seems to have come remarkably close to such an unaristocratic conclusion when he gave expression to his love for 'the one who is ashamed when the die has fallen in his favor and asks: Have I then been cheating?'[106] Certainly it would be unworthy of anybody who shares this lofty attitude to accept unearned privileges over his fellow-beings such as the ones granted by the 'accident of birth'.

Finally, even from the recent cult of heroic self-reliance, which would like to owe everything to its own efforts, it is not a far cry to the acknowledgement of the demand for an equal start.

But these alternative arguments are hardly conclusive to anyone who does not accept the ideals of charity, or noblemindedness, or selfreliance, as binding. It is largely for this reason that the argument based on the demands of justice seems to me to carry much more weight. Besides, all other arguments have to appeal to the additional premise of the 'moral chance' of our inequalities of birth.

105. *Republic,* Book X, 614B ff. (Myth of Er); also *Timaeus* 41 D.
106. *Thus spake Zarathustra.* Preface, 4; Old and New Tables, 4.

7.6 Conclusion

To restate the central idea of my principal vindication of human equality: The postulate of equality, as far as it is valid, has its ultimate basis in the demands of a fundamental human justice which requires equal consideration even of unequals who equally owe their factual inequalities to the 'chance of birth'. It is thus not equality of factual being but equality of ethical status, as indicated by the equal initial ethical score of each individual, which constitutes the foundation for the postulate of human equality. The paradox of the ideal of equality in the face of all the factual inequalities among men disappears once one discovers its basis in the need of redress for the unwarranted privileges and handicaps of our unequal stations at birth.

The most notable thing about this vindication of the idea of human equality seems to me that so little of it has entered into philosophical discussion. I am well aware that this vindication raises issues which exceed by far the scope of this paper. All I could hope to do was to point out a dimension of facts and problems from which new and deeper insights into the ultimate reasons for the postulate of human equality may be obtained. Such insight may help not only to solve a theoretical problem but also to strengthen those who, while still believing in the ideal of equality, seem to have lost its clear meaning and its reassuring support. Unless the ideal of human equality in its redefined sense can be justified from such a deeper conception of our existence, there seems to me little hope of defending it successfully against the present onslaught.

8. EQUALITY IN EXISTENTIALISM

8.1 Existentialism: Core and Fringe

All generalizations about existentialism, amorphous as this movement is in its philosophical, literary, and political expressions, are apt to be misleading. But if one limits its circumference to the core of what is sometimes called the Paris group, i.e., Jean-Paul Sartre, Simone de Beauvoir, Maurice Merleau-Ponty, Francis Jeanson, and most of the staff of Sartre's *Les Temps Modernes,* one statement about its political line needs no qualification: It is unequivocal in its stand for human equality. This stand is part of the struggle of these existentialists for the liberation of human existence from all types of discrimination and oppression based on class, race, and sex. Thus they have fought 'colonialism', old and new, in Vietnam, Madagascar, and Algeria. They have also denounced discrimination in the American South and in totalitarian dictatorships, both fascist and communist.

The situation becomes less clear if one includes, as most introductions to existentialism do, all those writers who have used the term 'existence' in a Kierkegaardian sense even before 1944, when the label 'existentialism' became the fashion, among such major inspirers of the core group as Kierkegaard, Nietzsche, and such contemporary philosophers of existence as Karl Jaspers, Martin Heidegger, and Gabriel Marcel, who violently reject the label of 'existentialism', and Nikolai Berdyeav, Martin Buber, and Paul Tillich, who seem to be allergic to it.

Søren Kierkegaard, who first gave the term 'existence' its existentialist ring, was for all practical purposes a *homo apoliticus*, even

Reprinted by permission from *Nomos* IX (1967), 193-213.

in his philosophizing; hence for him the question of social equality in existence did not arise. One might argue, however, that inequality in the form of aesthetic individuality belongs to Kierkegaard's aesthetic 'stage on life's way', while equality is at least compatible with the ethical and religious stages.

If Friedrich Nietzsche is to be included among the philosophers of existence (to my mind one of the more dubious inclusions, if only because the term 'existence' as such does not mean anything special to him), then existentialism would indeed be saddled with one of the most violent denouncers of human equality, the 'lie' invented by the envious resentment of the revolting slaves.

Karl Jaspers, politically a staunch antitotalitarian and democratic liberal, finds it necessary to reinterpret the idea of equality along Kantian lines: 'The idea of equality of all men is palpably false, as far as their specificity and endowment as psychologically knowable beings is concerned . . . The essential equality of all men resides solely in that depth where to each one freedom opens a way to approach God through his moral life . . . This equality means: respect for every man, which rules out the treatment of any man as means only and not at the same time as an end in himself.'[107] Besides, Jaspers' fascination with greatness and great men, not only in philosophy but in other fields as well, clearly expresses his aristocratic taste.

Heidegger's notorious, though short-lived, involvement with Nazism may well make him suspect of sharing its contemptuous rejection of the unity of the human race and its segregation into superior and inferior races. But even an examination of his most sickening pronouncements from that episode does not reveal any explicit repudiation of the doctrine of human equality. As to his philosophy and specifically his analytics of existence, one of the chief inspirations of the core existentialists, it is so absorbed in questions of the ontological structure of *Dasein*, rather than with concrete ontic existence, that anthropological questions such as that of human equality never arise. Heidegger's concern here is with the common plight of man as such in his relation to Being, not with men in their qualitative individuality and their differences.

---

107. *Der philosophische Glaube,* München, R. Piper & Co., 1948, p. 56 f; Engl. transl.: *The Perennial Scope of Philosophy* by Ralph Manheim, Philosophical Library, 1949, p. 69 f.

Another problematic case among contemporary philosophers of existence is Marcel. Whereas he is an unequivocal enemy of all totalitarian degradation of man, he denounces equalitarian 'fanaticism' as the basis for modern mass-mindedness and as originating not only from the sinister 'spirit of abstraction' but also from the egocentric envy of the masses toward the privileged, at which point he even invokes Nietzsche and his theory of ressentiment.[108]

8.2 An Existentialist Ousider: Vladimir Jankélévitch on Equality

I am familiar with only one case of an explicit plea for equality based on a concept of existence. It comes from a highly original French thinker, usually not associated with existentialism but clearly sympathetic to it in spite of his chiefly Bergsonian inspiration. His case is unusual enough to merit a brief digression. It occurs in an article of 1939, hence is still existentialism *avant la lettre*. It runs roughly as follows:

Being, which Jankélévitch identifies with 'ipseity', is absolutely contingent and in this sense a mystery. The 'that' of this being is also the foundation of *human* being and the true foundation of its dignity. It is also equal for all human beings:

> Being does not require any particular aptitude. Here is a chapter where everyone is competent, since all men are equally and sufficiently initiated in the affairs of destiny. All are specialists. There are no laymen, no more or less gifted ones — — for being represents the great equality of the unequals. Here everyone is housed under the same sign, and the hereditary princes are not ahead of the guardsmen. We are all equal according to our *being,* but doing makes us unequal (p. 25, my translation).[109]

Such equality proves to be the primary explanation of equality before the moral law of the 'ecumenical democracy of the men of good will. For the good is something which everyone can do without any handicap or initial privilege (p. 27).'

---

108. *Les Hommes contre l'humain,* Paris, La Colombe, 1951, p. 119 f.; Engl. transl.: *Man against Mass Society* by G.S. Fraser, Chicago, Gateway, 1952, p. 160 f. Also *La Dignité humaine,* Paris, Aubier-Montaigne, 1964, p. 172; Engl. transl.: *The Existential Background of Human Dignity*, Cambridge, Harvard University Press, 1963, p. 131 f.

109. 'De l'Ipséité', *Revue internationale de philosophie*, Vol. II (1939), pp. 21-42.

Certainly not all the steps of this sketchy argument are cogent. True, the fact that we are all equal in the contingency of our being is a plight worth remembering and considering. It is less clear whether it is sufficient ground for defending the kind of equality that is at stake in the philosophical and political debate about human equality. But what is most relevant in the present context is that Jankélévitch does not distinguish between being in the universal and classic sense and existence in the new Kierkegaardian sense of a specifically human way of being. Hence his equality of being in general is apt to 'prove' too much: It would make us equal to sticks and stones and every form of life, granting them equal rights. Besides, it is by no means clear whether the *fact* of being implies any *right* of being. The contingency of being may be a mystery, but hardly in a sense that gives it any special dignity and claim to our respectful awe.

Nevertheless, here is at least an explicit attempt to link an existential approach with the problem of human equality. What is more, the idea that contingency has something to do with the demand for equality is worth developing.

8.3 Equality in the Thought of Jean-Paul Sartre

However, the best defenders of human equality in social and political life remain the hardcore existentialists of Paris. It is all the more surprising that their theoretical writings do not seem to include any explicit pleas and arguments for equality as a principle. I have no ready explanation for their apparent reluctance to speak out on this issue. Is it because of their general rejection of absolutes? But then why is freedom such a basic concept of their ethico-political ideology? Nevertheless, their writings contain enough evidence of their implicit equalitarianism. This deserves explicating.

I shall attempt to do this chiefly in the case of Jean-Paul Sartre, the central figure of the Paris group, although he now seems to be ready to contribute his existentialism to a pool of diluted Marxism purged of its objectivism and materialism. I shall also comment on a pertinent elaboration of the general pattern by Simone de Beauvoir and on important variations by Merleau-Ponty. Next, I shall raise some critical queries about the foundation of this equalitarianism. And finally, I shall make some suggestions about possible ways of strengthening the existentialist case, even though these may not quite fit into the framework of orthodox existentialism.

Sartre's equalitarianism, as practiced in concrete situations both political and literary but not preached in his philosophical theory, can be derived as a corollary from some of his basic ideas. But before turning to his philosophical works, one might do well to seek them in his nonphilosophical writings. There is special reason for this, related to the strangely unfinished condition of Sartre's existentialist ethics. Sartre developed this ethics, and in fact proclaimed existentialism as a comprehensive philosophy, only after he had published the 'essay in phenomenological ontology', which still contains his major claim to philosophical fame, *Being and Nothingness*, of 1943. Its 'Conclusion' discusses some of the 'Ethical Perspectives' of his philosophy, which were to be further elaborated in a book tentatively announced as *Man (L'Homme)*, which never materialized and apparently is no longer expected to do so, for reasons never fully explained. In fact, Sartre's existentialism, in the sense of the term that developed after the liberation of France from the Nazis, has thus far been formulated mostly in literary documents, in such philosophical manifestoes as his lecture on existentialism as a humanism,[110] with its surprising changes in position,[111] and in his plays. The 'manifesto' and even the political essays are strangely unenlightening on the equality issue. But there is one play in which it is at least skirted, *The Devil and the Good Lord*. Using as background the revolt of the German peasants against their feudal lords in the Reformation period, Sartre introduced into his plot some of the levellers of the time under the leadership of a sinister character by the name of Nasty, who poses as a religious equalitarian;[112] but quite apart from his odd name, he is certainly not Sartre's mouthpiece. So too, the equalitarianism that the main hero, Goetz von Berlichingen, tries to espouse during one of his existential conversions, also turns out to be a failure. When he sides with the em-

---

110. *L'Existentialisme est un humanisme*, Paris, Nagel, 1946; Engl. transl.: *Existentialism* by B. Frechtman, New York, Philosophical Library, 1947.

111. See my 'French Existentialism: Its Social Philosophies', *Kenyon Review*, Vol. XVI (1954), pp. 446-462.

112. *Le Diable et le bon Dieu*, Paris Gallimard, 1951, p. 104; Engl. transl.' *The Devil and the Lord* by Kitty Black, New York, Alfred A. Knopf, 1960, p. 54.

battled peasants he first wants to fight alongside them as their equal but finally finds himself forced, in view of the incompetence of the peasant leader, to become their dictatorial general in the fight for the freedom of all men.

As happens only too frequently in Sartre's literary productions, the author's own explicit answer remains ambiguous and enigmatic. The only way to determine the foundation of Sartre's equalitarianism is to examine the principles of his earlier ontology. I shall try to present, as briefly and nontechnically as I can, those relevant for the deduction of equality and to show their significance for the equalitarian position.

Equality in Existence

Sartre's slogan for existentialism, 'existence precedes essence' (which incidentally is not acceptable to the other philosophers whom he wants to include) has a meaning that is anything but clear. One of its simplest interpretations is that man exists before he achieves a specific essence as a result of his choices. More specifically, there is no such thing as human nature before man 'chooses himself' and in choosing himself also chooses for all humanity.[113]

What does this imply for the problem of equality? In contrast to essence with all its diversities, existence is here conceived as an indeterminate stage preceding all differentiation. But such indeterminacy cannot fail to be equal for each existence. Consequently the doctrine of an essenceless existence preceding human nature implies indeed an original equality at the very start.

Equality in Freedom

Human existence, as Sartre conceives of it, is not a merely passive condition, as is mere being, the opaque and massive state of unconscious reality, the 'In-itself (en-soi).'[114] For Sartre, existence coincides with freedom. Now, according to one of Sartre's boldest pronouncements, freedom is either absolute or nonexistent. That it is indeed absolute is the challenge he flings into the face of scientific determinism. Now if all men's freedom is absolute, as Sartre asserts,

113. *L'Existentialisme*, p. 83 f.; transl. p. 20 f.

114. For a discussion of the *en-soi*, see my *Phenomenological Movement* (3rd ed.), The Hague, Martinus Nijhoff, 1982, pp. 484, 490, 493.

then it is hard to see how they could be anything but equal. There could be inequalities in freedom only if freedom were a matter of degrees.

It should, however, be added immediately that from the very start Sartre warned against certain misunderstandings of this doctrine. For example, he never meant to assert that human freedom is omnipotent and that all human beings are equal in such respects as physical strength or social opportunities. As it turns out, man's unrestricted freedom concerns not factual possibilities but meanings and values. For no matter what his factual limitations, man is always free to determine the meaning of the facts by choosing his projects and by relating the facts to these projects.

Equality in Responsibility

Whatever special meaning the term 'responsibility' may have for Sartre —and indications are that it has many— he makes it clear that man is responsible not only for himself but for the world as a whole. In this sense his responsibility is, as he puts it, total. Now totality does not admit of any degrees. Hence the responsibilities of different 'existers' would have to be equal.

Of course one may wonder how anyone's responsibility can be total, if everyone else is also totally responsible. But being totally responsible does not necessarily mean to be responsible to the exclusion of everyone else. Whereas everyone may have responsibility for everything and each one may be responsible with his whole being, everyone else may be coresponsible in much the same way as, in the case of multiple insurance, all insurers are liable for the amount of the total damage, although they will eventually distribute their liabilities. The important thing is that, no matter how many bear the burden of responsibility, the field for which they are responsible is completely covered by their guarantees.

Equality in Factivity

To the philosophers of existence, all being is contingent. There is essentially no way to base being on a necessary being. This is also true of human existence or, as Sartre puts it, human reality. In fact, the contingency of human existence is even more acute. Man's 'facticity', as Sartre, following Heidegger, called this condition is characterized by what the latter had called 'thrownness' (*Geworfen-*

heit), and what Sartre calls '*délaissement*', i.e., abandonment. Besides, there are other aspects of his condition, such as anguish or despair (better, 'non-reliance') that reveal the basic condition or facticity of human reality.

Now whatever differences there may be in the concrete forms of man's condition, basically it is the same for every exister. Each one is 'thrown' into the world like an orphan, is existentially abandoned, no matter on what coast he is shipwrecked. In this respect at least our facticity is the same, although the concrete facts of each one's existence will differ. Thus our fundamental plight is equal.

Equality and Situation

Despite his insistence on absolute freedom and total responsibility, Sartre has always made it clear that such freedom is only freedom in concrete situations. Some of these may be common and equal, but most concrete situations differ and change constantly.[115] How far do these differences affect human equality?

In order to answer this question, one has to take account of Sartre's peculiar conception of a 'situation'. For to him a situation is not simply an objective brute fact. Instead, he conceives of it as the joint product of the contingent 'in-itself' *(en-soi)* and human freedom *(pour soi)*. There are therefore no such things as objective situations by themselves. Mere facts become situations only by their relation to a human consciousness with its freely chosen projects. Thus a wall may be a barrier to my project of walking or a challenging hurdle in an obstacle race.

How far then are the situations of different existers equal? This will depend partly on the factual element and partly on human freedom. Some of the factual elements are sufficiently common to be equal, but most of them are apt to differ considerably. However, to Sartre the decisive factor is the use that freedom will make of them. Will it try to equalize or 'unequalize' the equal or unequal objective raw material of the situation? Even equal starting conditions can be 'unequalized' by the societal goal of maximum variety, which may call for slaves and castrates. Even unequal starting con-

---

115. It is significant that Sartre's essays on matters literary, aesthetic, and political have been republished under the title *Situations*, Paris, Gallimard, beginning 1947; Engl. transl. of Vol. IV by Benita Eisler, New York, Braziller, 1965.

ditions can be equalized by a society that grants equal votes even to citizens still uneducated. In other words, situations are essentially neither equal nor unequal. Their equality or inequality is in this sense a matter of choice.

But then what are concrete situations for Sartre's existentialism? In the main section on situation in *Being and Nothingness,* Sartre discusses five of them: my place, my past, my environment, my fellow-men, and my death. He omits 'my body', although elsewhere he assigns to it the role of a situation. Now for place, past, environment, and fellow-men there will certainly be plenty of differences in the factual elements. These differences will be less pronounced in the fact (though not in the form) of death, which however is for Sartre (in contrast to Heidegger) the situation discussed last and certainly not the ultimate 'sense' of, but rather the ultimate absurdity in human reality. But all these factors will always depend on their relation to the equalizing or 'unequalizing' projects of freedom. The place where I am born can be fitted into the project of a pre-fabricated standard existence and thus become a monotonous situation. By the same token, my past, however humdrum, can become part of extremely different situations as I choose and follow a career.

This, then, would appear to be the basic pattern of Sartre's implicit philosophy of human equality: There is no total equality as far as the concrete facts of human existence are concerned, especially not in a society divided into classes and in a world composed of oppressing and oppressed nations. Whatever factual equality may exist is restricted to existence as it 'precedes' essence and to freedom in its absolute power to decide upon the meanings of situations.

Such equality is certainly not enough to guarantee equal value and dignity to each man's existence. This will depend on whether men exist 'authentically', choosing freedom for themselves and for others, or 'inauthentically', escaping from it in bad faith and thus becoming cowards. But even then Sartre seems to believe that none of these choices is irrevocable. There are 'conversions' like the metamorphoses of 'Saint Genet', the kleptomaniac turned writer; yet according to Sartre's film *Les Jeux sont faits (The Chips are Down),* there are limits to this freedom of reversing one's fate.

What is most obvious is Sartre's assent to equality in rights and duties. The concept of equality of duties is included in the thesis of man's total responsibility, which, however, need not imply equality of rights, a phrase not common in the vocabulary of the existentialists. But Sartre's stand for the oppressed as part of the struggle for universal liberation makes it amply clear that the equal freedom he claims for everybody also includes equal rights to freedom.

8.4 Equality of the Sexes in the Thought of Simone de Beauvoir

As a philosopher Simone de Beauvoir reflects Sartre's position so completely that no special discussion of her version of existentialism seems to be called for. However, she deserves special credit for having spelled out, in her *For an Ethics of Ambiguity,* a little more clearly than had Sartre in *Being and Nothingness,* what his abandoned book on ethics might have contained —although the existentialist meaning of the term 'ambiguity' needs considerable explaining. What makes her voice important in the present context is her discussion of the problem of equality between the sexes, a point about which Sartre himself in his philosophy is strangely silent.

The Second Sex is, of course, also an indictment of actual inequalities. And one might easily interpret it as just another plea for the equality of the underprivileged sex on existentialist grounds. But this is certainly not the whole story. Simone de Beauvoir does not even raise the problem of equalitarianism as such and is anything but a mere feminist. Most of this huge and learned work is diagnostic. The main finding is that there remains an enormous amount of inequality between the sexes, especially in social relations. This inequality has its chief root in the fact that the woman finds herself, her life, and her world defined as 'the other' or second sex by males, even where she is recognized as equal. However, her role as 'the other' of man is by no means immutable and essential. On the whole 'it is as absurd to speak about 'woman' in general as of an eternal 'man'. This explains why all comparisons, if one tries to decide whether woman is superior, inferior, or equal to man, are idle: their situations are profoundly different'.[116]

116. *Le Deuxième Sexe* II, 454; Engl. transl.: *The Second Sex* by H.M. Parshley, New York, Knopf, 1952, p. 627.

There is thus a basic difference. But it is not a difference permanent in nature, 'not a matter of brain or hormones', but of the situation.[117] Some of these differences, such as anatomical and physiological organization, are clearly permanent. But the decisive factor remains the interpretation of these situations; it may emphasize or de-emphasize, equalize or 'unequalize' the meanings of these facts.

Even as far as the future and the ideal relation are concerned, Simone de Beauvoir raises no explicit demand for equality, and still less for uniformity. In fact, Stendhal's romantic offer of equality for women is one of those 'myths' which do not satisfy her. What matters to her is that woman should become an 'autonomous individual', able and entitled to define her own situation and not to have it defined for her by the 'first sex'. In the 'liberation' she envisions, there will be not only equality in differences but 'differences in equality'.[118] Both sexes will be themselves but also 'others' in reciprocity. In other words, each sex will be both first and second.

Thus even for the existentialist there will remain inequality in fact, based on different situations resulting from the free choices that start from the biological differences. But such inequalities will not interfere with the equivalence in value and dignity, and least of all with the equality of rights and responsibilities, as far as these are not grounded in relevant biological differences.

8.5 Human 'Universality' in the Thought of Merleau-Ponty

Maurice Merleau-Ponty, whose phenomenological existentialism differs so much from Sartre's that the two should never be lumped together,[119] shared with him an apparent reluctance to discuss human equality explicitly and to refer to it as a political argument.[120] But one of his most original discussions of existentialism, the one on Hegel's existentialism in *Sense and Non-sense*,[121] comes very

117. *Ibid.*, p. 422; transl. p. 597.
118. *Ibid.*, p. 576; transl. p. 731.
119. See my 'French Existentialism: Its Social Philosophies', *Kenyon Review*, Vol. XVI, p. 454 ff.
120. See, e.g., his 'Sur l'Indochine', *Signes*, Paris, Gallimard, 1960, p. 403; Engl. transl. by R.C. McCleary, Evanston, Ill., Northwestern University Press, 1964, p. 323.
121. *Sens et non-sens*, Paris, Nagel, 1948; Engl. transl. by H.L. and P.A. Dreyfus, Evanston, Ill., Northwestern University Press, 1964.

close to spelling out existentialism's equalitarian implications in a way that improves on Jankélévitch's incomplete case. A first indication of such an argument is implied in a sentence in which Merleau-Ponty supports what his friend Jean Hyppolite used to say to his students during the Nazi occupation:

> We are all Jews to the extent that we are responsible for the universal, are not resigned to merely being (*être*), and want to exist (*éxister*).[122]

Beyond this will to 'existence' as a foundation for a common existential equality, the very consciousness of others, even as enemies, implies equality:

> My consciousness of another as an enemy comprises an affirmation of him as an equal.[123]

But the most explicit linkage of Merleau-Ponty's conception of existentialism with the idea of equality can be found in the first part of his final revision of its definition:

> A more complete definition of what is called existentialism than we get from talking of anxiety and the contradictions of the human condition might be found in the idea of a universality which men affirm or imply by the very fact that they *are* and at the very moment when they oppose one another; by the idea of a reason immanent in unreason; and by a freedom which becomes what it is by binding itself, and to which the slightest perception, the faintest movement of the heart, and the least action bear incontestable witness.[124]

I submit that this assertion of a (Hegelian) universality in the very fact of existing, i.e., of being-in-the-world as Merleau-Ponty conceives it, constitutes a new and significant addition to the philosophy of human equality.

8.6 Some Critical Queries

This is not the place for a comprehensive appraisal of the existent-

122. *Ibid.*, p. 133 f; transl. p. 67.
123. *Ibid.*, p. 135 f; transl. p. 68.
124. *Ibid.*, p. 139 f; transl. p. 70.

ialist position, its claims and its foundations, or even of its social philosophy. I believe that in all of these respects it is incomplete. But it is capable of development, particularly if it strengthens its phenomenological basis and overcomes its penchant to stun philosophers and laymen alike by its insistence on paradoxical overstatements of its case.[125] It also deserves such development in view of the fact that a sane existentialism may well break through and transcend the stalemated debates between liberal and communist ideologies. Signs of such possibilities have not been wanting, particularly in the case of as independent a thinker as Merleau-Ponty, especially in his *Les Aventures de la Dialectique* (1955).

However, certain fundamental points that have specific bearing on the existentialist philosophy of equality as explicated in the preceding sections can be raised profitably in the present context.

(a) Sartre's conception of existence, linked by him with the scholastic distinction between essence and existence, rather than with Kierkegaard's conception, needs further probing. Not only ordinary usage and common sense but also conscientious phenomenology will balk at the idea that existence as the correlate of essence can occur, let alone act, by itself. This may at best be true of the 'exister', of the existing ego. But Sartre never distinguishes between existence as a property (or 'form') of a being and existence as the exister. It is on the latter that we would have to focus in order to make Sartre's view of existence as active tenable or at least plausible.

(b) The idea of such an existence as 'preceding' all essence is certainly odd, especially ontologically, implying as it does that even in time there has been existence without essence or 'nature'. 'The Man without Qualities' may be a suggestive and provocative title for a novel like Robert Musil's. But it certainly cannot mean that such a faceless being has no properties at all. How could such essenceless existence do any such thing as 'choose' without having at least potentialities and the kind of structures underlying them that would allow it to actualize them? True, these 'essences' could be fluid and impermanent. But they would have to be present all the same and allow a description of 'existence' with regard to what

---

125. See *Phenomenological Movement*, pp. 528 f.

it can undertake.

(c) Sartre's daring case for either absolute freedom or none at all is one he himself could maintain only with difficulty. Such statements as the one that the French had never been as free as under the Nazi occupation[126] when every action had the weight of ultimate commitments were so paradoxical as to seem perverse. Since then Sartre's increasing sympathy with a humanistic Marxism that includes the thesis of historical materialism has made him admit by implication that this freedom is severely limited, not only because of the lack of economic foundations for its free use but also because of the limited range of choices for the underprivileged. In this sense it would of course no longer be possible to assert the equal freedom of every exister. All one might still defend is the contention that, like the fearless Stoic, everyone always has the possibility, though hardly the equal strength, to say 'yes' or 'no' regardless of the odds that confront him.

(d) Sartre's invigorating appeal to human responsibility is apt to become meaningless when he tries to make it 'total'. As long as man is a finite being, any insistence on infinite responsibility is not only paradoxical but bound to be self-defeating and paralyzing. How can we ever dream of living up to it? Besides, in view of Sartre's assertion that all values are of our own choosing, it seems strange that he should make us responsible not only for these but also for the whole universe into which we were 'thrown' without having any choice. Responsibility in the genuine sense as expressed in ordinary language is bound to be proportionate to our actual powers. Any attempt to hold us responsible beyond these powers is not only unfair ('ultra posse nemo obligatur') but leads to the dilution of any genuine sense of responsibility. Thus our responsibilities will be equal only when our powers are equal. There is certainly no good reason for considering them 'total'.

8.7 On Chances for Strengthening the Existentialist Case for Equality

In making the following suggestions I do not want to imply that I

---

126. 'La République du silence', *Situations*, III, Paris, Gallimard, pp. 1-42.

consider myself an existentialist in any of the usual senses of the term. But I feel so close to some of the existentialist views that I would consider it a loss if their potentialities should remain undeveloped. I feel the greater right to say so since I once presented a plea for human equality even before 'existentialism' had appeared on the American scene, a plea in which I referred to a 'deeper conception of our existence than usual as a necessary foundation for a vindication of the idea of human equality'.[127]

But before connecting my earlier argument with the new existentialist position, I had better say in what sense and to what extent I am prepared to defend the equalitarian position.

a. Human equality as a fact, actual or potential, seems to me empirically indefensible (notwithstanding the intriguing exception of identical twins and doubles), even though I do not subscribe to Leibniz' principle of the identity of indiscernibles, which of course makes all absolute equality a metaphysical impossibility.

b. Human equality in value appears to me almost equally problematic, unless one is prepared to accept, as I am not, the position of complete subjective relativism, under which no objective comparison of value any longer makes sense. The only equality in value that I would admit is the potential equality of all moral agents with regard to those values based upon effort, where all depends on how large a portion of one's total energies, however unequal to those of others, has been spent on striving for the good within one's reach.

c. The case for equality of rights and duties seems to me strongest, at least as far as 'basic' human rights are concerned. What is to be included among these is not easy to tell, although the recent convergence in the field of human rights (Universal Declaration of Human Rights) is a good indication, at least for a certain period. 'Equality of consideration' and 'equality of opportunities' seem to be some of the clearest candidates for a more permanent place.

However, the real philosophical problem is to find valid grounds for supporting the postulate of equality in rights and duties in the face of inequality in fact and in value. I discussed the difficulty and the ways in which other ethical theories have tried to meet it in

127. See my 'A Defense of Equality', *Philosophical Review*, Vol. LIII (1944), pp. 101-24; this volume, number 7.

my paper just cited. I also suggested a solution that seemed to me partially new and, as I still believe, basically sound. What I want to do now is to show its possible connection with some of the theses of existentialism and to indicate how I think they may be strengthened.

Equality of the Existing Egos

In the preceding section I pointed out that one of the weak points of existentialism is not only its inadequate ontological conception of existence, but also its failure to distinguish between existence and the exister. For what really matters is not so much existence as the exister. Although it is impossible to present here a full discussion of who this exister is, I submit that the primary candidate is the ego of Descartes' *ego cogito*. If the existing ego, i.e., the concrete I-myself, is the real hub of a consistent existential position, then the question arises whether we have any right to assert the equality of all existing egos. Even the task of an epistemological justification of any assertion about the equality or inequality of such egos seems to be forbidding, considering the difficulty and limitation of all knowledge of egos other than our own. The difficulty is, by the way, quite different from that of knowing their individual personalities, their states and ideas. Perhaps the equal impossibility of certain knowledge in all these cases is one of the best reasons for the equal treatment of those whose inequality can not be accurately assessed.

A more basic difficulty concerns the distinction between the ego and its properties. How far is the ego distinct from its body, from its endowments such as intelligence, or from its personality, including its temperament? Only insofar as such a distinction is possible at all does it make sense to raise the question of the equality of egos. If it is not possible, the inequalities are obvious. However, I do maintain that the distinction is defensible, at least to the extent that each ego can objectify these properties by reflection, consider them as distinct from itself, and even conceive of having others in their place. As far as the body is concerned, even Merleau-Ponty, usually considered one of the main protagonists of the identification of the subject with his body, spoke on one occasion of the 'metaphysical hypocrisy' of the person 'who unreservedly pretends to be whatever it may be', for instance, a person who identifies with his hysterical symptoms to the extent of deceiving not only others but himself as well.[128] The clear implication is that even in hysteria the patient retains enough freedom to keep himself distinct from his condition.

How far can we then assert that the various egos, as distinguished from their properties, are equal or unequal among each other? If the ego itself has no actual qualities, has it at least potentialities that could be equal or unequal to those of others? I am afraid I cannot answer these questions with any confidence. However, there seems to me considerable evidence for believing that different egos have different 'ego-strengths' and even different powers for identifying with or dissociating from their 'personality'. But these differences are hardly as pronounced as those between different personalities in their entirety. Each ego is equal to every other ego at least in its plight of having to face its existence and its fundamental situation.

8.8 Equality in the Accident of Birth and Circumstance

I shall now turn to the argument for equality in rights and duties that I made in the previously cited paper and begin by restating it in a slightly amended form as briefly as I can.

Its major premise was: All undeserved distinctions call for equalizing redress; its minor premise: All inequalities of birth constitute undeserved distinctions; the conclusion: All inequalities of birth call for equalizing redress. I called this conclusion 'the moral postulate of equality'.

I placed the main stress of my argument on the minor premise's assertion that inequalities of birth are undeserved distinctions. This proposition seemed to me supported by the idea and existential experience of the so-called 'accident (or chance) of birth', which includes such circumstances as sex, race, class, and nationality. We refer to this accident even in our ordinary way of thinking and talking, without giving the matter much thought. But I submitted that it does deserve such thought. So in a later paper[129] I tried to

128. *Phénoménologie de la perception*, Paris, Gallimard, 1945, p. 190; Colin Smith's English translation, *Phenomenology of Perception*, New York, Humanities Press, 1962, of this passage (p. 162) is misleading.
129. 'Accident of Birth: A Non-Utilitarian Motif in Mill's Philosophy', *Journal of the History of Ideas*, Vol. XXII (1961), pp. 475-492; this volume, number 6.

show that what we mean by this phrase is actually a *moral* chance, a condition not based on moral desert.

What I would like to suggest now is that existentialism can give further weight to this conception. One of existentialism's most characteristic motifs is that of the contingency of all being. For Sartre, as for David Hume, the idea of a necessary being is a contradiction in terms. The most gripping expression of the experience of radical contingency occurs in Sartre's early novel *Nausea* (1938), especially in the episode at the root of the chestnut tree, where the realization of the complete irrationality of all being suddenly closes in on the hero:

> The essential thing is contingency . . . Contingency is not a delusion, an appearance of which one can get rid. It's absolute. Consequently it is absolute gratuitousness. Everything is gratuitous, this garden, this city, I myself. If one comes to take account of this, it turns one's stomach, and everything begins to swim . . . This is real nausea. The bastards try to conceal it from themselves with their idea of right. What a poor lie! No one has any right. They are completely gratuitous like everyone else. They don't get to feeling themselves as superfluous (*de trop*). (But) within themselves, secretly, they know that they are superfluous...[130]

Much of this is clearly literary overstatement. What seems to me significant about the passage is the emphasis not so much on general contingency as on gratuitousness, the absence of any moral right to existence.

Now what I mean by the accident of birth is actually nothing but a special form of this contingency. It is the contingency of the coincidence of two contingencies, the contingency of my being and the contingency of my 'birth', i.e., my sex, race, physique, and so forth. In this sense it is actually a double contingency, a contingency to the second power. I believe that the existentialist stress on contingency as such can further heighten the poignancy of this experience. What existentialism does not seem to have done is to incorporate the original experience of the accident of birth into its framework. Also, thus far it has failed to spell out the full moral and social implications of its doctrine of universal contingency and

130. *La Nausée*, Paris, Gallimard, 1938, p. 185 f.; Engl. transl.: *Nausea* by Lloyd Alexander, Norfolk, Conn., New Directions, 1949, p. 176 f.

gratuitousness.

Equality and Human Dignity

Recently the idea of human dignity has developed into one of the most powerful weapons in the struggle for equality, especially racial equality. Yet it is an idea about whose meaning there is surprisingly little clarity and agreement, both historically and systematically. There are after all senses of the term 'human dignity' that may be expressions of blasphemous pride or ridiculous self-importance. However, this is not the place to explore the entire range of this fascinating idea.

What can existentialism do to clarify it? There is little discussion of the issue in the key existentialist writings. Actually, in his *Nausea* and *The Flies* Sartre ridiculed the ideas of human dignity, among the bourgeois humanists. Only, for instance, in the lecture on 'Existentialism is a Humanism' does one find the claim that existentialism alone can give man dignity, inasmuch as it refuses to consider him a mere object, as materialism does. However, there is no real development of the idea of dignity in this or any other context.

Assuming that existentialism can add to the conception of human dignity, what bearing has this on the postulate of human equality? To suggest such a connection one might raise a few questions based on the experience of 'indignities', of which our age has provided so many appalling examples. Assuming that any treatment of a person which does not respect his basic claim to free development and expression offends his 'dignity', is there perhaps a basic indignity in the situation of a being from whom equality is withheld? Is his dignity violated if he is not treated on a par with others who have no better moral claims to their own preferential treatment? I submit that in this sense there is an element of indignity about every kind of inequality that is none of the victim's fault.

However this may be, all I want to suggest here is that a deeper consideration of the 'human situation' may result in finding new ground for the postulate of human equality. Existentialism is well on the way to finding them. But it is certainly not the only way. Some ground may be found in such surprising places as the writings of John Stuart Mill. Perhaps the most fitting expression of the approach I am suggesting may be a quotation from Mill's diary, showing as it does that even a liberal thinker in favor of individuality could also be a friend of equality. For he based this view not only on utilitarian grounds but also on an appeal to the kind of nobility of mind which I consider congenial to the best existentialist temper:

> The passion for equality is an attribute either of the most high-minded or of those who are merely the most jealous and envious. The last should rather be called haters of superiority than lovers of equality. It is only the high-minded to whom equality is really agreeable. A proof is that they are the only persons who are capable of strong and durable attachments to their equals; while strong and durable attachments to superiors or inferiors are far more common and are possible for the vulgarest person.[131]

8.9 Supplement 1982

Sartre's puzzling silence in his publications about his position toward human equality has now been broken by some explicit statements in his conversations with Simone de Beauvoir,[132] who in 1974 questioned him about the meaning of the ringing, but puzzling last sentence of his autobiography *Les Mots* (1963), in which he stated that what remained after the rejection of the seductive idea of an elite was: 'A whole man made of all men and as good as all of them and no better than any *(tout un homme, fait de tous les hommes et qui les vaut tous et que vaut n'importe qui).* In his reply Sartre now asserted that even during his early days he had 'the idea of an equality, an equality which I always wanted and have dreamed to establish between other people and myself. For ultimately each time that I have had strong relations with someone else, man or woman, I have perceived that this person was completely my equal, and that even if I could perhaps communicate better in words, in every case the primary intuitions the other person had were exactly the same as my own, and that he saw things from the same viewpoint as I did.'

131. From 'Diary', March 29, 1854, *The Letters of John Stuart Mill*, London, Longmans, Green & Co., 1910, Vol. II, p. 383.

132. Simone de Beauvoir, *La Cérémonie des adieux, suivi de Entretiens avec Jean-Paul Sartre*. Paris, Gallimard, 1981, p. 311.

9. HUMAN DIGNITY: A CHALLENGE TO
CONTEMPORARY PHILOSOPHY

This paper cannot 'and must not attempt a full-fledged philosophy of human dignity. All I propose to offer are prolegomena for such a philosophy. Specifically what I want to show is:

1. that the idea of human dignity plays a decisive role in today's social and political thought and action, even more so than commonly realized;

2. that this idea in its present sense is relatively new;

3. that our ordinary way of talking about it is confused and vague to the point of contradictoriness;

4. that the idea of human dignity is vulnerable to attack;

5. that the philosophical treatment of the idea thus far is inadequate;

6. that the way to a better philosophy of human dignity requires certain basic distinctions such as those between dignity in itself and the grounds of dignity;

7. that human dignity in itself is a phenomenon within our experience;

8. that the basis for human dignity can lie in several grounds related to different philosophies.

9.1. The Present Role of the Idea of Human Dignity

I can think of no better way to justify my insistence on the impor-

Reprinted by permission from *Human Dignity* ed. by R. Gotesky and A. Laszlo. New York: Gordon & Breach, 1971, pp. 39-64.

tance of the idea of human dignity than by referring first to some official documents.

(I) The Charter of the United Nations of 1946 in its preamble bases the new organization on the determination not only to save mankind from the scourge of war, but 'to reaffirm faith in fundamental human rights, in the dignity and worth of the human person . . .'

(II) The Universal Declaration of Human Rights of 1948, which in its own preamble refers back to the pledge of the Charter, begins with the words:

'Whereas recognition of the inherent dignity and of the equal and inalienable rights of all members of the human family is the foundation of freedom, justice and peace in the world.' And its very first article starts with the sentence:

'All human beings are born free and equal in dignity and rights'. Article 22 affirms man's right to realization of the 'economic, social and cultural rights indispensable for his dignity', Article 23 (3) entitles him to a remuneration ensuring for himself and his family 'an existence worthy of human dignity'.

(III) One other constitutional document from a nation not yet a member of the United Nations, also dating to the era after World War II, bears quoting here, since it reflects the urgency of this idea in a nation that had been implicated in some of the worst 'indignities' of modern history. Article 1 of the Basic Law *(Grundgesetz)* of the Federal Republic of (Western) Germany states: 'The dignity of man is unassailable *(unantastbar)*. To respect and protect it is the duty of all state power. The German people therefore profess inviolable and inalienable human rights as the basis of every human community of peace and justice in the world.'[133] This emphasis on the role of human dignity is all the more remarkable since the Weimar Constitution of 1919, which listed the 'Basic Rights and Duties of the Germans' only in its second part, contained no reference to human dignity. Article 1 also plays a part in the jurisdiction of the German Supreme Constitutional Court *(Verfassungsgerichtshof)*.

(IV) Moving from the international and national sphere to that

---

133. See John Ford Golay, *The Foundation of the Federal Republic of Germany* (University of Chicago Press) 1958, p. 218; see also the report on the preparatory deliberations, pp. 176 f.

of social issues, nowhere do we find the cry for human dignity raised more explicitly than in the struggle of the American Negroes for equality. This is all the more striking since in earlier emancipation movements, including that for the emancipation of women, there seems to have been little if any explicit appeal to this idea. The most outspoken voice pleading in the name of human dignity was that of Martin Luther King, whose fight for civil rights began in a revolt against the 'indignities' of segregation inflicted on the Negroes riding the public buses in Montgomery, Alabama, where it started when Mrs. Rosa Parks' 'personal sense of dignity and self-respect' rebelled against the order of the white bus driver to vacate her seat. This event also started King's 'struggle for human dignity'. This motif occurs over and over again in his speeches and writings, which present the 'achievement of human dignity' as the major aspiration of the American Negro. Thus his 'Letter from Birmingham Jail' proclaimed the 'dream of a positive peace where all men will respect the dignity and worth of human personality'.[134] While human dignity and human rights are not mentioned often in the decisions of the U.S. Supreme Court, Justices like William Brennan do mention them in their separate opinions.

(V) The revolt against the indignities of an increasingly computerized society spearheaded by the student movement in most countries of the world may not be in the habit of appealing to such old-fashioned ideas as human dignity. But it takes little imagination and interpretive violence to realize that the latest rebellion against all forms of technology attacks the anonymity of a civilization because it offends the dignity of the individual.[135]

(VI) The idea of human dignity plays a particularly striking role

134. It seems worth pointing out that in *Stride for Freedom*, Ch. VI, King credited the personalist philosophy of Edgar Sheffield Brightman with having given him 'a metaphysical basis for the dignity and worth of all human personality'. Actually, there seems to be little explicit emphasis on the idea of human dignity in Brightman's published writings.

135. Thus the Port Huron Statement of the 'Students for a Democratic Society' of 1962 proclaimed: 'We regard man as infinitely precious and possessed of unfulfilled capacities for reason, freedom, and love. In affirming these principles we are aware of countering perhaps the dominant conceptions of man in the twentieth century: that he is a thing to be manipulated and that he is inherently incapable of directing his own affairs. We oppose the depersonalization that reduces human beings to the status of things...' *The New Student Left*, an anthology edited by Michael Cohen and Dennis Hale, Beacon

in the *aggiornamento* of Catholicism through Pope John XXIII, especially in such documents as his Encyclical 'Peace on Earth' (1958), where it forms the basis of his entire social and international program. It found a major expression at the Vatican Council II, particularly in the Declaration on Religious Liberty ('Dignitatis humanae' and the 'Pastoral Constitutions on the Church in the Modern World' (*Gaudium et spes*, whose main author was Pope John Paul II, and *Humanae personae dignitatem*)).

(VII) The phrase 'human dignity' as such does not figure prominently in the original Communist ideology. But it is implicit in Marx's denunciation of the 'alienation' of labor. The new emphasis on humanism in twentieth-century Marxism of all shades, based particularly on Marx's early writings, comes even closer to proclaiming human dignity as its standard.[136]

9.2 The Newness of the Idea

'Human dignity' as a standing phrase and its equivalent in other languages is perhaps not older than two hundred years. It does not figure in the entry on 'Dignity' in the *Oxford English Dictionary*.[137] While the Latin *dignitas* occurs in a variety of contexts, signifying chiefly excellence and distinction it is not applied to man specifically.[138] At the beginning of the Renaissance Pico della Mirandola's famous oration is entitled *De dignitate hominis*, but neither

Press, 1966, p. 12. Also, Thomas Hayden concluded his report about 'SNCC in Action' in Mississippi by stating its goal as fightin 'for social justice, for freedom, for the common life, and for the creation of dignity for the enslaved, and thereby for us all'. (p. 85)

136. See, e.g., Leopold Senghor, 'Socialism is a Humanism', in Erich Fromm, ed., *Socialist Humanism* (Anchor Books, 1966), especially p. 64. The 'New Moral Code' proclaimed by the Communist Party of the Soviet Union in 1961 stresses 'the mutual respect between individuals'. (Richard DeGeorge, *Soviet Ethics and Morality*. Ann Arbor: University of Michigan Press, 1969, p. 83) – The topic of human dignity in Marxist thought was the subject of a paper by Helmut Fleischer (*Marxismus und Menschenwürde*) at one of the dialogues of the *Paulus-Gesellschaft* (Kellner, Erich, ed.) *Schöpfertum und Freiheit in einer humanen Gesellschaft. Marienbader Protokolle*. Wien, Europa-Verlag 1969, pp. 233-48.

137. An important article by Eugenio Garin entitled *La dignitas humana e la letteratura Patristica* in *La Rinascita* I (1944), pp. 102-146 may suggest that the phrase was current among some of the Church Fathers, but none of the texts quoted contains it.

138. The need for an analysis of the phrase 'the essential dignity of man' has been

this phrase nor *dignitas humana* appears in the text. In fact, according to Paul Oskar Kristeller[139] the original title was simply *Oratio* and the phrase 'on the dignity of man' was added by later editors. Apparently it was not until the Enlightenment that the 'dignity of man' became a current phrase.

The same thing seems to be true of equivalents in other modern languages, not to mention ancient Greek, which has no equivalent for the Latin expression. In German the compound *Menschenwürde* does not occur until late in the eighteenth century. It seems to be characteristic of the humanism of the *Aufklärung*.

But even if the term 'human dignity' should be recent, the idea itself may have had a much longer history. However, in order to trace it one needs a clear conception of the idea itself as distinguished from its varying labels. Now, it is precisely one point of this paper to show that our idea of human dignity is anything but clear.[140] If it simply means man's excellence, and specifically his superiority over other species of the animal kingdom and over sub-human nature in general, eulogies of man's dignity can be found from the dawn of man's consciousness of his own nature and status in the world. Psalm 8.v.5 'Thou has made him little lower than God' (or, in other translations, 'the angels') may serve as the earliest Biblical example. Sophocles' chorus in the *Antigone* 'Many wonders there are, but nothing is more wondrous than man' is one of the highest claims made for man's excellence in Antiquity. Even during the Christian Middle Ages, when man's corruption through original sin called for the new virtue of humility, the idea of man as the image of God was never effaced. It left to man a reason to put himself above all other creatures in spite of his 'miseries'. The main glorification of man was the work of modern humanism with Francis Bacon as one of its first 'trumpeters'.

---

pointed out before by Albert William Levi in 'Language and Social Action' *Ethics* 51 (1941) p. 311. Herschel Baker's *The Dignity of Man* (1947), which claims to be 'A Study of the Idea of Human Dignity in Classical Antiquity, the Middle Ages, and the Renaissance', is actually mostly an account of the various conceptions of man and the world up to the seventeenth century, with little explicit discussion of dignity, justifying the change of title in the subsequent Harper Torchbook edition to *The Image of Man*.

139. *Renaissance Thought and its Sources*. New York: Columbia Press, p. 173.

140. See Arthur O. Lovejoy, *Reflections on Human Nature*. Baltimore, John Hopkins University Press, 1963.

However, if by human dignity one wants to refer to the quality in man which, regardless of his various distinctions in comparison with other beings, entitles him to personal respect and certain basic rights, the matter is far from clear. Not until the idea of Natural Law came to be formulated in terms of subjective rights inherent in individual persons did it make sense to think of humans as worthy of respect simply on the grounds of their being human. I submit that this idea was born with the first declarations of the rights of man, as inspired by John Locke's *Second Treatise on Government*. However, even here the appeal to human dignity is at best implicit.

In the latter sense, then, 'human dignity' both as a term and as an idea is historically a very recent arrival. This should serve as a first warning against taking it for granted.

9.3 Inconsistencies and Vaguenesses in our Ideas about Human Dignity

Next, I want to show that our ordinary talk about human dignity is anything but clear and consistent and hence is by no means a philosophically safe point of departure. In pointing out such defects in our ordinary thinking and speaking about dignity and human dignity in particular, I have no intention of denying that it makes sense. On the contrary it may make too much sense, or better, too many (good) senses. The task is to take them apart and to clarify them in an effort to make them not only safer but more effective.

I shall begin with some examples from nonphilosophical talk.

1. Human dignity is described as inherent in every man. But it is also held up as a goal to be 'achieved' or even 'created' and hence not man's natural endowment.

2. Human dignity is proclaimed as 'unassailable'. Yet 'indignities' are denounced as flagrant violations of such dignity.

3. Human dignity is presented as independent of recognition by other people. Yet it is also fervently demanded by the disinherited, as something conferred on or withheld from them ('Give us our dignity').

4. Freedom movements aim at awakening in the suppressed a 'sense'

of their (inherited) dignity. But often they talk as if the suppressed are deprived of the very dignity of which they are to develop a sense.

5. Every man is supposed to be incapable of losing human dignity. Yet some seem to be losing it by doing things which are below human dignity.

6. Dignity is something that attaches to persons who are considered as ends in themselves. Yet in speaking of treating human beings 'with dignity' we seem to imply that dignity qualifies an action and is something like a 'means by which we handle them'.

Conceivably, in these cases we are speaking about human dignity in different senses. What are they? Distinguishing between them as I shall do in Section 9.6 will be one of our first tasks in making sense of human dignity talk.

9.4 Denials of Human Dignity

The idea of human dignity is not only novel, its beginnings have been far from easy. I have no intention of tracing its history and difficulties, but I do want to identify some of the objections to it which signal possible weaknesses of the idea and call for discussion and reply.

(1) I shall begin with the theological aspect. Recent statements by the churches and particularly by the leaders of the Catholic Church can easily give the impression that the belief in human dignity was basic in Judaeo-Christian religion. The reason given for this belief is usually the conception of man as an 'image' of God, who thus shares in God's perfection and 'dignity' (a term usually missing in the roster of divine attributes). But this must not make one overlook that this dignity had been severely damaged, if not effaced, by the Fall, according to Augustine to the extent that man had become totally corrupt and could be redeemed only through an extraordinary act of divine grace, of which he is unworthy on his own. In fact, according to the more sophisticated interpretations of the Fall, man's primary sin was pride, which may well be identified with an exaggerated sense of his own dignity as not being dependent on his creator. In any case, humility forms one of the

basic virtues of Christian theological ethics, in contrast to Aristotle's 'great-mindedness' (*megalopsychia*), i.e., the right sense of one's own worth. This humility implies 'humbling' oneself, if only for the sake of being raised again as a reward. In fact, the 'seventh step of humility' (Thomas Aquinas) demands 'confessing and believing that one is useless for, and unworthy of everything' (*Summa Theologica* II, 2 q. 161, a. 6). It is certainly no accident that the great theologians before the nineteenth century never seem to speak about man's dignity. The real question is whether man's finiteness and need of slavation is compatible with any boasting about his dignity. The answer will largely depend on a clarification of the meaning of human dignity.

(2) One might think that the threat to human dignity comes only from the side of theology. But human dignity is by no means safe from secular critics of human nature. Thus, the optimistic pride in the 'grandeur' of human nature (Pascal) has always been matched by the pessimistic bewailing of his 'misery', his meanness and imperfectibility, in the form of sober arguments as well as of satire and comedy. In fact, according to Pascal's *Pensées*, human dignity consists in thought; but this very thought is 'contemptible, ridiculous and foolish' (ed. Brunschvicg, 386). And even before Hobbes' downgrading of the rational animal, such humanists as Erasmus and Montaigne had seriously questioned the self-glorification of man. But the main attack on human pride, less as a sin than as a ridiculous pretension, developed precisely during the Age of Enlightenment with its progressive hopes, spearheaded by such satirists as Pope and Swift.[141] David Hume, in his little essay 'Of the Dignity or Meanness of Human Nature', takes a seemingly neutral stand, making the decision for or against dignity or meanness relative to the basis adopted in our comparisons.[142] But there is good reason to believe that his own estimate of man did not grant him any special dignity above the animals.[143] There is clearly no need to trace the pessimistic perspectives of man throughout the nineteenth cen-

141. See Bertrand A. Goldgar, 'Satire on Man and the Dignity of Human Nature', *Publications of the Modern Language Association* 80 (1965), pp. 535-41.

142. See *Essays Moral, Political and Literary*, eds. T.H. Greene and Grose, I. p. 151 f.

143. See Marvin Fox, 'Religion and Human Nature in the Philosophy of David Hume', *Process and Divinity: The Hartshorne Festschrift*, Wm. E. Reese and Eugene Freeman eds. The Open Court, 1964, p. 77.

tury in order to see that human dignity is anything but a universal creed in modern thought. Just mentioning the subject of the descent of man from lower species will suffice to show that the belief in man's unique dignity in the cosmos was rapidly losing its scientific credibility.

(3) But it is not only in the West that human dignity has been questioned. For instance, in Gandhi's interpretation of Hinduism, humility, one of its basic virtues, 'should make the possessors realize that he is a nothing. . . Our existence as embodied beings is purely momentary; what are a hundred years in eternity? But if we shatter the chains of egotism, and are melted in the ocean of humility, we share its dignity. To feel that we are something is to set up a barrier between God and ourselves. . .'[144] In other words, dignity belongs only to humanity as a whole, not to the individual in his essential 'egotism'.

Actually Heinrich Zimmer, one of the authorities on classic Indian philosophy, goes so far as to say:

> A basic fact generally disregarded by those who go in for Indian wisdom is this one of the total rejection of every last value of humanity by the Indian teachers and winners of redemption from the bondages of the world. . . 'Humanity', whether in the individual or in the collective aspect, can no longer be of concern to anyone striving seriously for perfection along the way of the ultimate Indian wisdom. . . For the Indian point of view, the special dignity of the human being consists solely in the fact that he is capable of becoming enlightened, free from bondage, and therewith competent, ultimately, for the role of the supreme teacher and savior of all beings, including the beasts and the gods.[145]

Surely, this is not the kind of dignity which can support the belief in the universal dignity and worth of the human person.

At this point I shall rest the case against the dignity of man. Enough if it has shown that it is anything but unchallengeable. It certainly needs clarifying and buttressing. Until then we had better be prepared for the objections and ridicule of those who point at the sorry sight of man in today's world. Certainly any pride man may still want to take in his cosmic rank or nobility is no longer

144. *Selected Writings of Mahatma Gandhi,* ed. by Ronald Duncan, Boston: Beacon Press, 1951, p. 52.
145. Heinrich Zimmer, *Philosophies of India,* Meridian Books, 1956, pp. 231 f.

safe. Human dignity had better be based on firmer foundations if it is to become the cornerstone for the superstructure of universal human rights.

9.5 The Philosophers' Case for Human Dignity

Philosophers have not been completely silent on the subject. But are their contributions sufficient to underpin human dignity? On the following pages I shall look into several such pleas: those of Giovanni Pico della Mirandola, Immanuel Kant, Leonard Nelson and a few existential philosophers.

(1) Pico may well have been the first to have tried to give arguments in defense of the dignity of man. Actually his 'oration' was meant as the opening 'trumpet' for a disputation that never took place. But it must be realized that what Pico meant by 'dignity' was the fact that man is a 'great marvel' *(magnum miraculum)*, 'most worthy of admiration' *(admirandus maxime)*. Such admirableness can hardly be identified with the kind of dignity which calls for respect even in cases where there is little, if anything, left to admire in a person, e.g., a psychotic patient or a 'human vegetable'.

Pico's reason for claiming such admirableness for man is new and highly original: man's 'chameleon'-like freedom to mold and make himself into lower or higher natures, or, to put it in more up-to-date form, into a superman or into a subman. But while this may give man a remarkable ontological distinction, anticipating Sartre's existentialism and make us 'gape', is it enough of a reason for paying him our respects in a moral sense? Besides, the validity of this reason depends on Pico's implicit indeterminism, something which a philosopher cannot take for granted. In fact, Pico's defense has to face the objections of the pessimist critics of human nature, especially those of evolutionalists who consider man a biological blind alley. The apologia for man's defects is by no means easier than the theodicy of the creator.

(2) Kant did not compose a special treatise on human dignity. But the few pages which he wrote about it, especially those in the second section of his *Foundations of Metaphysics of Morals,* may well have been the most influential text on the subject. Here he introduced dignity in connection with the second formula of his categorical imperative according to which man is to be treated as an

end in himself and never as a means only. As such, man possesses in Kant's sense 'dignity'. Dignity is here contrasted with 'price', the kind of value for which there can be an equivalent, whereas dignity makes an object irreplaceable. Only man can have such dignity. But this does not mean man as an empirical being. Kant focuses on 'the idea of a rational being which obeys no law except that which he himself gives at the same time'. In fact, dignity attaches directly to morality as based on moral legislation: 'Only morality and mankind insofar as it is capable of it' can have 'dignity'. Finally Kant goes so far as to say that the basis of morality, 'legislation itself, which determines all value, must have dignity, i.e., unconditional, incomparable value. Hence autonomy is the basis of the dignity of human and of all rational nature.'

Later, in the *Metaphysics of Morals,* which contains some very revealing developments of this view on the occasion of his discussion of 'servility', Kant even speaks of 'moral humility' as the 'consciousness and feeling of the insignificance of one's worth in comparison with the law'. This does not preclude that 'as a person, i.e., as the subject of morally-practical reason . . . he possesses a dignity (an absolute inner worth) whereby he exacts the respect of all other rational beings in the world, can measure himself against each member of his species, and can esteem himself on a footing of equality with them.'[146]

Impressive though this first sustained philosophical case for human dignity sounds, it makes full sense only in the framework of Kant's total philosophy. What it presupposes specifically is:

1. that all morality is related to laws;

2. that these laws must be 'given' in the sense of legislation;

3. that moral laws are given by man himself qua rational being.

But even granting these debatable presuppositions, it must be realized that this interpretation and vindication of human dignity restricts it to man as a rational and moral being, but does not include man as an empirical being with all of his additional characteristics. Also, it is far from clear that and why self-legislation ('autonomy' in Kant's sense) entails dignity in any ordinary sense of the word.

146. *The Metaphysical Principles of Virtue*, Translated by James Ellington (Bobbs Merrill, 1969), p. 97 f.

Legislating may have any number of desirable and even morally meritorious features. But is there anything about it that bestows a peculiar human dignity upon the legislator? Why should only the *making* of universal rules entail dignity but not other acts, especially those done from respect for such laws, let alone acts of spontaneous generosity or noble-mindedness? Even if it should be possible to absorb them into Kant's concept of autonomous legislation, the fact remains that Kant cannot claim more than conditional dignity for man the empirical being rather than man the rational moral being. Kant's moralistic plea for human dignity is not a defense of man in his entirety. As far as he is concerned, Kant made it clear that man 'in the system of nature is a being of little significance, and, along with the other animals, considered as products of the earth, has an ordinary value ('vulgar' price). Even the fact that he excells these in having understanding and can set up ends for himself still gives him only an external value for his usefulness, namely the value of a man in preference to another animal'.[147] Kant's primary interest in dignity concerns morality, and it is moral law 'that fills his mind with ever new awe', not man as a human being.

(3) A twentieth-century Kantian in whose philosophy of morals and law the concept of human dignity had a central role was Leonard Nelson. Actually he resumed the tradition of Jakob Fries, whose practical philosophy was dominated by the Kantian concept of personal dignity, but who added little to its development. For Nelson, the neo-Friesian, human dignity consisted primarily in his 'capacity as a rational being to raise himself to a level of education where he can overcome practical error'.[148] Later he pointed out that rational beings can give their lives a meaning which, depending on them, is identical with dignity (*ibid.*, p. 358 f.). Finally Nelson declared: 'The dignity of man lies in his self-determination'.

Again, Nelson's conception of human dignity cannot be fully understood and evaluated in isolation from his system. But even without it, its similarities with and differences from Kant's philosophy of human dignity are noteworthy. There is the same emphasis on autonomy in the sense of man's creative self-determination as

147. *Ibid.* p. 97.
148. *System der philosophischen Rechtslehre und Politik,* 1924, p. 115 f.

the core of his dignity. But there is no mention of moral legislation as the basis of morality. This could be an asset. But the whole treatment of the ideal of human dignity is much too incidental and incomplete as an adequate and convincing basis for a system of morality and human rights, which incidentally Nelson, the Socialist, develops courageously in considerable detail.

(4) To my knowledge the only contemporary American philosopher who has taken up human dignity explicitly is Abraham Edel in his article on 'Humanist Ethics and the Meaning of Human Dignity'.[149] Edel treats human dignity as a 'construct', comparable to the construct 'atom' in science, thereby rejecting its interpretation as a 'Platonic type of essence' or 'phenomenological quality'; he also rejects a mere linguistic analysis. But even as a construct, dignity can be given two interpretations, a 'realistic' and an 'instrumentalist' one. The realistic interpretation is based on phenomenal qualities, to be explored by what Edel calls a 'phenomenological psychology'. It finds dignity, for instance, in situations where people are treated with more or less 'dignity'. Such dignity appears to be changeable and differs in different people. Actually, dignity becomes here a matter of theory of personality, of individuals and social psychology. One may well wonder whether this does not result in psychologism, i.e., the conversion of non-psychic phenomena into psychic ones. Can we seriously think of describing dignity in psychological terms, even in terms of a phenomenological psychology?

Edel's 'instrumentalist interpretation' puzzles me even more. Its fair appraisal depends of course on a full presentation and critique of John Dewey's instrumentalism in ethics and social philosophy. In the present context Edel seems to think of human dignity on the one hand as a social ideal on a par with justice and well-being, which would make it more than a mere 'instrument'. On the other hand he suggests that it 'is evaluated by the type of life it makes possible, the human purposes it helps achieve and the human problems to whose solution it contributes' (p. 238). This ambiguity seems to me characteristic of the instrumentalist refusal to distinguish sharply between ends and means. No doubt the idea of human

---

149. *Moral Problems in Contemporary Society,* ed. by Paul Kurtz, Englewood Cliffs, Prentice Hall, 1969, pp. 227-40.

dignity can be and is a major weapon in the struggle for the ideal society. But it seems odd to make its evaluation dependent on this role. Actually my impression is that later on Edel himself is on the move to giving this particular tool a more dignified rank in his scheme. But in any case, the instrumentalist interpretation is no adequate answer to the question of the meaning of the ideal dignity and even less to that of its justification.

Edel himself considers his ideas as merely 'probing suggestions'. But even taken in this spirit they invite and deserve probing questions. To make dignity a construct seems to imply that prior to construction nothing definite corresponds to the phrase. Does this mean that the place of this construct could be taken equally by that of Nietzschean supremacy or Nazi racial 'purity'? What does construction mean in such a case? Furthermore, what does it really mean to subject such a construct to different interpretations? How are they related? Are they always compatible? Specifically, how can the realistic interpretation of dignity, which presumably discovers something 'real' underlying the construction, serve at the same time as an (instrumental) ideal?

All this would have to be much more fully developed before the claims of the construct-theory can be fully appraised. Meanwhile the idea that human dignity has a 'realistic' and an 'ideal' aspect is worth pursuing. But even so, there seems to be no good reason for postponing the empirical task of first exploring what we 'really' mean with human dignity at the risk that we should find out that it is nothing at all, and that we have to go into the construction business.

(5) Among other contemporary philosophies which show some concern about human dignity, existentialism must at least be mentioned. Thus Sartre, at the stage when he formulated his existentialist humanism, announced that 'this theory is the only one which gives man dignity and does not make of him a thing' (as supposedly do all forms of materialism), since it opposes the free consciousness to the brute fact of Being.[150] Heidegger's answer to Sartre in his 'Letter on Humanism' rejects all humanisms because even 'the highest humanistic accounts of the nature of man do not yet experience the authentic dignity of man'.[151] According to Heidegger this dig-

---

150. *L'Existentialisme est un humanisme* (Paris, 1946), p. 65.
151. *Brief über den Humanismus*, Frankfurt, V. Klostermann, 1949, p. 199.

nity is to be found in the fact that man has been 'thrown' by Being into the truth of Being, i.e., man's calling is something like that of a keeper of Being.

The only philosopher of existence who has devoted a full book to the topic is Gabriel Marcel in his William James Lectures at Harvard. However, this book is largely an intellectual autobiography and discusses the topic of its title explicitly only in one chapter, according to which human dignity is not rooted in rationality but in the 'mystery' expressed in the very weakness and finitude of human being (p. 128). It points at some 'living tie which unites all men'.

While all these ideas are suggestive, they are much too undeveloped to tell us what human dignity means, what is its basis, and whether it actually exists.

I conclude that even philosophers have thus far not given us a clear sense and a convincing defense of the idea of human dignity. How then can we improve on their cases? At this point I have to repeat that it would be foolish to offer a quick solution of the problems we have encountered thus far. It is precisely my point that more is needed than the approach by piecemeal discussions. All I can hope to do is to outline some of the steps which a further study of the problems must take and in so doing clear some of the ground for future solutions.

9.6 Some Basic Distinctions

My first approach to these tasks will consist in an attempt to dispel some of the semantic confusions which endanger the meaningfulness of human dignity talk. Such a cleanup can at the same time lay bare some of the phenomenal structures hidden behind the verbal screen.

I shall begin with the inconsistencies in our ordinary talk about human dignity as pointed out in Section 9.2.

(1) In calling human dignity 'inherent' and yet something to be 'achieved', we mean in the first case something which man need not and cannot strive for. By contrast, what we mean when we talk about achieving it is one of two things:

1. the manifestation of the inherent dignity by the attitude of its owner, who shows it in a way which cannot be ignored, or

2. the recognition of inherent dignity by its erstwhile deniers.

We should therefore distinguish

1. dignity itself,

2. the expression of such dignity in inward and outward behavior, and

3. the recognition of both by outsiders.

(2) In talking about human dignity as 'unassailable' and yet as 'violated', we really mean in the first case that in an ultimate sense human dignity itself cannot be destroyed by any attacks, specifically not by inflicting 'indignities' upon people. But this does not prevent such attempted violations from being actions which are in ('flagrant') conflict with such dignity, inasmuch as they do not fulfill the claim to respect issuing from the inviolable dignity. Thus we must distinguish the ultimate dignity in man and the claims issuing from it, which can be violated in the sense of not being fulfilled, though they can never be annihilated.

(3) Human dignity as being immune to nonrecognition or denial and yet something which is demanded must refer in one case to dignity itself, in the other to its realization in practical response by the community which may have ignored it. Dignity in the second case stands for the kind of treatment demanded by dignity in the first sense.

(4) A 'sense of dignity' presupposes indeed that there is an inherent dignity to which one is or is not sensitive. But it need not be a realized dignity. It could also be a dignity longed for, but not yet achieved. In the latter case what is at stake is again either the manifestation of dignity by its owner or its recognition by others, which has still to be realized.

(5) 'Losing one's dignity' in the sense of becoming deprived of it and of losing it by doing something which is beneath it refer to two different kinds of losing: in the first case to being henceforth without dignity, something which the thesis of universal human dignity considers impossible; in the second case to doing something which is in conflict with the demands of one's own dignity, which remains unaffected by such 'loss'. What is lost is merely the kind of attitude, the 'composure', demanded by dignity itself.

(6) 'Treating someone with dignity' does not imply that dignity

is a means or a way of using such a means. The true sense of this phrase is 'to treat someone with respect for his dignity'. Secondarily it may also characterize the way in which the agent manifests his own dignity by the way he acts, i.e., either with or without dignity (in a sense not to be identified with human dignity as such), for instance in 'dying with dignity'.

While such distinctions may remove the appearance of inconsistencies in our everyday talk by pointing out varieties of meaning of our words or phrases, such a method does not yet give us a complete picture of the phenomena. And, more important, it does not guarantee that what we mean is true. In order to make sure of this, we would need at least a complete phenomenology of the experience of human dignity, which would compare what we 'really' mean with what we 'really' find in 'going to the things'. In the present context this is out of the question. At best some groundbreaking work can be done which will lay out some of the dimensions for such research.

One such dimension could be a systematic collection of ordinary usage, not restricted to seeming inconsistencies, in the manner of John L. Austin's 'linguistic phenomenology'. But such an attempt, which would have to be extended to different languages and different phases in their history, is also impossible in this context.

However, I would like to draw attention to the fact that there is a considerable and significant difference in the way in which we speak about *dignity* in general and about *human dignity* in particular. Dignity in general, the only dignity which figures in such dictionaries as the *Oxford English Dictionary,* is a term of many meanings. It applies to all sorts of carriers, human and nonhuman, and indicates primarily certain distinctive qualities which give them a rank above others that do not have these qualities. In fact, dignity in the general sense is a matter of degree. It reflects a hierarchic picture of reality in the tradition of the 'Great Chain of Being' with higher and lower dignities. Such dignity is subject to change, to increase and decrease; it can be gained and lost. It finds its expression in such dignities as are conferred on 'dignitaries' through honors or titles, and can be expressed in dignified or undignified comportment.

Human dignity is a very different matter. It implies the very denial of a hierarchical order of dignities. For it refers to the minimum dignity which belongs to every human being qua human. It does not admit of any degrees. It is equal for all humans. It cannot be gained or lost. In this respect human dignity as a species of dignity differs fundamentally from the genus.

This is also the reason why most of the attacks on human dignity which alarmed us in Section 9.3 are really irrelevant to human dignity as here understood. The fact that man has lost through the Fall whatever likeness to divine perfection he may haved had does not affect his human dignity as long as he remains a human being. Even in total corruption the sinner remains a man. Likewise, whatever reason for pride or shame a person may feel considering his optimistic or pessimistic secular portrait of human nature, he is still a man. The question is whether this remnant is enough for the equal minimum dignity which is meant by human dignity. But what is this dignity? Finally, even the dignity denied humanity by Indian philosophy is mostly its cosmic rank, not its dignity qua being human.

Several other distinctions applying to all types of dignity may prove helpful:

(1) There is a difference between what may be called *intrinsic* and *extrinsic* dignity. The first means inner, self-sufficient worth of beings by themselves, which does not call for any outside complement. In this sense we may ascribe dignity not only to people but to things, natural and cultural: the majestic dignity of redwoods or the 'dignity of the sciences' (Francis Bacon) may illustrate the latter. But then there is the 'aggressive' dignity of being worthy of something else, to which what is worthy has something like a claim, e.g., to attention, to approval or to support. Such dignity is in this sense outward bound, extrinsic, demands a complement. The first is a matter of mere contemplation, the second calls for action, the fulfillment of a claim. In general we are much more aware of the second kind of dignity, since it puts demands on us. But there is certainly an intimate connection between the two. In order to be worthy of anything else the 'worthy' must have some worth of its own. And having such worth, it cannot fail to make demands on its context.

(2) The search for human dignity was in the beginning and is still largely a search for man's distinctive characteristics which set him apart and put him above his less 'dignified' fellow beings. Most of

the meanings in the *Oxford English Dictionary* suggest such hierarchic distinctions. Obviously, they are only a relative, or better, a *relational* dignity. But this attempt to give man a claim to superiority in the cosmic scheme, illustrated best by Pico's eulogy, differs from the less ambitious attempt to determine man's worth without boastful or 'invidious' comparisons with other beings. Here man is simply appraised on the basis of what assets and liabilities he may have by himself and in his own right. This may be called *absolute* dignity. Actually, even his relational or comparative dignity cannot be determined without an appraisal of his 'absolute' dignity, as well as that of those beings with which he is being compared.

(3) What is the relation between 'human dignity' and 'worth'? In the *Universal Declaration of Human Rights* and in some of Martin Luther King's statements the two are mentioned side by side. Is this merely a rhetorical redundancy, or do the two words stand for different ideas? There is no easy answer to this question, and it had better not be precipitated. There are at least indications that the two words stress different aspects of the same phenomenon, 'worth' standing more for man's value by himself, i.e., his 'absolute dignity', 'dignity' for the manifestation of this worth as it relates to a wider setting, i.e., his 'relational dignity'.

(4) Another general distinction which seems to be usually overlooked in connection with dignity is that between human dignity in itself and the *grounds* for such dignity. Saying that dignity 'consists in' personality may mean one of two things: either that dignity means nothing else but being a personality. Or it may mean that dignity is a peculiar characteristic of its own, but based on the fact that its owner has personality. Distinguishing between an entity and its grounds should make not only for clarity but deeper insight. In any case, before it makes sense to ask for the grounds of dignity, it is essential to know what it is in itself.

9.7 The Phenomenon of Human Dignity in Itself

Among the synonyms or connotational definitions of human dignity, thus far encountered more or less incidentally, two seem worth special consideration: dignity as intrinsic worth and dignity as worthiness of respect.

I shall begin with the second definition, because it shows human dignity in action; this is the way in which we are most likely to experience it.

(1) Can human dignity be identified with worthiness of respect? In order to answer this question one has to examine a little more closely than usual what is meant by such respect. Specifically, is respect something restricted to human beings? It is probably true that in ordinary language one would not, except facetiously, speak of having respect for mere material objects such as mountains, although one may have a 'healthy respect' for them or rather for the difficulties involved in climbing them. But especially in the context of conservation one may speak of respect for nature as a whole and particularly for plants and animals. Going to the other end of the spectrum, one would hardly speak of respect for God or even for human heroes, when worship or reverence seem to be the more appropriate responses. Respect seems directed mostly toward fellow humans on the same level with us. But one must not overlook respect for truth or the law. The question then would be whether such respect differs from the kind of respect accorded human beings.

What is really going on in the act or attitude of respect? The etymology of the Latin-based English word suggests a looking back at. But respecting means certainly much more than this. It involves at least a standing back from what is respected and at the same time an attitude of noninterference with it. But there are several kinds and degrees of such respect. For instance, to respect dissenting views or personal idiosyncracies (German: *respektieren*) does not mean to have respect for them. Mere respecting implies nothing but toleration, but respect-for suggests active approval and even looking up to the respected. However, such noninterfering support does not go so far as reverence or worship. For there is no implication that the respected is of a superior order, deserving admiration or awe. Respect or regard means mainly the willingness to leave the respected alone as deserving such independence. But even such respect has variations according to its object. Personal respect is addressed to a person and tends to be communicated, whereas impersonal respect is not addressed at all, and is expressed merely by further pursuit of the respected, e.g., of truth.

Now what kind of respect is meant by worthiness of respect in the case of human dignity? Certainly more than mere tolerance and impersonal respect. At least we should have to add worthiness of personal respect, i.e., the kind of respect addressed to a person with human dignity. Interpreted in this manner the definition of dignity as worthiness of respect, i.e., personal 'respect for' makes sense. But does it make enough sense? For the question is inevitable: What is it that makes man worthy of such respect? Claims such as the ones expressed in worthiness of respect have grounds. Why should man as man be worthy of personal respect? What should we respect him for?

The first answer to this question can be given in the form of a definition of human dignity in terms of intrinsic worth: Human dignity is the worth of a person who is worth being for his own sake, regardless of his usefulness for another. It is because of this worth that he is worthy of personal respect. However, it is by no means clear that what we mean by intrinsic worth in this nonrelational sense coincides with human dignity. A person may have such noninstrumental qualities as beauty, charm or saintliness, which all add to his intrinsic worth but which can hardly be identified with human dignity. Only certain kinds of intrinsic values qualify for the kind of dignity which is answered by personal respect. Is it possible to specify these values any further? All I can suggest at this point is that they must be values which make man 'respectable', in a sense differing from the conventional one. The clue to such a specification of social respectability has to be found from an analysis of what this 'respectability' means. I submit that respect in this sense depends on the fact that the value is to some extent under the control of the worthy person, who has a share in its realization. Thus beauty or other natural gifts are not under the direct control of the person. Hence they do not add to that part of personal worth which rates respect. It is different with such dispositions as honesty or generosity. Human dignity is the kind of intrinsic worth which attaches to a human being in his capacity of being a responsible person.

What else can be done to make this dignity more concrete? I can only suggest watching it in action. One of the best approaches to an exploration in depth of what human dignity means is to start from the experience of 'indignation' at the 'indignities' suffered by human beings in concrete situations and to ask: What is it that revolts us most in what they have to undergo? Consider, for instance, the following situations of human beings, taking vicariously the places of both the victims and the victimizers in turn:

1. being tortured and forced to make confessions;

2. having to grovel for scraps of dirty food;

3. being drilled into an automaton without one's consent, for instance, in a goose-stepping military formation, carrying out barked commands;

4. being packed into overcrowded prison cells or public conveyances (e.g., by special 'pushers' in subways);

5. being given meaningless jobs to be repeated endlessly;

6. being treated and referred to as 'material' and a mere number in an (educational) institution;

7. being segregated because of skin color or other native racial characteristics;

8. having to stand in line for hours when there are other means for securing fair treatment.

In each and any of these situations consider what is being done to the victim's personality and how this is reflected in both the victim and the victimizer. The revolting thing about it is not only the physical happenings but the attempt to break down the personalities of the victims and deprive them not only of the respect of others but of self-respect. Even though such indignities cannot destroy the person's inner worth and claim, they certainly represent an 'affront', i.e., confronting dignity face to face with something that is incompatible with it. What seems to be happening is that dignity, whatever it means, is prevented from manifesting itself. For dignity needs a way of expressing itself, of shining forth, of having a 'sphere of free unfolding'.

Such an analysis of the concrete experience ('phenomenology') of 'indignities' is merely an indirect approach to the full phenomenon of dignity. But before any more direct exploration it is of paramount importance to face the concrete situations out of which the present outcry for human dignity was born. This may not add up to a meaningful definition. But more important than a definition is the vivid experience of what it means to have the kind of intrinsic worth which is disregarded in dehumanizing treatment.

9.8 Grounds of Human Dignity

In distinguishing between two definitions of human dignity I suggested that the one, 'worthiness of respect', was really based upon the definition of dignity as intrinsic worth. For it was this intrinsic worth which provided the ground for the claim to respect. But this poses the question of whether this more basic human dignity is self-sufficient or whether it has grounds in turn. I maintain that dignity rests indeed on such grounds. Like any other value it is the dependent variable of certain value-determining grounds.

What could be such grounds? Some have been mentioned and discussed in Section 5. But these are by no means exhaustive. What we have to find are certain universal characteristics in humans as humans which make them worthy of personal respect. One might think at first of such characteristics as man's capacity to reason. But I submit that, while this may be one of his excellencies entitling him to admiration, it does not make him worthy of personal respect.

The search for grounds of human dignity presupposes a full-fledged philosophical anthropology, showing not only man's essential nature, its ingredients, its structure and its place in the cosmos, but also his values, rights and responsibilities. Only on such a basis will it be possible to make an adequate survey of the possible grounds for his dignity.

Here I would like to present merely an example of the kind of characteristics which I think may prove relevant for such an enterprise. Kant began his *Anthropologie* (1798) with the following sentences:

> The fact that man can have the idea of an 'I' elevates him immeasurably above all other living beings on this earth. This is what makes him a person . . . (my translation).

This observation, quite different from Kant's usual moralism, suggests possible grounds of a new type for human dignity. Saying 'I' to oneself may be the expression of an act of 'choosing oneself' (Sartre) and confronting the world into which one finds oneself born. Such acts and the stance based on them are no mean reasons for meeting man with personal respect. And even his mere capacity for them is worthy of a secondary personal respect for man's potentialities.

My last but by no means my smallest plea is this: Human dignity seems to be one of the few common values in our world of philosophical pluralism. But while our philosophies seem to agree on this conclusion, they display no agreement about its reasons. And there is little hope that they will agree on them in the foreseeable future. I see in this situation no reason for dismay. On the contrary, such a variety of reasons may be an asset.[152] The same conclusion can be reached from several independent premises. The main hurdle at the moment is that there is not enough clarity about the meaning of human dignity. To provide it is the responsibility of all philosophies.

This, then, is what I would like to see happen as a result of our first symposium: that the major philosophies of our time present and exchange their interpretations of human dignity and their justifications for it. We need the voices of Marxist as well as of Scholastic philosophers, whose dialogue is just beginning, of realists, idealists, personalists, pragmatists, naturalists, the various types of philosophical analysis and phenomenology, of essentialists and existentialists, of Heideggerians and cyberneticists. Even their disagreements can be an enrichment, as long as they agree on some of the conclusions. The challenge to all of these philosophies is to refine and to deepen a vital idea of our time, lest it degenerate into a mere slogan, soon to be discarded as outmoded and oldfashioned.

152. A title which promises such an approach in a restricted area is 'Philosophic Bases for Human Dignity and Change', in *Thomistic and American Non-Thomistic Thought* by Sister Sophie Simec, O.S.F. (Washington, D.C.: The Catholic University Press, 1953).

10. ETHICS FOR FELLOWS IN THE FATE OF EXISTENCE[153]

> 'A sense of justice is grounded in the men-
> tal operation by which a person puts himself
> in someone else's shoes.'
>
> *The New Yorker*
> January 6, 1973, Notes and Comments.

> Fellowship is heaven,
> and lack of fellowship is hell:
> fellowship is life,
> and lack of fellowship is death.
>
> William Morris
> 'A Dream of John Ball' (1885)

10.1 Basic Concerns

What follows is not a personal creed. I doubt that in my case such
a self-important profession, even if I could offer it in good faith,
would make sense to my fellow beings. I doubt even more that
this is the job of a philosopher in the Socratic tradition. What I
want to try instead is a first formulation of certain ideas which have
become increasingly important to me. They were sparked by experiences of my childhood during the First World War in my native Alsace, then on the German side of the battlelines. They have grown
in me since my adolescence in response to the circumstances into
which I found myself born and which I have encountered in my

153. Carl Wellman, my colleague and friend at Washington University, helped me
greatly by his constructive challenges.

Reprinted by permission from *Mid-century American Philosophy*, ed. by P. Bertocci.
New York: Humanities Press, 1974, pp. 193-210.

later life, including the expulsion as a German from Alsace, now French again, the rejection by Nazi Germany because of racial 'impurity', and the admission as an immigrant to the United States in 1938 on the French quota because of my birthplace in what was retroactively considered France. For these ideas I have found no real support in past and present philosophy and too little in recent existential thought. I believe that they contain the most relevant insights I can offer to my fellow humans at this time. Hence I no longer feel the right to withhold them, while still hoping for a chance to develop them more adequately, and particularly to put the proper phenomenological foundations under them. Much as I believe in the possibility and necessity of such foundations, this paper should not yet be considered as a valid sample of phenomenological philosophizing.

My title should speak for itself. But I would like to make it plain that by 'ethics' I do not understand a mere theory of moral conduct, let alone a meta-theory of ethical language, but an attempt to offer some guidelines for approaching the mounting problems of our day. I shall try not to dogmatize. But I shall have to appeal to the empathetic efforts of my readers, hoping that my attempt to present my findings will evoke in them similar experiences, or help them to think through those they have had thus far.

What will need most explaining is what I mean by the phrase 'fellows in the fate of existence'. Even before doing so I would like to account for the cumbersomeness of the expression 'fate of existence'. Why do I not speak simply of 'fellows in existence' or simply 'fellow beings'? Firstly, I want to make it plain that I consider the fate of 'existence' a special and ultimate basis for fellowship. Moreover, in talking about 'existence' I want to bring out the affinity of my thinking to existential philosophy. However, in so doing I do not want to subscribe to any specific form of 'existentialism'. In particular I have found no support for my position in Sartre's version of it. I consider his failure to supply the explicit promised ethics one of existentialism's sadly lost opportunities. This is true especially of Sartre's failure to spell out the ethical implications of his emphasis on the essential contingency of human existence.[154]

154. See also my 'Sartre's Last Word on Ethics'. *Research in Phenomenology* (1981), 90-107.

What to me remains the main significance of existential theory is that, thanks to Kierkegaard, the wonder and terror of man's way of existence has been highlighted in a new and sensitizing manner, something which the mere term 'being' or 'fellow being' cannot convey.

But why call 'existence' a fate? For at least two reasons:

1. Without implying fatalism, for which I hold no brief, the word 'fate' stresses the inexorableness of existence as the prime and ultimate fact about our being, which cannot and must not be glossed over.

2. Without identifying fate with 'blind fate' the word expresses the fact that the victims of this fate are totally ignorant of any possible meaning in it or purpose behind it. In this sense the mere fact of our existence is something that has befallen us, has happened to us as an 'accident' in a sense which does not imply a denial of cause. This is one of the meanings of the phrase 'accident of birth', which is basic for my present approach to ethics. However, what I would like to keep out, especially at this stage, is the connotation of a sinister power which has 'thrown', 'thrust', or 'flung' us into existence. These melodramatic terms, injected into the discussion without real clarification of their implications especially by Martin Heidegger, introduce a kind of anthropomorphism and Promethean revolt for which we have as little ground as for a more theistic interpretation implying a mission entrusted to us. Instead we had better face our situation and in fact our predicament soberly without such futile emotions as cosmic rage or exultation.

I shall begin with an attempt to clarify what I mean by the idea of fellowship and particularly by 'fellowship in the fate of existence'. I shall then simply state some of the general ethical premises which will form the basis for my subsequent ethical reflections, without trying to justify them. The balance of the paper will consist in an attempt to spell out some of the implications of my approach for the most burning moral issues in the present crisis of humanity, which can no longer afford its past provincialism. For mankind can survive only if it develops a sense of planetary fellowship without which the ideas of world citizenship and world government must remain powerless dreams.

10.2 Types of Fellowship

'Fellowship' is an idea which thus far seems to have had surprisingly little consideration in ethical literature. Only the phrase 'fellow feeling' figures conspicuously in Adam Smith's ethics as a synonym of 'sympathy'.[155] Even more noteworthy is the fact that in this context Smith stressed the need for putting ourselves imaginatively into the place of our fellow beings. But he supplies no clear and cogent connection between the fact of fellow feeling and the ethical duty of imaginative self-transposal.

One might think that the idea of fellowship is nothing but that of human brotherhood or 'fraternity'. But quite apart from the 'male chauvinism' expressed in this metaphor, its implications are different and more problematic. Already the expansion of the original meaning from the relation of brothers within the nuclear family unit to larger groups and finally to mankind as one family is far from obvious. Moreover, it makes sense only if mankind is a family with two common parents, one father of all mankind clearly not being enough, as commonly asserted, whether these be human fathers and mothers or superhuman ones. From this point of view the idea of fellowship is certainly less loaded than that of brotherhood, and certainly theologically neutral.

But what does the appeal to fellowship imply? The history of the English word with its etymological connotation of partnership in a business venture (from *feoh,* cattle, money, i.e., one who lays down money) hardly throws much light on the present ethical implications of this term. Even though there must be some historical connection between these meanings, at present it carries no live meaning. Here the main division is that between two types of fellowship. The one is based on choice, be it by co-optation, as in the case of academic fellows, or by free joining, e.g., through a financial contribution to an association, or the mutual 'good fellowship' of an informal group of more or less 'jolly fellows'. The other fellowship is none of our own choosing and doing but of finding our-

155. *The Theory of Sentiments* (1759) Part I Section I ('Of Sympathy').

selves 'in the same boat', of being caught in the same unchosen predicament. Coming from the earlier idea of fellowship as a voluntary association,[156] one might well wonder why such an involuntary condition can make any claims on us, let alone more valid claims than those based on voluntary association. But this is precisely what I maintain. To show this requires some more basic considerations not based on the mere study of words and their history. What is it then in the natural human condition that establishes a real bond among persons who have not chosen such a binding relation?

Fellowship in the basic sense is always fellowship in a certain respect. It does not make sense to speak of Tom, Dick and Harry as being fellows, except in the colloquial sense of being 'nice fellows', without saying *in what* they are fellows or what they share. Now this sharing can refer to practically everything under the sun (and in a sense even the sun and the universe beyond). It need not mean sharing identically the same object: even having different but equal or similar conditions in common may be the basis for such sharing. It can begin with such relatively trivial circumstances as sharing the same house or address or public conveyance, and extend to sharing the same country ('fellow countrymen'), the same planet, or the same time in history ('fellow contemporaries'). Fellows who in this manner share identically the same fate may be called *same-fated* or *fated-joined* fellows.

But there is also a very different kind of 'sharing'. Having the same height or skin-color, sex or class and ultimately human kind or simply being does not mean that we are connected by real contact with the same thing or situation. Here our sharing consists in having parallel, i.e., equal or similar, characteristics without being linked by them. Fellowship based on such sharing may be called *like-fated* or *parallel-fated* fellowship. It hardly needs pointing out that fellowship in the fate of existence is of this latter kind.

It seems noteworthy that not all fellowship is essentially con-

---

156. The seeming priority of voluntary fellowship or association may well be characteristic of the English language. Thus Greek *hetairos*, a word whose etymological roots seem to be far from clear, refers to all kinds of being joined, voluntary and involuntary; Latin *socius*, related to *sequi* (to follow), also does not presuppose an act of association; French *camarade* refers to sharing the same chamber or room; German *Genosse* is based on the relation of enjoying *(Genuss)* something jointly, such as a house *(Hausgenosse)*; similarly the common western word 'companion' expresses the sharing of the same bread *(panis)*.

scious. While choice-based fellowships are essentially conscious, this is by no means true of fellowship in fate. It may be relatively frequent in same-fated fellowships based on actual living together in relation to the shared object or situation. But this is not the case with parallel-fated fellowships such as the class-fellowship of the proletariat. To make us conscious of them takes comparing, pointing out and even awakening. No wonder that we are so little aware of our fellowship in existence.

10.3 Fellowships in Parallel Fate

Let us now consider some more momentous instances of such parallel fellowships.

There is the fellowship of those struck by the same disease like polio or cancer or by physical suffering in general —according to Albert Schweitzer the basis for a 'brotherhood of those marked by pain'. This should not rule out the possibility of a fellowship among those who 'struck it rich', i.e., those 'fortunate' few or many who have been spared disaster and suffering and enjoy the bliss of a great aesthetic or religious experience, as in a concert or on separate pilgrimages.

But while such instances of shared departures from normal experiences may stand out and give rise to a special kind of bond and fellowship, they are by no means the most important ones, since they are based on common accidents or coincidences. The basic instances are those grounded in our essential conditions. In ascending order of relevance I nominate here:

(1) our common fate of belonging to one rather than to another group of beings, such as:

1. being female or male (fellows in sex)

2. being young or old (generational fellows)

3. being black, yellow, brown, or white (racial fellows)

4. being in one particular place or time (neighbors)

5. being Chinese or American, Palestinian or Israeli (fellow nationals).

(2) But there are even more common and nondiscriminatory

parallel fates, predisposing to potential fellowships:

1. the fate of being born human, rather than animal (fellow humans), or being born alive (fellow living beings)

2. and finally of 'being', both in the form of 'mere being' (fellow beings) and of existing (fellow existers).

It is on this condition of sharing the fate of being human and of existing, with all its assets and liabilities, that I would like to base my approach to ethics.

10.4 Accidents of Birth as Parallel Fates

Why should such parallel fates have any ethical significance, establishing ethical relationships among us? After all, isn't it understood that in this case there is no direct social bond between us, as in the case of partnership and companionship?

It is probably true that in our usual lives we are not very ready to pay attention to our ethical bonds with parallel-fated fellows, something which we are almost forced to do in the cases of fate-joined fellows sharing the same real 'boat' with us. However, it takes not much sensitizing or reminding to see that the new situation is at least analogous —and infinitely more momentous. But we have to be awakened to it. What we have to appeal to for such an ethical awakening is what we at times casually, if not thoughtlessly, call 'the accident of birth' which assigns to each one of us a specific lot and no other. To take this phrase seriously is, I firmly believe, the lever which can move the dead weight of our social lethargy.

What specifically does it mean to take the accident of birth seriously? At first glance one may think that this phrase is nothing but a manner of speech which makes little if any real sense. After all, what sense is there to speaking about 'birth' as an accident? Even if we do not share the deterministic or fatalistic view that there are no accidents but only ignorance of definite causes, is it not obvious that scientifically there is nothing accidental about birth or, for that matter, conception, and in fact about all the accidents which threaten our lives, and against which we take insurance policies?

But it does not take much reflection to realize that something quite different is at stake when we begin to fully realize the accidental character of our situation. How else could it be that a determinist such as J.S. Mill was greatly influenced by this motif throughout his social and political thinking?[157] Here I shall not attempt to show the real meaning of our talk about the accident of birth. I shall simply submit that what is involved is not a mere denial of natural causation, but a fundamentally novel conception. Its thrust is to bring out the absence of any moral title to whatever accidental, nonessential position we find ourselves and others to be in, be it economic plight, sex or skin color, which were Mill's prime concerns.

And now for the positive aspect of the 'accident': In denying any moral claim to our congenital position I am pleading for a novel concept of existential justice (and injustice). I mean by this that existence as such involves for the exister certain basic claims, regardless of whether they are fulfilled or even fulfillable in fact and even in principle. Specifically, (1) the fact that 'I am me' is something not of my choosing or doing for which I can claim any credit or can be legitimately blamed. At best I can have some responsibility for my further becoming, for the 'nature' I shape by my choices and efforts out of my initial me-ness. My being-me is therefore an 'accident of birth', a fate into which I am 'cast' without my consent. I submit that whatever is done to a person without his consent is in principle an existential wrong, regardless of whether it is an objective benefit, a harm or something neutral: even benefits forced upon a beneficiary, in order to be valid gifts implying obligations, have to be freely accepted. And one cannot take it for granted that such benefits will be accepted, if only because such acceptance diminishes one's moral freedom, as even the proverb knows *(beneficia accipere est libertatem vendere)*. Hence the fate of one's own very self-being involves essentially an 'existential' wrong in the sense of a 'slight' to one's basic freedom. There is something morally incongruous about the lack of consent to one's own basic being. There is perhaps even an essential indignity in this predicament. To this extent the repudiation of his existence by the suicide is not only a defensible protest but an act of reaffirma-

157. See 'Accident of Birth: A Non-utilitarian Motif in Mill's Philosophy', number 6 in this volume.

tion of his dignity.

(2) The fact that I am or exist is likewise a condition on which I have had no say —and actually could not possibly have had any say. But this impossibility does not preclude the fact that to be exposed to being is a 'condemnation' without a prior hearing. Regardless of whether the infliction of a temporary existence with the attached price of having to die is a clear objective benefit, there is something morally objectionable about this situation and the implied imputation that I have to acquiesce to it. To be, to exist is in this sense an affront to one's freedom. In this sense it means: being an innocent victim, a pawn, at least at the start of one's career.

(3) The fact that whatever one is at the start by way of one's congenital endowment, from one's genetic heritage to one's intellectual and emotional constitution, is a condition one never asked for or could have asked for, notwithstanding Plato's telling myth of Er in the *Republic,* 'telling' because it concedes that on moral grounds we really should have had a say about our 'lot' and even our character. This applies particularly to

1. being a human. The very idea of the migration of souls (metempsychosis) emerging independently in several cultures (e.g., in Greece and India), is an indication that being oneself is by no means identical, and experienced as identical, with being human. Totemism, animal worship and even plant (tree) and mountain worship is another confirmation. There is simply no essential, let alone morally necessary relation between being a self and being cast in human shape. *A fortiori* this is true of
2. being male or female,
3. being of one race or another,
4. being of one constitution or temperament or another, including various kinds of physical 'beauty' or 'ugliness',
5. being born normal (healthy) or with various 'handicaps'.

(4) The fact that our initial station, i.e., our belonging to any particular (historical) time, (national) culture and (social) situation is none of our choosing. There is therefore an essential moral imbalance in being born into any such station, whether it turns out that this station is one of overprivilege, as in being born into the aristocracy or into the most powerful nation, or into the proletariat,

or an underprivileged (underdeveloped) nation.

Whatever pride (or shame) we may feel, and may be exhorted to fell and display on such occasions by our current education, is therefore morally and existentially indefensible, apart from being socially disruptive. There is no moral basis and no excuse for pride and shame over congenital conditions, which are all accidents of birth.

10.5 Some Premises for Ethical Implications of the Fellowship in the Fate of Existence

In outlining some of the implications of fellowship I am clearly making some general and specific assumptions about ethics which I shall not spell out in detail, let alone justify explicitly. They include the following beliefs:

1. There are 'objective' qualities and conditions which, regardless of our whims and wishes, demand our respect (usually called 'values', 'worths', 'dignities'), such as harmony, fairness, freedom.

2. Our freedom and power to 'realize' them in the sense of both noticing them and actualizing them involves for us a responsibility, however limited, for their reality and survival in the world.

3. The accident of birth involves for its beneficiaries and victims the duty of imaginative self-transposal and empathy.

10.6 Ethical Implications of the Fellowship in the Fate of Existence

(a) Why fellowship in fate commits us
It is relatively easy to see that fellowship in the sense of a companionship freely entered by mutual promises or consent involves mutual obligations and responsibilities. These are the obligations based on free commitments. But the situation is quite different where we find ourselves as fellows who never asked to be matched together, caught willy-nilly in the same predicament. And here there is an additional important difference between the situation where we share identically the same plight and that where we find ourselves merely in a parallel but separate plight. In the former case we are tied together by the bonds of neighborship among individuals depending on one another, receiving aid from or giving it to one an-

other, since we have a joint stake in the preservation of what we share. But such a comradeship or mateship of people thrown together by circumstance is very different from the fellowship of those who 'share' merely a similar situation in different corners of this planet. 'Why on earth' should they be at all ethically related to one another?

Perhaps the best way to show that they are indeed so related is to imagine a case where, among people of roughly similar condition, one were struck by a tornado, while most or all others remained safe and perhaps even profited from the misfortune of the one less 'fortunate'. It is certainly no accident that witnessing such scenes and even hearing or reading about them, we cannot suppress the thought: How come that the twister struck him rather than me? Can we then simply shrug off such ideas and rejoice in our better luck or fortunes? True, Lucretius wrote:

'Tis sweet, when, down the mighty main, the winds
Roll up its waste of waters, from the land
To watch another's labouring anguish far.'[158]

The very revulsion we may feel against such moral smugness is an indication that there is a tie between us and those in conditions parallel to our own, such as equal physical and economic distress, the basic human condition, and even being itself.

Why? I submit that there is something like a moral imbalance if people sharing similar situations are subject to a 'discrimination' which favors those more 'fortunate' by the mere 'happenstance' of 'good luck', and disfavors the 'unfortunate' victims of 'bad luck'. There is clearly a special sense of injustice behind our words when we say that it was 'unfair' that a person struggling under a physical handicap should also be struck by the loss of his supporting friends. Something, we feel, is basically wrong about such a fate and, what is more, something ought to be done about it.

In a different context I have asserted by way of a tentative premise that unearned advantages call for redress, and apparently this 'axiom' has appealed even to such original thinkers on justice as

---

158. *On the Nature of Things,* translated by W.E. Leonard, Book II. But even he added:
'Not that we joyously delight that man
Should thus be smitten, but because 'tis sweet
To mark what evils we ourselves are spared.'

John Rawls to the extent that he seems to take it for granted.[159] I consider this as additional support for the belief that fellow beings are tied to each other by the similar fates of their very being to the demands of a compensatory existential justice.

Lately, there has been a poignant confirmation of this belief in the case of the so-called Hibakusha, the survivors of the manmade cataclysm of Hiroshima. Robert J. Lifton in his study of the after-affects of the atom bomb concludes his chapter on 'The Atomic Bomb Experience' with these italicized sentences:

> 'The survivor can never, inwardly, simply conclude that it was logical and right for him, and not others, to survive. Rather he is bound by an unconscious perception of organic social balance which makes him feel that his survival was made possible by others' deaths: If they had not died, he would have had to; if he had not survived, someone else would have.'

And he ends (without italics):

> Such guilt, as it relates to survivor priority, may well be that most fundamental to human existence.'[160]

Moreover, I maintain that such compensatory existential justice requires our putting ourselves vicariously into the places of our fellow beings whether privileged or handicapped. Without such imaginative self-transposal we could not adequately realize what it means for the fortunate or unfortunate to experience their fates and make appropriate amends. Such an operation is actually nothing new in philosophical ethics, and even less so in everyday ethical thinking. Consider how often in our discussions or in our appeals to others we introduce such fictions as:

> 'Suppose you were black (or yellow or white) . . .'
> 'Suppose you were poor (or rich) . . .'
> 'Suppose you were young (or old) . . .'

In fact, such invitations to 'supposals' and especially to imaginary self-transposal occur not infrequently in the thought experiments of moral philosophy. Even the golden rule makes full sense only if

---

159. 'A Defense of Human Equality', *Philosophical Review* 53 (1944), 113, as quoted in John Rawls, *A Theory of Justice*, Cambridge: Harvard University Press, 1971, p. 100.
160. *Death in Life: Survivors of Hiroshima*, New York: Random House, 1976, p. 56.

interpreted as: 'Do unto others what you would want them to do unto you *if you were in their place*' (otherwise you might inflict your taste on them). Similarly, thinking through the implications of the greatest happiness principle commits us to determining the quantity and equality of other people's pleasures, which ultimately requires our imagining how we would feel in their places. Thus, self-transposal is a basic part of our moral thinking. How far has moral philosophy paid real attention to it?

However, one might object: Does it make sense to attempt such self-transposal? After all, it is based on assumptions not only contrary to fact but impossible to perform in reality. For 'I am I and you are you; and nothing can be done about it. And I can't ever be anything else but me, and you can't ever be anything else but you'.[161] Moreover, the request for such a supposal sounds at first like a noncommittal invitation to our imagination to participate in an intellectual or aesthetic adventure. Is this really all there is to it? Suppose we decline this invitation? Isn't there something much more serious behind it: a duty to accept the invitation to put ourselves into the place of the other? If so, how can we account for it and justify it? I submit it is again the accident of birth and the existential imbalance implied which commits us to compensation, beginning with an effort of imagining ourselves in the place of the other, realizing that we might have occupied it, were it not for the accident of our actual birth.

(b) To what fellowship in fate commits us
But now for a more specific consideration of the ethical implications of the accident of birth as characterized above:

(1) The fact that 'I am me' —and of course on equal terms also that 'you are you', (only that I have no comparable access to and insight into you and your world except by way of your letting me in on it)— points to a dimension of personal existence whose full depth and richness can here merely be asserted. The fact and experience of this rarely realized and fathomed 'wonder' seems to give each self a unique 'dignity' in a sense which certainly calls for

161. Carson McCullers, *Member of the Wedding*. Boston: Houghton Mifflin Co. 1946, p. 138. See also Alfred Tennyson: '...this main miracle, that thou art thou..." *De profundis* II.

much more clarification. It calls for a respect approaching awe. This is one of the reasons why we feel or ought to feel the 'unconditional regard' (postulated by Carl Rogers but never justified) for everyone who shows signs of such consciousness of selfhood. In the light of this realization all treatment of human beings as numbers, as 'material' or as bodies (to be 'counted' as measures of military success) stands condemned as a crime against human dignity. So does all 'rubricizing' of human beings, i.e., treating them primarily as specimens, as 'one of those . . .' or rather as representatives of a type rather than themselves.[162] J.

(2) The fact that I *am* —and on equal terms that you *are*— while rarely fully experienced in its stark irrevocableness, establishes at the same time a right to continued existence regardless of whether I had a right to come into existence at the start.[163] Once I have been put into existence and am now a personal self capable of realizing and taking charge of my being, no one else has a prima facie claim on this my existence. Such being, which is more than mere life, has a claim to unconditional respect —(unless waived or forfeited) perhaps to the degree of reverence (for life), although the latter term and feeling may be excessive for a being as imperfect as man.

One may well hold that being in itself, no matter what it is that has this being, has value *('omne ens qua ens est bonum')* and a claim on our respect, and that destruction, even of 'worthless' things, is a kind of cosmic 'misdemeanor'. All the more is any interference with personal existence an attack on basic values.

(3) The fact of the 'accident' of our congenital 'nature' calls for a primal tolerance for and patience with one another's natures. It is very easy to get impatient, critical and contemptuous of the characteristics of people other than ourselves (at times even with our

---

162. W. James, *Varieties of Religious Experience*, N.Y.: Mod. Lib., 1902, p. 10: 'Probably a crab would be filled with a sense of personal outrage if it could hear us class it without ado or apology as a crustacean, and thus dispose of it: 'I am no such thing', it would say: 'I am *myself, myself* alone'.' See also Abraham Maslow, *Toward a Psychology of Being*. Princeton: Van Nostrand, 1962, 126-130.

163. Recent discussions of the wrong we may inflict on future generations by exposing them to the prospects of nuclear disaster, overcrowding and pollution may well imply that they as nonbeings have a moral right to non-being violated by bringing them into this world, a right which can perhaps be construed in less paradoxical, e.g., hypothetical terms. See Joel Feinberg, 'Is There a Right to be Born', in *Rights, Justice and the Bounds of Liberty*, Princeton University Press, 1980, pp. 216-220.

own), as if they were to blame for them. But at least congenital characteristics are by definition those for which no one is to be blamed except those parents who could have known the high probability that these characteristics were hereditary. Otherwise we are all the victims or beneficiaries of accidents over which we have had no control. None of us has earned or deserved his endowment or lack of it.

Race may be at the moment the major occasion for this reminder. Once all of us realized that being born black is as much of an accident of birth as being born white, we might be more ready to transpose ourselves into the places of our alternates in racial fate. But it does not hold any less for such characteristics as being born into either sex or into another physique.

Realizing the origin of these congenital differences may seem primarily a reason for deepened patience with the other's differing characteristics, though not necessarily for resignation to them. It might be one reason for compassion, only that there is something much too pharisaical about this attitude if it is practiced by the self-righteous haves toward the have-nots.

What must also be realized, harder though it be for handicapped victims of existential imbalance, is that the targets of their understandable envy and resentment did not ask for the silver spoons they discovered in their own mouths. To this extent even the fortunate ones are victims of fortune, and it is usually not even in their power to divest themselves of their congenital advantages without committing suicide. All they can do and should do for everyone's benefit is to try to make up for their better luck. This is why we might hope that even the handicapped, or those who rightly or wrongly believe themselves to be handicapped, will eventually come to realize that their opposite numbers are not villains, that they could not help being privileged and that even each born 'aristocrat' deserves to be looked upon as a new human being.

(4) The most urgent need may be to become aware of the ethical implications of the accidents of our congenital status. For it is these accidents that keep us apart on the social, national and particularly on the international level. To begin with the last: realizing the accident of our national birth as Americans or Asians, as Palestinians or Israelis, as French or Germans, should remove all occasion for one of the most fateful obstacles to international union, the pride

of national birth, now considered almost the most basic feature in one's social nature to the extent that 'I am an American' not only takes precedence in consciousness over 'I am a world citizen', but colors one's view of human nature; to put it in the form of a pun, man seems to be a national rather than a rational being. Pride of being born as a member of one nation rather than another is just as misplaced (if not silly) as the pride of aristocracy for 'having taken the trouble of being born' (Beaumarchais, *Marriage of Figaro*). The same is true of being ashamed of being born in a nation humiliated by defeat or disgraced by collective guilt.

Such an approach should also allow us to break the stalemate in our hereditary national blood feuds and hatreds. Once we are fully aware that each new generation is born without any doing of its own, and is, as a matter of historical accident, either a Montague or a Capulet, a Greek or a Barbarian, a prince or a pauper, it becomes morally indefensible to hold one another responsible for such differences. By the same token each new generation could and should make a fresh start by challenging these accidents. In fact, the best hope for reconciliation —or rather conciliation, since the new generations have never been in conflict— is the replacement of one generation by another ready to dissociate itself from its predecessors and to realize that both sides are the innocent victims of a history they did not make. This is the place where the generation gap is one of the greatest opportunities for all mankind. It could imply a call to the new generations of the world to unite; for they have nothing to lose but the heritage of a fratricidal history bequeathed them by their elders.

Realizing that the generation gap is a matter of the accident of birth could also be a means for bridging it. The older generation, deploring the decline of authority and damning the younger one as immature and irreverent, might do well to realize that its 'riper' age and greater experience (not always such a blessing anyhow) are matters of an accident of earlier birth entitling it to nothing. But also the younger generation might consider that the older generation is older not of its own choosing but can't help belonging to another age and is powerless to cross the gap. Both are captives of the accidents of chronology. But they can liberate each other to some extent by mutual imaginative self-transposal.

Such a new approach to the generation problem may also offer hope for a novel solution of such tragic historic conflicts as the one between Palestinians and Israelis. There was little point in contesting the legal international right of an Arab majority to their territory and even to keeping out immigration that would make it a minority. Compared with this right the millennia-old claim of the Jews to their ancestral home may have weighed little. What did weigh was their claim to *some* place on this globe where they could escape oppression by those who tried to deprive them of their chance of survival and their very right to existence, particularly when the rest of the world refused to give them a haven of safety. Their best hope was and still seems to be a return to their ancestors' underdeveloped land, which they may be particularly well qualified to develop. On what basis can this moral issue be adjudicated? What I submit is that once the new Palestinian and the new Israeli generations come to realize that it was merely the accident of birth which made them Palestinians or Israelis respectively, they should be able to make a fresh start: realizing that they are fellow victims of one of history's most tragic conflicts, who ought to forgive each other for sins they themselves never committed. Besides, they as well as every other group and individual must come to realize that no new generation has a birthright to the soil on which it is born, that we all, not only our ancestors are settlers, if not squatters, in new land, and that we have no moral right to exclude those who have as little claim as we have to any part of the earth where we happen to be born. Even inheritance is no unconditional and unlimited right of the heir, but at best a right of the testator if he does not harm others by his dispositions.

The mutual realization of the accidents of birth may also build new bridges across the generation gap in its primary area, the modern family. It is obvious that no child chose his parents and his entire family. This fact should make it clear that his mere birth does not put him under any obligations to his family until he has accepted them freely. It is less obvious that even parents have a choice only as far as the *existence* of the new generation is concerned. But even if they knew all about genetics, they could not 'make' and 'create' their children in 'procreating' them. What these children are is to that extent an 'accident'. Such a coexistential understanding of the contingencies of the basic existential constitution of the family may well be the basis for authentic tolerance combined with the effort to mutual respect and cooperation.

Realization of the accident of birth also throws a new light on membership in one religious denomination rather than another. Actually it is not so much the ignorance of the truth or untruth of religious beliefs and dogmas, but the obvious accident of being born Muslim or Hindu, Catholic or Protestant, which is the deepest argument for genuine tolerance. Reconsider John Bradford's exclamation on watching a 'heretic' being led off to execution: 'There, but for the grace of God, go I.'

At least equally serious is still the matter of social and economic class, now that this fate has become a matter of 'class consciousness'. Granting, what should not be granted as a dogma but only after much more critical examination, the fact and necessity of the class struggle as the basic social reality of our society with the rigid division between the exploited proletariat and the bourgeois exploiters: How much is the division a matter of accident or of choice for the class strugglers? Under a rigid historical materialism there clearly is no real choice anyway. Being born a bourgeois is an unalterable fact and there is no chance for him to ever change sides. All the revolution can do is to liquidate the exploiters, never convert them. (Apparently Marx and Engels, the born bourgeois turned fathers of the revolution, are in a special class.) But even so, being born in either class was an accident of birth. One is a proletarian, but also a bourgeois, as a matter of a blind fate. In that case, is there no reason for 'mercy' with those bourgeois who make an honest effort to repudiate their capitalist past and their inherited capital by joining the 'disinherited'? Or is this as impossible as a change of sex or color?

The basic truth of the matter is that there is no such thing as a moral birthright to nationality, creed or class, even though to a limited extent some of these can become a matter of choice by change of allegiance, granted grudgingly and disapproved by the native groups as a case of 'disloyalty'. Unless we believe in original sin in the sense that the children inherit the guilt and possibly the merits or grace of their forefathers, we must reject the idea that we have any right to any 'native headstart'.

10.7 Final Pleas

This leads me to some final pleas. As an attempt to sum up some key principles of the ethics of fellowship in the fate of existence I shall put them in the form of simplifying imperatives not meant as commands, but as appeals to spontaneous 'realization', both in the sense of insight and of actualization in practice.

1. Approach every human person as a being who has been cast into his lot without his own doing. In particular think of him as a person who has not chosen (a) to exist, (b) to be himself or herself, (c) to be whatever he is as far as his congenital characteristics such as race are concerned, (d) to occupy his station in life as far as national, religious or class differences are concerned.

2. Whether handicapped or privileged, consider all human beings as fellow victims of a morally unaccountable fate.

3. Considering his basic condition, treat every human person as a new being in his own right, never merely as a continuing extension of his biological ancestors and never as a specimen only.

Put more succinctly:

1. Respect each new being in his own dignity.

2. Transpose yourself in imagination into his plight which is his merely by the accident of birth, but could have been yours as well.

3. Be patient with, and tolerant of, his congenital differences, however alien to you.

4. Be compassionate with those who do not know what they have done to you and others.

5. Have mercy with others and yourself threatened by our self-righteousness and callousness in pursuing a collision course in the name of national honor or similar traditional ideals, which can lead only to the victimization of innocent new generations.

6. Redistribute burdens and privileges rather than take revenge on and exterminate those equally victimized by the accident of birth.

Accident of birth is not the last word of the new ethics for fellow beings in fate. But it is the first word. The second word is the free choice by which we can respond to and redeem this accident. The way from chance to choice is the path of human reclamation of a 'universe we never made'. Hence we ought to consider human beings not only as fellow victims of the accidents of birth but also as fellow agents capable of accepting and rejecting this fate by converting their congenital endowment into a new order based on choice.

What, then, is the significance of this new approach to ethics? It tries to make us face the fact of our existence in all its inexorability, cosmically and morally. Against this background we can best plot our course individually and jointly as coexisting fellows, each one for himself, but not alone, and develop the kind of ethics that makes sense where before there was no sense or only potential sense. Such an ethics may provide a way out of the impasse in which we victims of history find ourselves caught at this juncture. It may also help us to develop the sense of planetary solidarity instead of the nationalist provincialism which seems to doom us to reciprocal suicide.

What fractured mankind needs desperately now is a fresh start. The new generation must really begin as a new set of human beings, not identified with their inherited past, free to reject and accept the lot into which they were cast. As fellows in the fate of such co-existence they have something in common that allows them to throw off the shackles which their predecessors have bequeathed them. We all are victims of this past, but we are not enslaved by it. On the contrary: The fact that we are new existences gives us the chance and the obligation to confront it as an alien accident and to redeem this old world of chance by innovating choices.

11. GOOD FORTUNE OBLIGATES: ALBERT SCHWEITZER'S SECOND ETHICAL PRINCIPLE[163]

Until now the public image of Albert Schweitzer as an ethical thinker has been that of a single-track mind absorbed by the one idea that came to him in a flash on the Ogowe River in Lambarene during the First World War: reverence for life. True, Schweitzer himself promoted this image, last and most impressively in his spoken message of 1964, which began with the sentence 'I summon mankind to the ethics of reverence for life'.[164] Urgent though this final appeal remains, I shall not discuss its adequacy and its short-comings. But it would be unfortunate if this emphasis were to divert us from another part of Schweitzer's message, which not only was more basic in his life but may have even greater significance for social ethics. I shall call it 'Good fortune obligates'.

What I propose to do here is to

1. present the main textual evidence for what Schweitzer himself once called his 'other thought';

2. point out its originality;

3. clarify its meaning;

4. show its source in our moral consciousness;

5. try to determine some of its deeper foundations.

163. A shorter and slightly different version of this article was presented at the Fifteenth World Congress of Philosophy in Varna, Bulgaria, under the title 'Albert Schweitzer's 'Other Thought': Fortune Obligates', and was published in *Africa: Journal of the Philosophical Association of Kenya* I (1973): pp. 11-17. Especially in the reformulation of the article I have been aided by my colleague Carl Wellman.
164. 'Mein Wort an die Menschen' (1964), *Berichte aus Lambarene*, vol. 30 (Basel, September 1967). English translation in Albert Schweitzer, 'My last Message to Mankind', *Pax et Libertas* 32 (1967): p. 9.

Reprinted by permission from *Ethics* 85 (1975), pp. 227-234.

11.1. Textual Evidence

In Schweitzer's publications during his lifetime this principle first
occurs explicitly in 1924 in his memoirs of childhood and youth.[165]
Here, toward the end, he mentions 'the second great experience'
(next to that of suffering in the world): the constant crushing concern about the question of the 'right to good fortune (*Glück*)' as
he had experienced it in his own happy youth in a well-situated and
loving family'.[166] This experience is described more poignantly in
his autobiography of 1931: 'On a brilliant summer morning —it
was in 1896— when I was spending the Pentecost vacation in Guns-
bach, the thought overwhelmed me that I must not accept this good
fortune as a matter of course but had to give something in return,'[167] a thought which then led to his decision to become a medical missionary in the African jungle. But the experience found its
most explicit statement as an independent 'other thought' in a short
autobiographical address which Schweitzer gave in 1932 over the
German radio, published only recently by Erwin R. Jacobi.[166] It
extends over two paragraphs, beginning with this sentence: 'Another
thought besides that of reverence for life which has dominated my
life is this: that we must not accept what comes to us in our life
by way of good luck as a matter of course, but have to make a sacrifice of thankgiving (*Dankopfer*) for it by some act of help or service'.
In this stress on the independence of this 'other thought', Schweitzer's statement differs from his writings on ethics, where it appears
as one of the demands implied in the principle of reverence for life,
but without any attempt to derive it.[169] But even where the new

165. *Aus meiner Kindheit und Jugendzeit* (Munich: C.H. Beck, 1924) (*Memoirs of Childhood and Youth*, trans. C.T. Campion, New York: MacMillan Co., 1949, pp. 6–62). Page references in English translation are hereafter given in parentheses. For a first for-mulation in a sermon of June 16, 1919, see Albert Schweitzer, *Was sollen wir tun?* Heidelberg: Verlag Lambert Schneider, 1974), pp. 119-20.

166. *Ibid.*, p. 57 (97).

167. *Aus meinem Leben und Denken* (Munich, C.H. Beck, 1931), p. 70 (*Out of my Life and Thought*, trans. C.T. Campion, New York: Henry Holt & Co., 1949, p. 85).

168. 'Aus meinem Leben: Ein Vortrag', *Schweitzer Monatshefte* 50 (1970): 1-7. Also 'Albert Schweitzer spricht', *Cahiers Européens* (1975), pp. 11-13 (with English and French translations).

169. *Kultur und Ethik* (Munich: C.H. Beck, 1924), pp. 242-46 (*Civilization and Ethics*, trans. John Nash. New York: Mac Millan Co., 1960, pp. 269-70). It is of some interest that in 1961, when Gerald Götting prepared a condensation of Schweitzer's doc-trine of reverence for life with Schweitzer's active cooperation, Schweitzer himself se-

thought appeared as a special principle on a par with reverence for life, Schweitzer did not develop it sufficiently to attach a special label to it. He described it simply as negatively forbidding us to accept good fortune as a matter of course and positively bidding us to compensate for such luck by an equivalent sacrifice.

11.2 The Novelty of the 'Other Thought'

Schweitzer himself did not claim any originality for his second principle beyond testifying to the spontaneity and strength of his own experience. But such a claim could very well be staked out and defended. As far as I can see, even after checking with some of the specialists in the history of ethics, there is no explicit precedent.

One might think that its spirit is expressed in Jesus' maxim 'Of him to whom much is given, much will be required' (Luke 12,48). But even though this saying, which occurs inconspicuously in the middle of a three-sentence verse, has often been interpreted in the sense of an obligation of the privileged toward the underprivileged, the original context, the parable of the faithful servant, makes it clear that there is no immediate thought of good fortune at the start and that the obligations involved are primarily those toward the divine master, not toward one's fellow beings.

Another possible anticipation might be suspected in the much-quoted French adage *noblesse oblige*. This saying occurs first as a separate item in a collection of aphorisms by a French aristocrat of the Restoration period, the Duc de Lévis (1764-1830), in the context of his attempt to justify the renewed privileges of the nobil-

lected from Götting's longer proposal the following three items in the context of the section 'Man and Man': (1) 'No one has the right to take for granted his own advantages over others in health, in talents, in ability, in success, in a happy childhood and congenial home conditions. One must pay a price for all these boons. What one owes in return is a special responsibility for other lives'. (2) 'All throught the world, there is a special league of those who have known anxiety and physical suffering. A mysterious bond connects those marked by pain. They know the terrible things man can undergo; they know the longing to be free of pain. Those who have been liberated from pain must not think they are now completely free again and can calmly return to life as it was before...' (3) He who has experienced good in his life must feel the obligation to dedicate some of his own life in order to alleviate suffering' (Gerald Götting, *Die Lehre der Ehrfurcht vor dem Leben*. Berling: Union Verlag, 1964. *Albert Schweitzer: The Teaching of Reverence for Life*, trans. Richard and Clara Winston. New York: Holt, Rinehart & Winston, 1965, pp. 40-41).

ity.[170] No obligations are specified. The next aphorism talks about the children of noble families as expected to duplicate the merits of their ancestors, 'since nothing is more gratuitous than the respect paid to birth' (no. 51). This, then, is clearly a maxim of class ethics. And although the concept of nobility has since been expanded to include even the noble-mindedness of Nietzsche's superman, the vague implications of such an ethics for a special group of human beings do not include any compensation to the less than noble.

Schweitzer's principle knows of no such distinction of class, feudal or mental. It applies to every human being who finds himself endowed with a natural advantage by birth or circumstance and asks him to make up for it. It would be a mistake to present Schweitzer as an ardent advocate of democracy in politics. But it is all the more appropriate to point out his remarkable plea for social equality among unequals, both in his living and in his teaching. The episode from his childhood when, in open rebellion against his parents, he refused adamantly to wear any dress that would distinguish him from his fellow pupils in the village school for the reason that 'I did not want to be different and be better off than they' is perhaps the most telling expression of Schweitzer's ethical egalitarianism.[171] With or without label, his 'other thought' strikes a new chord in social ethics.

11.3 Clarifying the Meaning of the New Thought

But precisely the novelty of the 'other thought' requires its fuller development and buttressing. This should begin with a clarification of its major concepts. In questioning the right to luck '*Glück*' in his radio address, Schweitzer made it plain that luck included 'not only possessions and other favorable life circumstances but also health, ability to work, a happy disposition . . . and even healthy sleep'. What he did not seem to include is happiness in the utilitarian sense of a pleasure-filled state of mind. In any case, with all his thankfulness for his excessive luck, Schweitzer himself denied any particular happiness in his own life, chiefly because of his thought

170. Pierre Marc Gaston, Duc de Lévis, *Maximes et réflections sur différents sujets de morale et de politique* (Paris, 1808), no. 50.
171. *Aus meiner Kindheit und Jugendzeit*, p. 13 (9).

of all the suffering around him.[172]

One must, of course, realize that even luck is not completely an objective fact. It depends to a large extent on how it is experienced, accepted or rejected, and in what framework it appears in a person's existence. But such a phenomenology of good or bad luck does not alter the fact that such meanings conferred by the subjects are based on a hard core of objective facts which are not of the subject's own doing. These are the 'luck' of our lives that Schweitzer is talking about.

What, then, is to be included under 'fortune' beyond the specific examples in Schweitzer's own list? More important than a complete enumeration would seem to be a clear criterion which would enable one to identify instances. The decisive factor in all these cases is that all the lucky circumstances are not of our own doing and are in this sense unearned. If this correct, then any circumstance in life, beginning with the accident of birth in a particular place, time, physical, social, and religious situation, if it is in our favor, would qualify as 'luck'. This calls for a fuller exploration of the concept of accident of birth and circumstance as basic for Schweitzer's 'other thought'.[173]

Next, what does Schweitzer imply by the obligation of sacrificing an 'equivalent in help and service'? How far does this obligation reach? In his own case Schweitzer interpreted it as allowing him to spend his first thirty years, that is, possibly the average length of one generation, in the pursuit of his scholarly and artistic ambitions before turning over the balance to the exclusive service of his less fortunate fellow beings by taking up the study of medicine, which he began practicing as a missionary doctor in the jungle at the age of thirty-eight. However, he did offer limited services to the handicapped along with his other activities long before. While it would be questionable to make this one example a model for all others, it seems clear that Schweitzer did not want to deny the individual a right to enjoy his gifts, which after all had come to him without his asking; merely sooner or later he has to do something about

172. 'Only in very rare moments have I been really happy in my life'. (*Aus meinem Leben und Denken*, p. 208, p. 204).

173. See my article 'Accident of Birth', *Journal of the History of Ideas* 22 (1961): pp. 475-91; this volume, number 6.

compensating his less fortunate fellow beings, perhaps with interest, for the delay in doing so. The main point is that at some time we have to make up to some of the deprived for unearned benefits (received without our own doing).

Now one might feel that the new principle, even if it is not restricted to the aristocracy of birth, is not a universal one but is limited to only one-half of mankind, that is, to its upper half, which is under an obligation to compensate the other half. While at first sight this seems to be true, closer consideration shows that in some regards the new principle applies to almost everyone for the following reasons:

1. Good fortune is not an absolute condition. It is always good fortune with regard to specific conditions, such as health, wealth, talent, or disposition. These 'regards' are by no means interdependent. Whoever is fortunate in one regard is likely to be unfortunate in some others. This does not exclude the sad truth that some people seem to be unfortunate in almost all regards. But for all others the ethics of 'fortune obligates' has at least some application.

2. There is also a sense in which even the most unfortunate is fortunate by the very fact that he is unfortunate in the first sense. He may not be born on the right side of the tracks. But on the scales of justice it is precisely those who are born on the wrong side who have claims to compensation and have moral, if not legal, rights against those who are favored. This too is a privilege, though a privilege of a different, and in a sense even a higher, order. It is unearned in the same sense in which being born on the right side of the tracks is a privilege, never to be taken for granted. This privilege, without stopping the otherwise underprivileged from pressing their claims for compensation to the utmost, obligates them all the same to some understanding of, and even patience with, the overprivileged, who were born 'in the wrong' without any personal fault. This may also be one of the insights expressed in the Beatitudes of the Sermon on the Mount, with their commendation of the poor in body and spirit and of the suffering.

After this attempt to clarify the meaning of Schweitzer's 'other thought', it makes sense to consider a more impressive label for it than his primary negative injunction 'not to accept one's luck as a matter of course', matched by the positive obligation to compensate the less fortunate by service. As a quick formula one might consider, in analogy to 'noblesse oblige', 'bonheur oblige', and render it in English, as I did in my title, as 'good fortune obligates', though it is not so euphonic as the French phrase. More important than such a slogan would of course be a proper formulation of the principle involved. I suggest: The more fortunate owe to those less fortunate a compensation in proportion to their handicaps.

11.4 The Evidence for the New Principle

There should be no mistake about the fact that at first sight such a principle will be anything but self-evident to the common sense of the proverbial man in the street. His immediate reaction may well be: 'Why shouldn't we be allowed to enjoy whatever is our lot instead of worrying about those less lucky than we?' Such a reaction would be even more natural in the case of those who happen to believe that our lots have been assigned to us by a superior, wiser, and fairer power. No wonder that our traditional ethics, including our moral philosophy based on moral common sense, has no place for Schweitzer's principle. In its light the principle can only appear as extravagant. What, then, was Schweitzer's evidence for the validity of his new thought? How far did he try to communicate it to others not yet convinced?

Clearly, what is needed here is not merely an interpretation of ordinary moral sense but an attempt to push out its boundaries by widening and deepening it. This task calls not for mere reasoning but for an appeal from one's everyday opinions to one's 'better knowledge'. This is actually what Schweitzer's approach to ethics involves: an appeal to modern man to develop his ordinary moral consciousness to the level of 'better knowledge' once he has been awakened and sensitized to it.

One way in which Schweitzer tried to achieve this consciousness-raising was by telling us about himself. The most impressive example is, of course, the story of his decision to go to Equatorial Africa as told in his autobiography and, perhaps even more directly, on the first pages of his first book-size report about his Lambarene enterprise.[174]

But Schweitzer did not leave it at setting an example putting others to shame without directly tackling their consciences. At the very end of the book, in chapter 11 of the first edition, he made a general appeal to the 'fraternity of those marked by pain' to assume responsibility for those not yet relieved from the bondage of physical suffering: 'Whoever has been delivered of pain must not think he is now free again and can return to life as if nothing has happened to him. Now that he knows about pain and anxiety he must help to meet pain and anxiety as far as human power can and bring deliverance to others as he received deliverance'. And he added: 'Sooner or later the idea which I am proclaiming will conquer the world because in its merciless logic it compels men's thoughts as well as their hearts'. And in a later plea for aid to blinded soldiers Schweitzer wrote: 'We who lived through this ghastly time and who have suffered no or merely minor injury cannot get rid of a certain embarrassment at having fared so much better than they. It forces us to resolve to offer them a little more than some ordinary sympathy. They have the right to expect that again and again we meet them with reverence and with a kindly, understanding, patient readiness to help in everything —we who have been spared the heavy fate that has been laid upon them'.[175]

Thus, Schweitzer appeals not simply to ordinary moral common sense but to something that a person 'must' feel or ought to feel. This does not mean that his appeal is simply an attempt to persuade. It is based on the 'merciless logic' of the idea of fraternity among fellow-sufferers. He aims at awakening and developing a moral sense that is usually dormant but that on special occasions can be brought to the surface. This is the way in which prophets have tried to shape the moral consciousness of mankind. In this sense Schweitzer too does not simply engage in moral philosophy but attempts to create a new moral consciousness, not by commandments or suggestion but by proclamation and 'summons' leading a person to

174. *Zwischen Wasser und Urwald* (Bern: Haupt, 1921) (*On the Edge of the Primeval Forest*, trans. C.T. Campion. New York: MacMillan Co., 1948).

175. Translated from Schweitzer's foreword to *Kriegsblindenjahrbuch* 1958 (Wiesbaden, Selbstverlag, 1958), p. v.

see by himself what he has not yet consciously 'realized' in the full sense of this term, expressing seeing and doing at the same time.

How far is such an ethics of moral appeal able to expand moral common sense? How far can it bring it to accept the principle of 'fortune obligates?

11.5 The Foundation of the Second Principle: Justice Reinterpreted

There is perhaps one more consideration that may help. Schweitzer does not make an explicit attempt to lay any deeper foundations for the new principle. As he proclaims it, there does not seem to be any other reason for this obligation with its enormous practical implications than its direct appeal. Only in a few places does he intimate that it has something to do with a compensatory justice that not only gives the fortunate a duty but gives the unfortunate a moral right to claim compensation.

One might well ask whether in the last resort it is not this sense of justice which underlies Schweitzer's new principle. But what kind of justice? What is needed to this end is a wider and deepened concept of justice.

John Rawls, in his new theory of justice as fairness, provides a first opening for such an expanded conception of justice. Ostensibly he maintains merely, in accordance with his contractual theory, that the partners in such an imaginary 'original agreement in a situation of equality'[176] would agree on 'two rather different principles:

1. that of 'equality in the assignment of basic rights and duties' (principle of equality), and

2. social and economic inequalities are just only if they result in compensating benefits for everyone, and in particular for the least advantaged members of society' (principle of difference).

But he also suggests that such an agreement is not a matter of arbitrary choice and accidental accordance of choices. It may be

---

176. John Rawls, *A Theory of Justice.* Cambridge, Mass.: Harvard University Press, 1971, pp. 14-15.

'expected . . . if reasonable terms are proposed'. Thus, the agreement on the principles of justice may itself be considered as fair if 'those better endowed, or more fortunate in their social position, neither of which we can be said to deserve, could expect the willing cooperation of others . . . Once we decide to look for a conception of justice that nullifies the accidents of natural endowment and the contingencies of social circumstances . . . we are led to these principles. They express the result of leaving aside those aspects of the social world that seem arbitrary from a moral point of view' (p. 15).

Now it seems to me that here Rawls distinguishes actually two types of fairness, (1) that of the principles of equality and differences agreed upon and (2) that of the criterion by which he thinks we can decide that these principles themselves are 'fair' in the sense of nullifying accidents of natural advantage. While even the second fairness seems to be a matter of 'decision', that is, the decision to look for a fair conception of justice, it is actually anything but left to arbitrary choice. More important to me is that this precontractual fairness implies a consideration of natural or cosmic, not merely of human, distribution, for which, however, man is to compensate. To me this makes it clear that Rawls acknowledges not only a principle preceding all contracts but that this principle implies a different, more basic kind of fairness and unfairness in natural relationships. But this conception has to be developed far beyond the few hints that can be found in his book. Our ordinary concept of justice applies only to human actions and social arrangements and concerns such questions as the fairness of distribution or 'rectification of wrongs' as developed in Aristotle's classic theory of justice. Such a theory can hardly account for the sense of justice or injustice that applies to natural conditions, particularly to the fair distribution of good or bad fortune at birth.

What I would like to suggest, then, is that the ultimate foundation of Schweitzer's principle can be found in such a concept of cosmic justice under which good and bad fortune are cases of nonpersonal justice or injustice which, though not asking for any sanctions in the form of punishment, call for restoration and compensation as exemplified in the legal institution of unjust enrichment. Connecting the principle of 'good fortune obligates' with such an enlarged theory of justice would give it additional strength.

11.6 Conclusion

I do not want to contribute to the kind of Schweitzer worship which he himself tried to discourage, with only partial success. What I have tried to show is that his ethics contains at least one more thought than that of reverence for life that has not been sufficiently appreciated. Properly developed, his principle of 'good fortune obligates' could become one of the strongest levers for breaking down the worst divisions of mankind by undermining the immoral pride behind nationalism, racism, sexism, 'classism', and all kinds of orthodoxies. Schweitzer himself in his own life transcended such divisions by rising above Franco-German nationalism, the denominationalism of the Christian churches, the iron-curtain mentality between West and East, and finally by his unique ecumenical interest in both Indian and Chinese thought. In approaching these differences as basically matters of fortune putting special obligations on the privileged toward the underprivileged, Schweitzer buttressed the case for the solidarity of a humanized humanity.

12. WHY COMPENSATE THE NATURALLY HANDICAPPED[177]

A Case for a New Conception of Compensatory Justice

> We who have lived through this cruel time
> and came through it with no or only little
> harm cannot overcome a certain embarrass-
> ment toward the handicapped of the World
> War over the fact that we are so much better
> off than they are. It compels us to vow that
> we meet them with more than ordinary com-
> passion. They have a right to expect that we
> meet them again and again with reverence,
> with friendly understanding and with the pa-
> tient readiness to help them in everthing —we
> who have been spared the heavy lot that has
> been laid upon them.
>
> Albert Schweitzer (1958)

> It is our wish to delude ourselves that those
> who are severely handicapped are not ex-
> cluded from living, that we therefore do not
> owe them a compassion much deeper than
> words, which would express itself in deeds.
>
> Bruno Bettelheim
> *The New Yorker*
> August 4, 1980

177. My main helpers and constructive critics in the preparation of this paper were my colleagues Professors Carl Wellman and Stanley L. Paulson of the Department of Philosophy, Professor Martha Storandt and her graduate student Chris Hager Feeley of the Department of Psychology, and Professor Ralph E. Pumphrey of the School of Social Work, all of Washington University, St. Louis. I also received important advice from Dr. Richard Goldbaum of the St. Louis League of Handicapped Children.

12.1 Natural Inequalities and the Human Rights of the
Naturally Handicapped

The late William T. Blackstone, one of the keenest thinkers on the problem of reverse discrimination based on race and sex, in an Appendix to his paper on 'Social Justice and Preferential Treatment'[178] entitled 'Compensation and Natural Inequalities' included the following sentences:

> When the inability to compete is not due to invidious past discrimination of the social system but to natural inequalities, the accident of birth, the luck of the draw —however one wishes to put this— what is required by the equalitarian commitment to equal rights? . . . In the long run the answer to this question may be far more significant for social justice than the answer to the question of compensation for past invidious discrimination.[179]

In this essay I propose to take up the challenge implied in these sentences. In particular I hope to justify the prediction that a full understanding of the problem of compensation for natural inequalities will not only complement but undercut the present controversies over compensatory justice for manmade discriminations. I believe that one of the best levers for this refocusing can be a philosophical reflection on our rapidly expanding practice, though not yet on our ethical theory, of compensation for the naturally handicapped. I also believe that a full consideration of their case requires a phenomenological investigation of the subjective experience that goes with these handicaps and their compensations. Such an investigation may allay Blackstone's apparent apprehensions lest the compensation of natural inequalities will have 'tremendous' consequences that could result not only from my own, but especially from John Rawls' more developed considerations. My underlying concern in this essay is to help ethics keep up with the growing edge of moral consciousness and cooperate with it by going beyond the range of the phenomena considered by traditional ethical theory. I hope that in this way I can contribute to developing our

---

178. *Social Justice and Preferential Treatment*, ed. W.T. Blackstone and R.D. Heslep. Athens: The University of Georgia Press, 1977, p. 78.
179. *Ibid.*, p. 79.

moral consciousness and break some of the deadlock in current ethical and social theory.

The International Year of the Handicapped in 1981 may be a fitting reminder of the fact that philosophy has not yet paid proper attention to them and to their case.[180] I believe that the plight of the handicapped, whether child or adult, is a challenge to philosophy. Its almost total neglect is all the more surprising since the liberation of the handicapped, initiated first by the nonhandicapped, and more recently by a powerful civil rights movement of the more articulate victims of handicaps, is one of the more significant developments in the recent social history of mankind. What is particularly remarkable about it is the ease and rapidity in the progress of the handicapped to the extent that the nonhandicapped never seem to have questioned their claims in principle, even when their fulfillment requires unusual expense and offers only limited 'rehabilitation'. Why was the victory of the cause of the naturally handicapped so much smoother than that of the socially disadvantaged? Why should the nonhandicapped feel more responsible for the victims of nature than for those of society?[181] In focusing on the problem of compensation for the naturally handicapped I want to make it clear that I shall not discuss the wider question of equalization of natural inequalities in general. As I intend to show, compensation does not always mean equalization. Whether or not all natural inequalities should be abolished seems to me a debatable question, which I am inclined to answer in the negative, especially if it means penalizing those with superior endowments. Instead I want to concentrate on a case, largely neglected, where at least some compensation for the unfairly disadvantaged is within our reach and has become an increasingly urgent demand of our social conscience.

180. In fact, not even the Universal Declaration of Human Rights of 1948 mentioned them explicitly. Only the 'Declaration of the Rights of the Child' of 1959 does so in its Principle 5: 'The child who is physically, mentally or socially handicapped shall be given the special treatment, education and care required by his particular condition'.

181. This differont is pointed out in the article on 'Poverty' by Jack Roach and Janet K. Roach in the *Encyclopedia Britannica* (15th ed.) Macropaedia vol. 14, p. 936, which states that whereas the 'socially handicapped' are often 'stigmatized', the physically and mentally handicapped are usually regarded sympathetically.

12.2 The State of the Question About Natural Inequalities

The more general question of the ethical implications of natural inequalities has not been completely ignored. It is beginning to surface especially in some recent work dealing with human equality and inequality and their ethical and social implications.

One of the most striking new motifs in John Rawls' traiblazing study of justice and particularly in his support of the 'tendency toward equality' is his concern for those unequal by nature in talents and skills. In dealing with them he at times speaks of them as victims of a 'natural lottery in native assets'[182] and refers to differences in the players' good or bad luck as 'accidental from the moral point of view'. This almost sounds as if some 'a-moral', if not malicious, power were responsible for our natural lots. In any case, for Rawls the resulting glaring injustices in the assignment of our initial positions call for 'nullification' of the resulting 'contingencies and biases of historical fate',[183] terms which however are never explained in detail.

Actually Rawls' suggested remedies are not as sweeping as this radical language may suggest. In particular, Rawls rejects the 'principle of redress', an expression for which I may have been responsible when in an article of 1944 I postulated that all undeserved inequalities call for 'redress', i.e., a restoration of the natural balance, a postulate for which at the time I failed to give an adequate foundation.[184] All that matters to Rawls is that something has to be done about the wrongness of the initial distribution. His criterion for such a redistribution is his second principle of justice, the 'principle of difference', according to which every remaining inequality must improve eventually 'the long-term expectancy of the least favored'. This principle is called the expression of an agreement to regard the distribution of natural talents as a common asset and to share in the benefit of this distribution whatever it turns out to be.[185] Now the agreement here proposed is based on Rawls' theory of a contract among the partners of a hypothetical 'original' state of nature. Apart from other doubts about its meaning and

182. *A Theory of Justice.* Harvard University Press, 1971, pp. 73, 104.
183. *Ibid.,* pp. 36, 378.
184. 'A Defense of Human Equality'; see Essay number 7, in this volume.
185. *A Theory of Justice,* p. 101.

our right to postulate such a fictitious settlement, do we have any good reason and right to assume the consent of the least favored group to it? Certainly a special appeal would have to be made to them as the immediate losers of an unequal distribution. Without it, how can they be expected to agree to such generosity? Cannot they as the immediate victims of the 'natural lottery' expect some explicit respect for their actual view? Otherwise I cannot see how they can be persuaded to adopt the universalistic perspective of the difference principle, even though this may be good prudential advice.

Furthermore, what about the underlying assumption that the difference in 'natural assets of unequal talents and skills' is the result of a natural lottery, ·accidental from the moral point of view? It is not surprising that Robert Nozick[186] challenged this initial assumption. In fact, in examining Rawls' thesis Nozick generously constructed two sets of arguments as possible support for Rawls' position: (1) that 'the distributive effects of natural inequalities ought to be nullified' and (2) that the counterarguments to the effect that they ought *not* to be nullified can be refuted.[187] But since he finds both of these arguments wanting, I see no point in rehearsing and appraising them here, leaving this task to their obvious defender, Rawls himself, who, to my knowledge, has not yet done so in print.

Nevertheless, Nozick's objections show that Rawls' ideal of equalizing natural inequalities is anything but universally accepted. His case against total equalization, formerly called leveling, is shared by other recent anti-equalitarians, among whom I shall mention merely H.J. McCloskey,[188] omitting the recent French 'New Right'.[189] Thus even today the case for human equality and especially for total equalization is far from established. What is now needed is a clear demonstration that our present moral consciousness supports it at least in one major area. Even more important will be the identification of the grounds for such 'equalization'.

186. *Anarchy, the State and Utopia.* New York: Basic Books, 1974.

187. *Ibid.,* pp. 213-224 (positive argument) and 224-227 (negative argument).

188. 'Equalitarianism, Equality and Justice', *Australasian Journal of Philosophy* 44 (1966), 50-69.

189. See Thomas Sheehan on Alain de Benoist, *Vue de Droite,* 1977 in *New York Review of Books* 26 (1980), Jan. 24, 1980.

My main thesis in this essay will be that there is indeed such an area in connection with our treatment of the naturally and otherwise accidentally handicapped. Here the degree of apparently unquestioned agreement on the need for coming to their support is all the more remarkable in view of the continuing dissent about compensation for handicaps based on social discrimination, in particular race- and sex-based handicaps, as expressed in the controversies and legal battles over reverse discrimination as a means of compensating the victims of past injustices. This makes it all the more significant to examine the much simpler case of the naturally handicapped.

12.3 The Problems of Compensation for the Naturally Handicapped

By way of introduction to such a study I shall present first some factual information about the significance of the problems of natural handicaps. I shall begin with some facts about the magnitude of the issue:

1. According to the official statistics 'perhaps one-sixth of the population of the United States is mentally or physically impaired with urgent unmet needs,[190] which would amount to some 35 million persons, making the handicapped the largest minority, exceeding even the Blacks with their 26,488,218 persons out of a total population of 226,504,829 (1980 census).

2. In 1978 nearly eight million children of school age could be classified as handicapped in some way, of whom only 50 percent were served by educational services.[191]

3. According to the World Rehabilitation Fund established by Dr. Howard E. Rusk, the handicapped are also the largest minority on the globe, estimated at 300 million.

Concerning the qualitative distribution of these handicaps the classification of the White House Conference in 1977 gives at least

190. *The White House Conference on Handicapped Individuals.* May 23-27, 1977, U.S. Government Documents Y3 W58/18; 1/977 vol. II, Part I, p. 7.
191. *Statistical Abstract of the United States* 1978 (Department of Commerce, Bureau

a preliminary idea. Here the handicapped were divided into 27 groups with an additional slot for 'other' handicaps, presumably on the basis of their different needs to be discussed at the conference. The handicaps were in alphabetical order: (1) Amputation, (2) Arthritis/Rheumatism, (3) Blindness, (4) Visual Impairment, (5) Cancer, (6) Cerebral Palsy, (7) Congenital Malformation, (8) Deafness — Hard of Hearing, (9) Near-blindness, (10) Diabetes Mellitus, (11) Epilepsy, (12) Heart Disease, (13) Language Disorder, (14) Learning Disability, (15) Little Person, (16) Mental Retardation, (17) Mental/Emotional Disorder, (18) Multiple Sclerosis, (19) Muscular Dystrophy, (20) Myasthenia Gravis, (21) Parkinson's Disease, (22) Poliomyelitis, (23) Respiratory Condition, (24) Speech Impairment, (25) Spinal Cord Injury, (26) Stroke, (27) Multiple (specify:), (28) Other: (specify).

The U.S. Center for Education divides the handicapped children into eight major groups: (1) speech impaired (ca. 29 p.c), (2) learning disabilities (ca. 23 p.c.), (3) mentally retarded (ca 19 p.c.), (4) emotionally disturbed (ca. 17 p.c.), (5) deaf and hard-of-hearing (ca. 5 p.c.), (6) visually handicapped (ca. 1.5 p.c.), (7) crippled and other health impairments (ca. 1.5 p.c.), (8) multihandicapped (ca. 1 p.c.).[192] It should also be realized that the condition of the very young and the very old constitutes at least an equivalent of these specific handicaps. Adding them to the minority of the technically handicapped would probably make them a majority of the total population.

All these handicaps are clearly 'natural' in the sense that they are not the result of any personal or social action, even though by mistakes or neglect the patients or society may have contributed to their development. In this respect such handicaps differ from conditions like addictions, e.g., alcoholism, which are at least in the initial stages 'manmade'. Yet the eventual disease is no longer under normal control. Thus, with an estimated number of alcoholics of over five million in 1979, and considerably more in other countries like France, even such handicaps must be considered in apprais-

of the Census), p. 363. See also the MacNeil-Lehrer Report on 'Handicapped Education' of October 11, 1978.

192. *Statistical Abstract of the U.S.* 1978. Department of Commerce, Bureau of the Census, p. 363.

ing the total of natural handicaps. It should also be realized that in a wider sense temporary disabilities like those produced by acute illnesses show some of the features of natural handicaps. Tuberculosis, fortunately no longer an incurable disease, could, but no longer does, figure among natural handicaps.

Finally, it should be realized that all of us when transposed into a new environment, especially one with a new language, are temporarily handicapped. In this sense everyone is handicapped in some respects all during his life. The realization of such universal relative handicaps may serve as a reminder that handicaps are part of the human condition in its finitude. They may also help to establish a bond between the severely handicapped in the standard sense and the nonhandicapped, paving the way to one-sided and even mutual understanding and aid among them. But for the purpose of the present study it will suffice to focus on the hard core of the handicapped in the legal sense.[193] In asserting that there is today surprising agreement on the need of compensatory measures for the naturally handicapped, I do not mean to imply that there is no reason for examining the meaning and the justification of this principle. On the contrary, this makes it all the more urgent

(a) to clarify the exact meaning of the phrase 'natural handicap';

(b) to find its referents in the phenomena and its origin;

(c) to test our belief in the connection between natural handicaps and the need for compensation;

(d) to determine who is responsible for such compensation;

(e) to fix the limits of such responsibility;

(f) to discover the ground for it.

Not all of these tasks can be fully discussed here. The important need, as I see it, is to raise these problems on a philosophical level. For thus far little has been done by philosophers to examine them.[194]

193. For the United States see especially the Rehabilitation Act of 1973 (*Public Laws*, 93-112, September 16, 1973), and its 'Definitions' in Section 7 regarding the term 'handicapped children' as meaning 'mentally retarded, hard of hearing, deaf, speech impaired, visually handicapped, seriously emotionally disturbed, crippled or other health impaired children who by reason thereof require special education and related services'.

194. I know only of three incidental treatments of the subject:

(a) The Phrase 'Natural Handicaps': Its Meaning and Its Origin
All handicaps and their counterparts ('headstarts', privileges, or preferments) represent human inequalities. But not all human inequalities are handicaps; some may simply be varieties which merely add to the colorfulness of the natural or cultural scene. They become handicaps only if one of the unequal partners is put at a disadvantage or advantage in relation to his fellow humans. Some of these may be self-inflicted, some inflicted by others, either purposely or negligently. Such socially caused handicaps or headstarts are of primary concern for social legislation and policy. But there

(a) Ronald Dworkin in his reinterpretation of 'Liberalism' in an essay under this title in Stuart Hampshire, ed., *Public and Private Morality* (Cambridge University Press, 1978), who in contrasting the liberal with the conservative attitude, mentions the liberal's preference for 'some form of redistribution of natural handicaps in talents in the name of justice' (p. 1370), but without developing and justifying this preference.

(b) Alan H. Goldman in the context of his analysis of *Justice and Reverse Discrimination* (Princeton University Press, 1979) briefly discusses the justification for funding 'special programs for the blind, deaf or otherwise physically handicapped' in the context of the attempt to achieve equal opportunity by attacking not only social but natural inequalities, which he carefully distinguishes (pp. 171-182), but decides that the entire question of natural inequalities, important as it is for social philosophy, need not be debated for his purposes. What he does say is that 'we can recognize rights to special treatment in their (the handicapped's) behalf, satisfaction of which may be demanded as just.' He also mentions three reasons for the recognition of such rights: 1. benevolence, 2. our own wish for special treatment if we were in the place of the handicapped, 3. the right to the fulfillment of basic needs: 'for the handicapped special programs may be necessary to accomplish even that much'. The first reason sounds like an appeal to charity, the second comes close to an appeal to the golden rule applied to the contrary-to-fact condition of our being handicapped ourselves, by itself hardly a convincing argument. The third is the only reason that amounts to a right for the handicapped, while the two others refer only to feelings and wishes. Clearly, these reasons need unfolding before they can be evaluated critically.

(c) Richard B. Brandt in his *A Theory of the Good and the Right* (Oxford: Clarendon Press, 1979) Section XVI ('Justice, Equality and the Maximization of Welfare') devotes subsection 3 to 'Why Supplements for the Ill and the Handicapped?' (pp. 316-318), in which he tries to refute A.K. Sen's assertion in *On Economic Inequality* (New York: W. W. Norton, 1973), pp. 16 f.) 'that a welfare maximizing system would assign less income to the crippled, on the ground that such a person would get less utility from it than would the normal person'. While Brandt claims that Sen is mistaken, and that in general special supplements to the handicapped would maximize welfare, he finally concedes that 'in the case of the imbecile Sen's argument might work, but the result is not outrageous. It would be stupid to spend much money when more than a little will add no further enjoyment'. And he concludes that the maximization of welfare which he advocates 'would require different interpretations of various kinds of handicaps . . . with different conclusions about the size of the supplement' (p. 318).

are also handicaps and headstarts totally or mostly unrelated to social causes. It is these not man-caused or 'natural' handicaps which are at stake in the present study. They may be congenital, like birth defects, e.g., Down's syndrome, and even prenatal, like malformations. They may also occur or become manifest only long after birth. Some may affect merely individuals, others also smaller or larger groups. But even natural accidents after birth due to 'natural causes' like diseases or natural catastrophes are natural handicaps in this sense. What they all have in common is that they are not caused by individual or social actions, which may at most have a contributing effect when the handicaps could have been prevented or mitigated. In a concrete case it may be impossible to draw a line between socially and naturally induced handicaps. The important thing is that there is a conceptual difference between them.

What corresponds to the expressions used above as referents are certain conditions in human subjects in their relations to other subjects. These conditions arise in connection with situations where they compete. The special condition of the handicapped is that he lacks certain prerequisites for the competition, whereas his privileged competitor possesses these qualifications and possibly even an exceptional amount of them. Neither one need be aware and conscious of this difference. This applies particularly to the mentally handicapped. Further investigation would reveal not only different types of handicaps, such as central and peripheral, severe and light, permanent or temporary, simple or multiple ones. There are also different modes of consciousness of these 'objective handicaps', which will have to be considered later. At the moment all that matters is to obtain a first idea of the variety of the phenomena to be considered.

Indications are that the *concept* of handicap as distinguished from the odd *word* is fairly recent. In western civilization it apparently did not exist or was at best merely implicit up to the nineteenth century. There was of course always a realization of differences in opportunities and abilities for different individuals. But these differences were merely of a factual nature. The idea that there is something amiss about them and that something could and should be done about it accrued to the concept probably quite late.

According to the *New Oxford Dictionary* the word 'handicap' has an 'obscure history'. Apparently it originated from the phrase 'hand-in-cap', which referred to a game of chance in which forfeit money was put in a cap. It is not without interest that the word 'handicap' was thus originally related to a kind of lottery. Closer to the present use is its eighteenth-century application to horse racing 'in which an umpire decrees what weights have to be carried by different horses entered according to his judgment of their merits in order to equalize their chances', a meaning which in the later nineteenth century was extended to any race or competition where an equalization of chances of the competitors was attempted by giving a headstart to the less able and/or imposing a 'hind-start' upon the better qualified. Finally, after 1895, the word 'handicap' stood for the weight or condition imposed on the superior in order to favor the inferior competitor. Thus it became a means for correcting natural inequalities and making up for them. In fact, up to this point, it was the superior, not the inferior party who suffered the handicap, i.e., a disadvantage, which was imposed on him on purpose. Only later was the handicap ascribed to the inferior, the initially disadvantaged or 'handicapped' by his natural condition.

At first sight this etymological story, which traces the origin of the term to an English betting game and then to horseracing or other competitive sports, may seem to be without ethical significance. Presumably the primary purpose for imposing handicaps on superior competitors was to restore the excitement of an unpredictable score instead of the foreseeable outcome of a competition among naturally unequal partners. However, I submit that quite early in this equalization of unequal chances among naturally unequal competitors in sports a sense of fairness entered according to which it was simply 'unfair' to the participants that from the very start one of them should have to cope with more difficulties than the other. This standard of 'fairness' seems to me one of the most significant contributions of the competitive sports to ethical evolution. This contribution also included the introduction of special 'umpires' (i.e., etymologically 'not of a pair of contestants') and 'handicappers', who had to guarantee 'fairness' and prevent 'unfairness'. Thus it is simply unfair that a person with a weaker constitution has to compete with an athlete unless he is given a headstart. It could well be that here are the roots of our social sense of fairness and of the feeling that something ought to be done to make up for the social disadvantages of the less fortunate by handicapping the more fortunate partners in society.

In the light of this story it is particularly instructive that by now we no longer apply the old term 'handicap' only to a human operation, but also to the natural condition which precedes it. Furthermore, interestingly not until 1976, did the *Supplement to the Oxford English Dictionary* add to the verb 'to handicap': 'Hence handicapped . . . of persons, especially children, physically or mentally defective, also as substantive'.

It may also be illuminating to trace the genesis of the concept of natural handicap corresponding to the expression. This concept has had quite a history in our moral development. It may well have originated in the English-speaking world, judging from the fact that other western languages borrowed it from the English (.e.g, French *'handicapé'*, German *'gehandikapt'*). However, in the present context I can offer only an outline of this history.

1. Presumably, in a society struggling for survival under conditions of extreme hardship there was little chance and inclination to pay attention to the needs of those who 'could not make it', i.e., particularly the handicapped. There was no alternative to abandoning them to their fate, sometimes of 'exposing', killing, and even eating them. Under some conditions this may even have been the equivalent of 'mercy killing'. In any case at this stage there was no room for any special concern for the handicapped.

2. On a more advanced level the attitude of the lucky survivors was determined largely by certain magical or even theological ideas according to which natural handicaps were ordained by superhuman powers beyond our jurisdiction. Theirs was the responsibility for such seeming misfortunes. In the framework of a predestinatarian theology the naturally handicapped could even be 'vessels of the wrath' of the Creator made for destruction, compared with the 'vessels of grace' which He had selected in His absolute discretion.[195] Thus there was no reason for special intercession or even regret for the handicapped.

3. A first concern for the naturally handicapped developed out of the growing care and aid for the sick. Since this tended to include help for any human being suffering from whatever cause, even the

195. St. Paul, Letter to the Romans 9, 21.

permanently handicapped could not be excluded. Refuges for them as well as for others were such institutions as hospitals (i.e., guest houses) in India, in Greece (temples) with its Hippocratic morality and especially in a monastic order, committed to works of 'charity' in the Middle Ages.

4. Another group of naturally handicapped taken care of by charity were orphans and especially foundlings. In fact orphanages in Italy went by the name of 'hospitals of the innocent' (e.g., the *Ospedale degli innocenti* in Florence).

5. The largest group of handicapped were probably those mixed in with the 'poor'. Relief for the poor was one of the major obligations in all major religions, primarily by way of almsgiving, i.e., of giving because of pity *(elemosyne),* often more for the sake of the almsgiver's record than of the recipient. But who are the poor? Primarily those in economic distress, no matter for what reason, whether because of their own fault or because they were naturally handicapped. Again, they were at best the objects of compassion, at worst of contempt.

6. A new stage was reached in England with the first attempts at legislation for the poor under Queen Elizabeth I (1601). However, one thing that should be realized about this first major attack upon the evil of poverty is that the new 'overseers of the poor' in the parishes were primarily to provide work for children whose parents were unable to keep and maintain them, secondly to set to work all such persons, married or unmarried, without means of support, and only in the third line to provide the necessary relief for the 'lame, impotent, old, blind and such others among them being poor and not able to work'. Thus among the poor in the sense of this legislation only some could be considered handicapped and especially naturally handicapped, namely the 'lame', the blind, and others unable to work, whereas the 'impotent' include also the young and the aged. But there was no special group of the handicapped as such. Moreover, this new legal approach did not establish any rights for the handicapped but merely obligations for the overseers in the parishes toward the Crown. Anyway, merely as poor people unable to work did the naturally handicapped have a chance for relief as a matter of public bounty.

7. This is not the place to trace the development of social service in the following centuries, especially during the age of Enlighten-

ment, of philanthropy and of humanitarianism. It certainly changed the spirit of the relief given to the poor including the handicapped. But even under enlightened rationalism and finally socialism relief remained a favor, even when it tried to respect the poor as persons by helping them to rehabilitate themselves. The beneficiaries of the new approaches still had no claims for relief on legal and moral grounds.

8. Such a change may be implied in the introduction of the Social Insurance System, particularly when not only the potential poor but their employers and the State were to carry part of the burden. Schemes for the insurance of the sick, the aged and the unemployed on the Continent and, more sweepingly, in the U.S. Social Security Act of 1935 were major steps in this direction. But even at this stage the naturally handicapped were not yet included under the new scheme. For their possible claims could certainly not be based on their own contributions.

9. The legal recognition of the handicapped has been achieved only in the legislation of the sixties and seventies in the United States and elsewhere. At this point the development of a civil rights movement by and for the handicapped including the naturally handicapped marks the explicit recognition of a special group different from the poor.

The development I have tried to sketch means one of the most remarkable evolutions in the social consciousness of mankind. I do not think that one could and should characterize it as a mere change in social attitudes and beliefs. What has happened — and what should be studied and documented much more fully — is an awakening of a new social sensitivity which discovers and responds to demands previously only dimly sensed. In this awakening not only the social imagination but also consistent thinking through of the implications of our incipient insights has played and is to play a major role. This is clearly the task of moral education rather than of dogmatic preaching. A major step in this evolution of social consciousness seems to me the development of our sense for handicaps and particularly for natural handicaps. Our first reaction, one which we can still trace in ourselves, is to look upon congenital defects, such as blindness, deafness or palsy, as unfortunate and unpleasant abnormalities which we would like to ignore, especially since we do not have to feel responsible for their occurrence. It takes not only the development of sympathy but of empathy to become aware of what a handicap means. Before that, we see an objective defect. But it takes entering into the life world of the handicapped to appreciate the existential wrong he is suffering. 'Handicap' may be an odd word for it, but it signifies the rise of a new sense of fairness in our relations with our fellow-beings.

(b) Need and Types of Compensation for Natural Handicaps

Do natural handicaps call for compensation? Conceivably the answer to this question would have been 'no' if it had been asked at all at an earlier stage in the moral development of mankind. Such a negative response could be understood partly in view of the primitive economic conditions of earlier man and of the lack of development in his moral sensitivity. Today's widespread, if not yet universal, conviction that something ought to be done about the condition of the naturally handicapped is indicative of, but not yet conclusive for, its justification. In order to buttress it I would suggest a kind of thought experiment by imagining our moral reaction to a situation where the handicapped would be simply abandoned (as they were in primitive society and even in ancient Greece and Rome) or hidden from view (as they still are too often). I submit that such an approach would awaken our indignation, if not outrage against such callousness. In other words, I am suggesting that by an appeal to the imagination it is possible to awaken our sense for the necessity of some kind of compensation for the naturally handicapped, an approach which could develop and reinforce a sentiment which perhaps is not always quite developed, but which is capable of such development and education. This means an appeal to moral intuition by means of imaginative variation.

In the present framework a complete enumeration of the possible kinds of compensation for the naturally handicapped would be impossible. It would also be unnecessary and possibly diverting from the main objective of this study. Suffice it to list here some of the compensatory attempts.

1. Equalization with the nonhandicapped by removal of the defect (which is actually more than compensation). In the case of physical handicaps this can be done to a remarkable degree by modern surgery, particularly through its transplants. As far as it cannot be fully accomplished, substitutes such as protheses or elec-

tric wheelchairs can restore to the handicapped some of the major functions of his body. Likewise visual or hearing aids can return to him the power of the original organ and even improve it.

Theoretically such equalization with normal people could also be brought about by depriving the nonhandicapped of some of their special advantages, for instance by withholding educational benefits. But such destructive equalization, coming close to King Solomon's notorious justice by threatening to cut a baby claimed by two mothers in half, is unacceptable to all those concerned with the maximizing values rather than uniform equality. Even the equalization of taking an eye for an eye in criminal cases no longer satisfies our sense of penal justice.

2. Where equalization is impossible in principle or in practice, as particularly in the case of mental handicaps, at best 'equivalents' for the handicap can make up for it. The most suitable equivalent would be the 'rehabilitation' of the handicapped by special opportunities, making it possible for him to compete effectively with the nonhandicapped, for instance by giving him a sufficient headstart. Actually this is not always a matter of rehabilitation, since especially the congenitally handicapped never had the *habilitas,* i.e., ability for achieving. Thus this type of compensation had better be called 'habilitation'. In most cases such compensation has to be achieved by the development of special equivalent skills. Thus the ability for lip-reading or the acquisition of a special sign language in the case of the deaf or hard-of-hearing, and the ability to read and write Braille in the case of the blind provide for these handicapped new skills of expression and communication different from those available to the nonhandicapped. The development of such substitute skills requires special instruction, mostly provided by special schools.

3. Wherever such equalizing restoration or compensatory 'rehabilitation' is impossible or insufficient, other equivalents have to be designed. Thus sheltered workshops for those who cannot compete in the open market, and special homes for those who cannot live in a family of their own have to be provided.

4. While most legal and social measures concentrate on helping the handicapped to secure as much economic and social independence as possible, some attempts have also been made to give them direct access or compensation for cultural deprivation. Special

libraries for Braille literature, free supply of records and tapes give some of the culturally handicapped at least equivalents and substitutes for what they miss. So does the recent use of sign language at public events and of special captions on television for the hearing impaired. Even special scent gardens have been built for the blind to give them some recreational equivalents for their visual loss. Free trips by planes, ships and buses for those deprived of free mobility try to make up for some of their deprivations (Norway).

(c) The Responsibility for Compensation to the Naturally Handicapped

The requirement for compensation would remain a dead letter if someone would not take responsibility for implementing it, since 'nature' clearly is deaf to any such appeals. The proper approach to answering this question may be to consider possible addresses of such responsibility, beginning with those closest to the scene, and gradually enlarging the circle of possible intercessors. As a preliminary answer I would suggest that those closest to the need, i.e., the neighbors of the needy, may be best qualified to step in when the need is a 'local' one, and that this circle will widen as the need affects wider groups, until in the case of universal needs it is society as a whole which has to be called upon. Much will clearly depend on the resources available to the interceding agents.

(d) The Limits of the Responsibility for Compensation

Clearly it would be senseless and unjustified to make everyone responsible for taking care of unlimited needs of compensation. Thus the main problem will be to determine what can be reasonably expected from agents who have not only many other responsibilities but also have a right to live their own lives. Thus the limits of strict responsibility will depend on the degree to which the responsibility for compensation interferes with the lives of those responsible. This does not prevent their right to sacrifice spontaneously some of their resources 'beyond the call of duty'. In fact, it adds to the meritoriousness of their charitable actions.

There are, however, also more essential ultimate limits to the chance of full compensation. They will be taken up in the final appraisal of compensatory justice.

12.4 Grounds for the Compensation of Natural Handicaps

Usually it it taken for granted that the naturally handicapped should receive all possible assistance in their efforts to achieve equality with their nonhandicapped fellow beings. No special justification for this right is demanded and none is offered. But this belief was by no means always self-evident. The classic principle since Aristotle was that equals should be treated equally and unequals unequally. Now the naturally handicapped and especially the mentally handicapped are clearly unequal to normally nonhandicapped persons. Why then should they be treated equally?

What is needed here is not only to show that the naturally handicapped have rights to compensation, thus allaying possible doubts of their existence, as I have tried to do in section 3.2. It is also necessary, and may add to the persuasiveness of the case, to demonstrate that the claim for the compensation of natural handicaps rests on definite and understandable grounds. Once we can determine these grounds we should also be able to understand why claims to compensation for the naturally handicapped are necessary.

On the following pages I shall discuss a number of such possible grounds, which are at least relevant even when they are not compelling, presented in ascending order of relevance. These grounds do not exclude each other. In a sense they may be considered as cumulative. The importance of the issue makes it advisable to approach the goal by all promising avenues. As such I shall consider the grounds of charity, utility, need, equality of opportunity, and what I shall call existential justice.

Charity

The most generous attitude toward the victims of natural handicaps is clearly charity, provided that charity means more than the institutionalized charity bestowed by charitable organizations. However, the attempt to base our attitude and compensating action toward the naturally handicapped on charity alone suffers from several weaknesses.

How far is charitable love under our control? Specifically, how far is it under our control in the case of the naturally handicapped, who are not always particularly lovable? If it is not, then any duty to compensatory action would be, to say the least, precarious.

An even stronger appeal to our spontaneous love for the naturally handicapped could be made in the name of compassion understood as a variety of sympathy or pity. But even such a more 'passionate' form of charity is hardly a matter of duty. Besides, compassion may easily imply a certain condescending attitude on the part of the compassionate givers in their superior safety. It may even express a 'Pharisean' self-righteousness, which the sufferer may very well resent.

But even more important: What is the moral status of the handicapped as the recipient of such compassionate charity? Can he do more than appeal to 'pity' in claiming compensation for his disadvantages? Certainly, as a mere beneficiary of charity he has no claims on the dispensors of gifts of love.

Utility

A more rational social ethics could base the case for compensating the naturally handicapped on the principle of utility to the effect that the social benefits of such compensation would exceed the costs involved. A possible difference between rule-utilitarianism stressing the effects of a general rule for compensation for the naturally handicapped and act-utilitarianism concerned primarily with the utility balance in concrete cases could be ignored at least at this stage.

Now it is indeed true that the past thoughtless neglect of the naturally handicapped by giving them at best mere relief is a social waste. 'Disabled is not unable.' But this does not mean that the balance between the 'utility' of compensation and its cost is always positive. Thus in the case of the totally paralyzed or the mentally retarded to the extent of feeble-mindedness it is difficult to imagine how they could be economic assets. Even Richard B. Brandt, the major advocate of rule-utilitarianism who advances this argument, admits in the end that in some cases utility does not justify special supplements to the handicapped. Moreover, is utility a sufficient foundation for a strict obligation on the part of the privileged, and even more of rights on the part of the handicapped? This question has often been answered in the negative. More recently a good case has been made for an affirmative answer on the ground that obligations and rights for compensation could add to general welfare. In particular, this seems to have been the position of John Stuart Mill as interpreted by David Lyons.[196] Nevertheless, I wonder whether conduciveness to general welfare is a conclusive reason for duties and corresponding claim-rights. Certainly it is not an intrinsic part of the idea of general welfare. This can be defended only if there is an essential of a priori connection between conduciveness to welfare and obligation. I have no objection to acknowledging such a relationship. But I am not sure that more analytically minded philosophers would agree.

Perhaps even more serious is the problem posed by the fact that very often the handicapped are in a hopeless minority, sometimes a minority of one. Considering the classic maxim of utilitarianism stressing 'the greatest happiness of the greatest number', how far would the maximization of welfare require that the benefit accruing to the handicapped would exceed the cost to the privileged majority? Chances are that the extraordinary cost of complete compensation for the handicapped would outweigh the benefits to the welfare of the community. In most cases in order to justify a decision in their favor more is needed than a positive balance of welfare on their side.

Basic Need

One particularly appealing ground for special compensation to the naturally handicapped is their special need and particularly their basic needs interpreting basic need with Joel Feinberg,[197] as a good 'in whose absence a person would be harmed in some crucial and fundamental way'. This will of course vary with the specific handicap from which a person suffers. Thus for a hemiplaegic a wheelchair and architectural access to educational facilities would be a basic need, for a blind person instruction in reading and writing Braille and perhaps a sonar device or a seeing-eye dog.

While such special rights may have a prima facie appeal at least under the circumstance of a society which can afford such special aids, even if it should not be able to afford dialysis machines for all patients with kidney malfunctioning, it may still be asked whether such basic and even less basic needs alone are sufficient and con-

---

196. 'Human Welfare and the General Welfare', *Philosophy and Public Affairs* 6 (1977), 113-129.
197. Joel Feinberg, *Social Philosophy* (1973), p. 111.

vincing grounds for the necessary compensation. Certainly a merely subjective need expressed however urgently by repetitive assertions of 'I need it' would not yet convince us of the validity of such a need in contrast to Feinberg's case of the 'hungry, sickly, fatherless infant, one of a dozen children of a desperately impoverished and illiterate mother in a squalid Mexican slum'.[198] A right to fulfillment does not follow from the mere presence of a need. Something else is required to account for such a right, a ground which makes this need one that deserves attention, quite apart from the fact that the mere presence of a need does not yet imply an 'ought' calling for its fulfillment.

Equal Opportunities

The closest to an explicit reason given for treating the naturally handicapped on an equal level with the nonhandicapped is that they deserve at least an equal chance with everyone else. In fact, the phrase 'equal opportunity' is the major battle cry of the new organizations advocating the rights of the handicapped. It is also the main rationale given for the legislation in support of their cause. But what is the real meaning of the phrase 'equal opportunity'? It must be realized that many of the concrete demands raised in its name require much larger than equal expenditures in order to put the handicapped on the same footing with their nonhandicapped competitors. Consider only the often multiple cost of the special education they require.

In fact, the very expression 'equal opportunity' is ambiguous. At first sight it may mean that each person receives the same treatment or support by the community as any other, regardless of whether this will give him an equal chance to compete in the race for success. In this case the competitors are considered in their actual condition without any previous adjustments of their unequal equipment, making sure only that their lanes are equally unobstructed. But equality of opportunity may also mean that both competitors must be in equal condition at the start of the race, which implies that their opportunities have to be equalized before the race can begin, no matter what the cost involved. This would amount

198. *Rights, Justice and the Bounds of Liberty*. Princeton University Press, 1980, p. 140.

to anything but equal treatment. Here equality of opportunity has the meaning of an ideal condition contrary to fact which has to be realized first. But why? And why in particular should the other members of society be held responsible for changing the 'natural' condition, since they had nothing to do with bringing about their own headstarts? Hence for them the responsibility for securing equality of opportunity is anything but self-evident. And yet it seems to have a strong, if not compelling, appeal for all those who support special aid to the handicapped.

Actually, the idea of equality of opportunity has had quite a history. In the beginning it was the equivalent of the slogan of the 'open road for talents' (*'la carrière ouverte aux talents'*). Thus, this Napoleonic slogan merely cleared the way for the laissez-faire policy of Manchester liberalism and capitalism as pictured most provocatively in Michael Young's 'meritocracy'. Only later in the nineteenth century this individualistic interpretation of the principle of equal opportunity was replaced by a 'socialist' one, which took account of the fact that without equalization of the unequal opportunities of wealth and education at the start of the race opportunities are anything but equal.

But even after such equalizations the concept is not yet without difficulties. Among recent searching studies I shall mention only those by John Schaar, Charles Frankel, and T.D. Campbell.[199] However, the problems they discuss do not bear directly on the possible justification of compensation for the naturally handicapped, but are concerned mostly with the socially induced differences between different individuals and require their abolition as a matter of social justice.

Why then should equal opportunity be allotted to competitors unequally endowed by nature? And why should we be responsible for equalizing opportunities for the naturally handicapped? These questions may have been even more in order in ages when such natural inequalities were attributed to 'acts of God', i.e., to God's providence, if not to His predestination, which were considered just in ways inscrutable to men. For no one should quarrel with the will

---

199. John Schaar, 'Equality of Opportunity and Beyond', *Equality*, eds. Roland Pennock and John Chapman, *Nomos* XI (1967), 228-249; Charles Frankel, 'Equality of Opportunity', *Ethics* 81 (1971), 191-210; T.D. Campbell, 'Equality of Opportunity', *Proceedings of the Aristotelian Society* 25 (1975, 51-68.

of God, even though such theological justification of natural handicaps does not exclude corrective human actions such as almsgiving and the maintenance of 'almshouses', if only for the sake of the moral credit accruing to the givers, regardless of the effectiveness of such measures.

As far as I know, thus far the naturally handicapped have not stated explicitly what they mean when they claim that they are not being given equal opportunities with the nonhandicapped unless they receive special compensation. What is puzzling about this claim is that they do not think that they are given an equal chance when they are simply treated the same as everyone else. By what right can they ask for 'privileges'? And yet, they clearly do no consider it a privilege if they receive special compensation for their disabilities.

The most plausible explanation for this attitude is that in their own eyes their handicaps are not part and parcel of their personalities. They consider themselves as fundamentally equal to the nonhandicapped and dissociate themselves from their handicaps in a similar way in which others dissociate themselves from such outer handicaps as extra weight or an obstacle in their way. In a sense this makes them think of themselves as split beings divided between their 'true' (equal) selves and their (unequal) handicaps. But by what right can they disown their disabilities in this manner. How can they expect others to respect this distinction? All I can suggest is that at least the most self-conscious handicapped experience a certain alienation from their handicaps, which they reject emotionally. Such an alienation would be certainly understandable for a nonhandicapped outsider putting himself empathetically into the place of the handicapped. Moreover, such handicaps are likely to be experienced as 'accidents of birth' that have befallen their victims. Granting this particular perspective on their own existence it makes sense that they feel their 'real selves' are not treated equally if they are not granted the same status as the nonhandicapped by the addition of full opportunities. And it is certainly understandable that they will desire such equalization.

But this wish does not yet make it clear that they also have a claim to its fulfillment. It leaves it even less intelligible that others who had nothing to do with depriving them of equal opportunities should be responsible for taking care of their needs. Hence, no matter how much one can sympathize with their wish and demand for equalization, this does not yet give them a moral, let alone a legal, right to compensation by their fellow beings.

The right to equal opportunity requires more than the recognition of the appropriateness of compensation for missing equal opportunities. What claim does it give them on others who had nothing to do with their predicament?

Existential Justice

What I want to suggest is that the best and potentially most impressive ground for compensation to the naturally handicapped is justice, yet not justice in the ordinary sense, but a kind of justice which has not yet been sufficiently identified and explicated. In order to do this I shall introduce first some typical situations in which it is exemplified and then contrast it with the traditional types of justice.

Consider the case of a child struck by polio, by the sudden loss of his parents in an accident or by some other blow with which he or she is unable to cope. Our immediate reaction to such cases is not only grieved sympathy, which we might also try to express through exclamations like 'How terrible!' or 'How heartbreaking!' But very soon we might also respond with reflections such as 'Why just this poor little victim?', 'How utterly unfair that an innocent child should have to suffer such a fate'. We might try to look for some theological consolation if we are religious. But even the pious cannot ignore the fact that prima facie such a child has been subjected to a terrible wrong for which there is no human excuse. The same feeling on a larger scale is apt to accompany our experience of large-scale natural disasters like earthquakes or flash floods. Here it seems in a peculiar sense unfair that one survivor lose his entire family and all his possessions, while his neighbor next door remains completely unharmed.

But this is not yet our entire response. The sense of the 'unfairness' of such events also involves the spontaneous sense that something ought to be done about relieving such conditions by some distribution of the damage or some kind of compensation. I submit that the spontaneous use of such terms as 'unfairness' in such situations is not just a misuse of the English language or at best an analogical use of the word. True, in ordinary situations where we speak of 'unfair treatment' we also think of its perpetrator, and here a personal cause of the misfortune is essential. But even when no such villain can be found, and particularly when we have no basis for blaming it on a personal supreme being, there remains the shocking fact that here an innocent being has been subjected to misfortunes which to all appearances he has not and cannot have deserved by his own conduct. It is this moral disproportion which is at the root of our outrage about the unfairness of undeserved suffering. Perhaps it would be more appropriate to speak here of unfairness in a wider or impersonal sense. But the main thing is that our response to such natural events leads us to the experience of a phenomenon that deserves to be investigated for its own sake and which is perhaps even the basic phenomenon in our experience of injustice.

Incidentally the wider use of the terms 'fair' and 'unfair' as applied to situations rather than to persons and actions like that between handicap and compensation is even etymologically justifiable. In fact, originally the words 'fair' and 'unfair' had not specifically ethical significance.[200] Note that e.g. Montaigne, in commenting on the paradox of Socrates' physical ugliness, wrote: 'Nature did him an injustice'.[201] These nonethical meanings have survived even in today's common parlance. Hence there is no good reason for objecting to the extension of the current use in moral philosophy to natural situations and specifically to fairness or unfairness with regard to a person's fortunes.

However, unfairness in natural situations cannot be the last word. The sense of unfairness is also intrinsically, though not analytically, connected with a sense of requiredness directed toward an appropriate compensation for this imbalance: *Something* ought to be done about restoring a new balance, and, if possible, *someone* ought to do it. (Consider the case of a person born with a harelip that

---

200. According to the *New Oxford Dictionary* the adjective 'fair' stood primarily for (I) Beautiful, (II) Desirable, (III) Free from blemishes and (IV) Favorable, with a great variety of submeanings, none of them ethical. The substantive 'fair' signifies (1) that which is fair, (2) one of the fair sex, (3) a person with a fair complexion, and (4) beauty. Only in connection with the adverbial use of 'fair' is the meaning 'equitably, honestly, impartially, justly' mentioned as the fourth submeaning. As to the term 'unfair' the first meaning is again 'not fair or beautiful', and only the second is 'not fair or equitable, unjust'.

201. 'Nature luy fit injustice', *Essais* III, Ch. XII (ed. Pierre Villey, 1965, p. 1057).

'unfairly' interferes with his social chances, who could be helped by surgery.) This is the normative implication of the apprehension of natural unfairness. It is in this sense that the more fortunate nonhandicapped owe to the less fortunate handicapped the kind of compensation that makes up as far as possible for their undeserved disadvantages.

In order to appraise properly the novelty of this type of justice and specifically of compensatory justice here involved, one has to compare it with the traditional Aristotelian distinctions.[202] Here distributive justice refers to situations in which a distributing agent dispenses benefits or burdens *de novo*, prior to any previous assignments. It thus presupposes the existence of a distributor. The same is true of the usual conception of rectificatory justice which deals with the readjustment of a balance upset by disruptions of the initial distribution pattern. One subspecies of this type of rectificatory justice is compensatory justice in the usual sense of making up for losses suffered by a wronged party. Another subspecies is penal justice imposing an additional disadvantage on the criminal in order to balance his criminal deed and especially intent. I shall omit here other subdivisions of the theory of justice such as commutative justice and equity since they introduce merely modifications of the basic distinctions.

All these types of traditional justice presuppose personal acts by a distributor, rectifier or compensator. By contrast, in the case of compensatory justice for natural handicaps nothing like this is required in order to judge the unfairness of a natural handicap and

202. In so doing I refer to the succinct account of these distinctions by Joel Feinberg and Hyman Gross in their *Introduction to Justice: Selected Readings*. Encin: Dickinson Publishing Company, 1979, p. 5 f. Even more explicitly Ronald Dworkin dealt with the problem of handicaps, without differentiation between natural and social handicaps in his two-part essay on 'What is Equality' in *Philosophy and Public Affairs* 10 (1981) in special sections on 'Handicaps' (pp. 240-44, and on 'Luck and Insurance' (pp. 299-302). In the earlier discussion he points out that the first form of equality, equality of welfare, cannot justify 'why the handicapped should sometimes have more natural resources than the healthy' (p. 241). Under his preferred interpretation of equality as equality of resource someone born with a serious handicap faces his life with fewer resources than others do. This justifies compensation under a scheme devoted to equality of resources, and though the hypothetical insurance market does not right the balance – nothing can – it seeks to remedy one aspect of the resulting unfairness.

its compensation in the relation between the naturally unfortunate or fortunate. Here the primary question is whether the relation between the two is or is not in accord with their original moral score, a score which is given with their very existence as persons capable of acquiring moral merit and demerit. Since the unfairness and fairness here involved is based on this fundamental condition of personal existence regardless of their individual differentiation, I am using for it the expression 'existential justice'. I shall not try to determine here how far this use of the term 'existential' can be based or related to any of the better known existential philosophies.

The next major step in the attempt to base the claims of the handicapped on the assertion of a basic existential unfairness in their plight will have to be the exposition of this basic phenomenon in much greater detail and showing its phenomenological and epistemological foundations. In the present context it may suffice to exhibit it and appeal to the spontaneous response experienced and voiced by sensitive witnesses to people's fates, particularly those of the handicapped, even before these witnesses acknowledge anyone's responsibility for the 'cruelty' of these misfortunes and charge any personal agent for it.

Natural handicaps as here conceived are only a special case of the kind of natural evil which have been a major theme in the historic debates about theodicy. But while there the emphasis has been on the facts of pain and suffering in general, handicaps are a novel case not considered there explicitly. Also, the problem of theodicy with its theological implications is irrelevant here where the major issue is that of what other fellow beings and society as a whole are to do about them.

If the present attempt to establish the phenomenon of fairness and unfairness in the relation between a person and his life circumstances is sound, then we might be in a position to tell the ground for the claim of the handicapped to compensation: The realization that something is wrong and unfair about this situation implies, if not analytically, at least by some kind of 'synthetic judgement' that something ought to be done about it, wherever possible. Here considerations of whether the restoration or equalization is conceivable will lead to an examination of the alternatives I mentioned before, particularly of such measures as rehabilitation (or rather 'habilitation') or the provision of equivalents, financial or otherwise.

But these additional insights do not yet imply a ground why some personal agent ought to do anything about such compensation, whether individuals, society as a whole, or any particular group in society. Assuming that no individual or group had anything to do with the occurrence of congenital handicaps —an assumption which is certainly mistaken insofar as some genetic defects are predictable— why should the nonhandicapped be under any obligation to do something about them?

At this point I shall have to fall back on some general principles of deontological ethics which I can state here only in a dogmatic fashion.[203] The one most relevant in the present context may be put as follows: Whenever a particular situation ought to be or not to be as we encounter it and it can be remedied by personal action, then whoever is in the best possible position to do so is under a moral obligation to step in. Now in the case of the naturally handicapped not only ought something to be done to compensate them most appropriately, but anyone in a position to do so, particularly a privileged position, is responsible for such compensatory action. I submit that normally this would be the person or group closest to the handicapped and, in the case of more widespread handicaps, privileged society as a whole. This sense of social responsibility for compensating natural handicaps on a larger scale is exemplified best by our attitude and actions in the case of natural disasters. Why is it that in the case of extraordinary catastrophes (*force majeure* or 'acts of God' not covered by insurance policies) the whole community feels a responsibility for distributing such damage by public disaster relief. One may base such a duty on the suffering of the victims, since other people's and even animals' suffering implies our duty to relieve it. This is clearly the line of Hippocratic medicine and especially of Albert Schweitzer's ethics of reverence for life. But meritorious though such active sympathy with all suffering may be, why would we in our feebleness feel called upon to relieve all suffering in the world unless we had a special obligation to do so? What I submit is that what makes our decision to help in certain

203. I have tried to show this in an unpublished German manuscript of 1937, of which I have giv_n an English sample in a paper on 'Rules and Order: Toward a Phenomenology of Order' for the ideal ought-to-be in Paul Kuntz, ed., *The Concept of Order*, The University of Washington Press, 1968, pp. 290-308.

cases and to relieve some suffering really urgent is our spontaneous sense of unfairness if in the case of an accident not attributable to human fault the innocent victim should carry the burden alone. In such a case we have a strict duty to compensate him according to our ability. This claim for fair compensation for nature's discrimination, for instance in the case of geographically disadvantaged nations without access to the sea as the 'common heritage of mankind', is at the root of the demands of the developing third world. This might also be the ultimate reason why certain needs command our help more than others, and why some suffering has a particularly urgent claim on us.

Finally, I would like to mention one more existential ground for our ethical responsibility to the naturally handicapped, which I have discussed in greater detail elsewhere.[204] I am referring to the deep-rooted, though often submerged, sense of the accidents of our births, which tells us also that the deprivations of the naturally handicapped are accidental from the moral point of view. Hence the beneficiaries of such accidents should feel an obligation to make up for them to those unaccountably disadvantaged. In fact, this sentiment may even lead to a comparative sense of shame. This is what Albert Schweitzer voiced in the motto which I put at the head of this paper. I submit that his experience can be another expression of an 'existential' obligation toward the naturally handicapped and can become a powerful lever for overcoming our moral inertia in activating it.

12.5 The Dilemmas of Compensatory Justice for the Handicapped

Thus far my case for compensation to the naturally handicapped as based on a deepened and widened sense of fairness extended even to natural assets and liabilities may seem to be radical indeed involving 'tremendous' consequences (Blackstone). For it calls for the eradication not only of social but also natural injustices, even though it does not call for a uniform leveling. It certainly would put enormous burdens on all those better off than the average of

---

204. See especially 'Equality in Existentialism' (this volume, number 8) and 'Good Fortune Obligates' (*Ibid.*, number 11).

mankind. I make no apologies for this impression, and I even think it is important to spell out these implications as bluntly as possible.

However, it seems to me equally important to realize that any attempt at complete compensation for all natural handicaps would run into severe difficulties as grave and possibly graver than would any attempt at absolute fairness in the distribution of benefits in the original situation. I shall call these difficulties dilemmas in the sense that any attempt to solve them directly would lead to insoluble problems. I shall distinguish four such groups which I shall call respectively phenomenological, epistemological, ontological, and practical.

Phenomenological Dilemmas

Thus far only the 'objective' equivalents for 'objective' handicaps and compensations have been considered. What such considerations ignore is the 'subjective' aspect of these facts in the experience of the handicapped themselves. Without implying that these aspects are all-important, I maintain that they are essential parts of the total situation.

How do the handicapped themselves experience their handicaps? The most obvious way to answer this question would be to consult a representative number of handicapped individuals. However, not all of them, especially not the mentally handicapped, are articulate enough for a meaningful response. But for the articulate ones questionnaire studies may make good sense. I am not familiar with any such previous studies. In their absence I could only, in consultation with Professor Martha Storandt of the Department of Psychology at Washington University, one of her students, Chris Hager Feeley, and an unnamed blind graduate student in History and Law (Phi Beta Kappa), draw up the Questionnaire added in the Appendix. But, short of the necessary expert help, I could not yet administer it.

There is also some valuable material in literary works, especially in autobiographies of the handicapped, beginning with Helen Keller's classic accounts (who, however, was not handicapped from birth), which would have to be analyzed critically. At best such case studies would add to a collection of phenomenological *observations,* not yet to a phenomenology of handicapped experience in general.[205] There is, however, room for more systematic phenomenological studies based on minor and mostly temporary handicaps experienced by practically everyone, which, with the help of imaginative variation, may yield some insights about the essential features of the consciousness of handicaps and their compensation. All I can attempt here is to raise relevant questions about these aspects and suggest some plausible answers using several of these sources.

The case of the blind may serve as an entering wedge. How far does the congenitally blind person experience the lack of his sight? Certainly not directly, since he cannot even know what it is that he lacks. His sense world, comparable to that of a sightless animal (like some moles), is simply restricted to the data of his functioning senses. He knows of his blindness only indirectly when he hears other people refer to some properties of the world like colors by words whose direct meanings escape him. This realization, the connected poverty of his information about the world, and the resulting restriction in his mobility are of course enough of a deprivation. Yet it should also be realized that if a congenitally blind individual gains sight (rather than regains it) by an operation this is for him by no means a particularly satisfying or liberating addition to his experience of the world. In fact, he has the greatest difficulty in correlating the new world of colored shapes to that of his previously merely tactile and audible universe. He might even feel more handicapped by the confusion which this unrelated dimension adds to his earlier picture of the world.[206] What has to be realized is that, as far as emotional reactions are concerned, many handicapped suffer most not from their primary deprivation but from the attitudes of others toward them, or rather from what they think others think of them. What they resent particularly is being ridiculed or being pitied and treated as inferior, e.g., 'crippled' persons. It is apparently this secondary handicap in their relations with the non-

205. As an example for such observations I refer to my 'Visual Perception Before and After a Cataract Operation: Phenomenological Observations' in *Journal of the British Society for Phenomenology* 8 (1977) 2-14.

206. V.M. von Senden, *Raum und Gestaltungsauffassung bei operierten Blindgeborenen vor und nach der Operation.* Leipzig, 1932, translated by Peter Heath as *Space and Sight.* London: Methuen, 1960.

handicapped which is foremost on their minds.

While it would be illegitimate to extrapolate from the example of the congenitally blind to that of all other sensorily deprived persons, it does indicate the problem of how their privations are experienced by the handicapped. How far do they really feel deprived? And how do they become aware of their deprivation? This experience may be much more acute in those with a mobility problem. It may be least noticeable to those who are mentally handicapped, especially the feeble-minded, supposedly the happiest of all human beings. Dickens' Tim Cratchett is a comparable case. The real discovery and suffering for the handicapped may arise only when they are in competition with the nonhandicapped and know about it. In any case it is anything but obvious that the handicapped suffer from their handicap in proportion to the amount of objective deprivation. They do so only proportionately to their inferred deprivation.

Besides, it has to be realized that even subjective handicaps can mean very different things to different subjects depending on their total perspective of the world and their life plan in it. It is even conceivable that in some contexts their very handicaps mean assets, an opportunity and an exemption from certain responsibilities and expectations. Thus the handicapped's inability to hold a full-time exhausting job may give him the leisure that eludes the fully employed. It may free him from public and private duties not of his choosing. And he might discover outlets and skills beyond the range of the routine-bound 'normal' person.

There is a parallel situation with regard to *compensation* for the handicapped. What does it mean for them to be compensated? The same objective compensation may have very different significance for different handicapped individuals. Comspensation as such is a mere external fact unrelated to the compensated person and his life.

In this light some fundamental differences in attitude toward one's life and one's lot have to be considered, which can be found among the handicapped as well as among the nonhandicapped. There is the pride of the self-made man who feels diminished in his self-respect if he accepts a favor that he could have provided for and by himself. Some handicaps do not affect the handicapped's ability to help himself, to rehabilitate himself and to compensate for his defect. He might resent any outside support. He might enjoy showing off his independent achievement and rejoice in it, even though the seriously handicapped persons will require some first aid from others before they can start on their own. They may object particularly to being treated differently and set apart from the nonhandicapped majority. The present demand for 'mainstreaming' handicapped children into the normal channels of education and breaking down the walls of segregation which have separated them from public life can be interpreted as an expression of this desire not to be compensated by a new kind of discrimination, however wellintentioned.

While thus the determination of the appropriate compensation for a handicap requires consideration of the perspectives and preferences of the handicapped themselves, this is not the only consideration that enters. Thus the handicapped cannot always judge and foresee the significance of the compensation he is to receive. This applies particularly to the mentally handicapped. Here only an empathetic outsider can estimate halfway what kind of compensation would be in the best interest of the handicapped, and particularly what would make his life as tolerable and meaningful as possible. For instance, even if the handicapped himself should reject rehabilitation and schooling, a good and sensitive 'guardian' of his interests might be able to anticipate what meaning the handicapped himself will derive from a certain kind of compensation in the long run.

It is also relevant that, regardless of the handicapped's personal interest, society as a whole has an interest that the handicapped are compensated appropriately. There is the danger of increased burdens to the community if the resources left to the handicapped are wasted, and the common advantages for the greatest possible rehabilitation of the handicapped are lost. Something would be basically wrong in a society that would completely neglect the unfortunate victims of natural injustice.

The preceding observations about the phenomenology of handicaps and compensations should not be understood as more than a first attempt to open up a new dimension for the investigation of the 'phenomenon' of handicaps. A fuller exploration would have to include not only a more complete description of the original experiences, but a study of what is essential to them. Furthermore, what has to be explored are the different ways in which they can appear both to the handicapped 'from the inside' and to the non-handicapped 'from the outside', for instance, dimly and clearly, constantly or only intermittently, the way a handicap is constituted in our consciousness by gradual or sudden realization and how it can be interpreted hermeneutically in relation to the total meaning of human existence. How much does the handicapped identify himself with his handicap, how far does he reject it as an alien intrusion into his self?

Even without such studies it should now be clear that any attempt to assess handicaps and compensations in their full meaning has to take account of the different aspects they display to different subjects. This makes it practically impossible to make any meaningful generalizations about the relation of any one handicap to the appropriate compensations. The best we can hope to achieve is to approximate a liveable solution in particular cases. This is enough to present any outside judge with serious dilemmas.

Epistemological Dilemmas

If we include the subjective aspect of handicaps and compensations among the essential features of the situation of the handicapped, the question arises how and how far we are able to know about them reliably. Assuming that each one can know what his own handicaps are and mean to himself in his historical setting, and what kind of compensation would meet his needs, how far are we able to tell this in the case of others than ourselves? How far can we know it directly? This is obviously a problem for our knowledge of other minds. How much can direct perception or empathy achieve this? How much can we rely on inference? This becomes particularly difficult in the case of the vast number of mentally and emotionally handicapped or of psychotic individuals like the schizophrenic and depressive. As far as we can attempt to obtain information by communication on the basis of specific questions, how far can we trust it? How far are the handicapped able to predict the meaning of possible compensation for them?

I therefore submit that our knowledge of handicaps, especially those of other people, and of the appropriate compensations for them is highly problematic. This too creates a dilemma for anyone who tries to reach definite conclusions on the proper relation between natural handicaps and compensations in a particular case.

Certainly in most cases we cannot aspire to more than probability, not knowledge.

Ontological Dilemmas

But even if we could achieve sufficient knowledge about the subjective aspects of handicaps and compensations for individual subjects, and even if we could approach divine omniscience of the 'hearts and minds' of each particular subject about his handicaps and the fittingness of specific compensations for them, there remains a much graver dilemma regarding the correlation of handicaps and compensations. Once complete equalization and removal of the handicap is no longer possible, is there one precise equivalent compensation for a particular handicap? Are there such equivalent at all? And how exactly can we determine them quantitatively? The question becomes particularly acute if only monetary compensation for a physical handicap or mental suffering remains possible. What amount of money corresponds to the loss of one's sight or hearing or physical or mental pain? This is of course not a merely theoretical problem. It concerns equally any areas where quantitative equivalences have to be established, beginning with economics, where the question of fair prices and fair wages arises, to criminal law after it had abandoned the principle of an eye for an eye and the problem was to determine what exact punishment would 'fit' what particular crime and specifically what fine or what time of imprisonment would correspond to such offenses as theft or fraud. The question of what is fair compensation for handicaps is not any easier. At best in such cases one can attempt to reach relative fairness by treating objectively equal handicaps equally. But the objective aspect would in this case not be considered. 'Fair discretion' is not much more than an admission that there is an inevitable element of arbitrariness in establishing such equivalences. I am calling this dilemma 'ontological' in the sense that it is neither phenomenological (concerning experienced appearances of handicaps and compensations) nor epistemological (concerning our reliable knowledge of them), but that it concerns what the handicaps and compensations and their relations are in themselves. What is at stake here is the 'ontic' or 'ontological' relation between them.

Practical Dilemmas

Finally, we must be under no illusion that the goal of perfect compensation of natural handicaps is in our power, even in our relatively affluent society. I mentioned before that in a 'primitive society' struggling for the bare minimum of food and shelter, there is simply no room for ordinary charity, let alone compensatory justice. But it must be realized that, although we have made progress in reducing scarcity, we are still a long way from sufficiency, let alone abundance. Only greater approximation to this goal has become possible, allowing us to provide more and better compensation for natural handicaps. At the moment the often forbidding cost of equal access for the handicapped to educational and recreational facilities can remind us of how much remains to be done.

Such limitations raise the question of what compensatory need is to take precedence, if not all can be satisfied simultaneously. Whose needs are more urgent, those of the blind, the visually impaired, the deaf, the mentally retarded? Or are they all to be met equally, even if their shares should dwindle to the vanishing point? What could be the criteria for ranking them, if this should be possible at all? Severity of actual suffering? Chances of effective remedy?

I am not suggesting that these types of difficulties exhaust the range of possible dilemmas. Nor do I want to imply that they are beyond a practical solution. But I do think that they have to be faced. Certainly the first impression is that when thought through radically existential justice is unworkable. The best that can be hoped for practically is to reduce the unfairness suffered by the naturally handicapped, but never to abolish it.

12.6 Toward an Alternative: The Co-existential Fellowship of the Handicapped with the Nonhandicapped

Is there no escape between the horns of these dilemmas? All I can do in this context is to prepare the way for it. I would raise the following questions: Could the naturally privileged have helped being privileged? Aren't they too caught by an accident of birth, only that in this case it worked in their favor? Even Karl Marx was born a bourgeois. These privileges include natural endowments, talents, native skills and even one's character. This implies that we can and do distinguish between our innermost selves and the properties of our personality with which and into which we find ourselves born. We express this by talking of them as 'gifts'.

Now if the privileged person could not help being born 'with a silver spoon in his mouth' (as little as the proletarian could help his 'tin' spoon), why should he be penalized for it? Would not depriving him of his advantages forcibly inflict on him undeserved suffering? Consider only the special hardship imposed on someone used to privacy, comfortable living and sleeping quarters, proper food and health care when he has to share the Spartan life of equalitarian conditions in an internment camp or in prison, which means luxury to the tramp, who may even seek it out by committing some misdemeanor in winter? Isn't it unfair to deprive the nonhandicapped of his native advantages into which he found himself born without having been asked or asking for them? Under these circumstances neither does the privileged have any good reason for pride in his headstart nor does the handicapped have any cause for blaming the privileged for his own 'hindstart'. It is understandable and excusable enough that he should feel envy and even resentment toward the privileged. But even so, this 'natural' reaction is no basis for reproaching the nonhandicapped.

Now it would be of course unfair simply to acquiesce to the status quo. It is clearly unfair to leave the naturally handicapped without any compensation. But there would be a corresponding unfairness in compensating him exclusively at the expense of the nonhandicapped. Here right stands against right: it seems impossible to do full justice to the handicapped without doing some injustice to the nonhandicapped. This too is a dilemma which almost amount to an antinomy.

But this very situation can be the starting point for overcoming the apparent stalemate. Realizing the insolubility of the conflict if approached only in the spirit of strict compensatory justice, the two partners should be able to see that they both are caught in the same plight. This realization might create a new sense of fellowship and solidarity between them. It should also be an incentive for trying jointly to reshape their relationship in a spirit of cooperation and harmonization which would remove or at least reduce the unfair imbalance between them. More concretely, compensation for the unfairness of natural handicaps must not consist in penalizing the nonhandicapped, in leveling all the differences between them and in trying to heal all the wounds of the past inflicted mostly by former generations. Instead, a mutually fair compensation should be limited to restoring to the handicapped the amount of 'unjust enrichment' still enjoyed by the naturally privileged, in analogy to principles which have been developed in the law of torts.[207] Obviously the privileged will have to make the major material sacrifice in such an adjustment. But the handicapped too can make an essential contribution to a conciliation by giving the privileged credit for these sacrifices and avoiding vindictiveness. The major purpose of such compensation cannot be to undo the past but to overcome it.

How could such a solution help in coping with the dilemmas lined up in the preceding section?

1. The phenomenological dilemma due to the divergence of perspectives on handicaps and compensations could be approached by a concerted effort to share these perspectives in mutual communication. While this will hardly lead to attuning the differences, it may help to take care of the remaining discrepancies in the spirit of good will and the greatest possible harmonization.

2. The epistemological dilemma could be reduced to the extent to which the uncertainty about the perspectives of handicaps and compensations can be removed by communicative verification or falsification as the partners accept or reject one another's diagnoses. Even this test may not provide reliable knowledge, but it can at least approximate it, a solution which an impartial arbitrator may facilitate.

3. As to the ontological dilemmas it may be a help if both sides can be led to realize that there is no way to determine accurate quantitative equivalents for qualitative differences between work and wages, goods and prices and, specifically, between handicaps and compensations. All that can be hoped for is to find equivalents relative to similar cases in the context of historical situations. As

---

207. Under the name of *'ungerechtfertigte Bereicherung'* this principle has been developed for instance in the German Civil Code (B.G.B.) paragraphs 812-822. For its place in French and British law see H.G. Gutteridge and R.J.A. David 'The Doctrine of Unjustified Enrichment' *Cambridge Law Journal* 5 (1933-35), 204-229. Also, *Words and Phrases* 43 (1969), 528-536 and John P. Dawson, 'Erasable Enrichment in German Law' *Boston University Law Review* 61 (1981), 271-314.

to the dilemma of comparing the perspective of the handicapped with that of the nonhandicapped, mutual transposal into the accidental positions of one another should help toward fair compensation in the spirit of the fellowship of the involuntary occupants of each one's lot.

I realize that this alternative to strict objective compensatory justice yields no clear and easy solution either. But I hope that its appeal to the spirit of solidarity and the common concerns of both the handicapped and the nonhandicapped may make it easier to find and agree upon solutions which are acceptable to both.

What I have been proposing in this section as an alternative to compensatory justice for the naturally handicapped is not to be ininterpreted as a rejection of it. The experience of natural handicaps and the demand for compensation remain basic to any attempt to transcend them. The new principle of attunement by an appeal to the fellowship of the accident of birth is rather a supplement to the original perspective, a level of experience on which it becomes possible to overcome the dilemmas which the strict standard could not solve. Realization of the fellowship of fate shared by both the handicapped and the nonhandicapped is a higher level of social consciousness, in a sense a corrective of justice comparable to, but by far exceeding equity.

How to achieve it? How utopian is this hope? While the answer to these questions is no longer up to the philosopher, this is certainly the much harder and more urgent task. To solve it calls for new attitudes that cannot be taken for granted. I submit that the first move toward their realization is up to the non-handicapped. Only then is there some legitimate hope that even the handicapped will respond in a spirit of co-existential fellowship. It will be particularly hard to persuade them to muster the kind and degree of magnanimity needed to see the position of the nonhandicapped in this new light. I can only think of reminding them first of analogous situations where they themselves have been blamed for congenital privileges they could not help, such as superior physique or health, by less privileged members of their own group. This seems to me the best realistic hope to awaken the spirit of solidarity and common concern of both the handicapped and the nonhandicapped. Only then will it be possible to find and agree upon practical solutions which are more constructive and humane than any blind mechanical justice and the irresolvable power struggle to which it will lead.

Corollary: *Implications of the Findings about Compensation for Natural Inequalities*

At this point I would like to return to William Blackstone's suggestion mentioned at the start of this essay that 'the answer to the question of natural inequalities may be far more significant for social justice than the answer to the question of compensation for past invidious discrimination'. I believe that I can now spell out some of this significance in a preliminary form.

1. Why is it unjust to treat different and thus unequal sexes and races unequally? The most obvious reason is that in the main relevant regards they are naturally equal and that any deliberate departure from equality in their social status should therefore be compensated. This makes it necessary to explore first the *natural* equality or inequality between them before raising the question of *social* justice and social discrimination. In this sense natural justice based on equality is the foundation for social justice and social discrimination.

2. Even for 'reverse discrimination' as far as it is justifiable, the ultimate foundation has to be traced to violations of previous natural equality and fairness.

3. The case is somewhat different where such naturally unequals as the mentally retarded are involved. Here natural justice requires compensation even for unequals. But on this basis social justice too demands of society that it take some care of the unequal. Here again the social injustice of neglect of the mentally handicapped can be assessed only on the basis of exploring the natural unfairness of his condition. Only once the fairness or unfairness of natural equalities has been established does it make sense to look for social defenders and offenders responsible for causing or failing to prevent social imbalances and to expect them to make amends for their offenses. In other words, the justice (or injustice) of the natural relationships is the foundation for the justice (or injustice) of social justice (or injustice). Its exploration is therefore the necessary if not sufficient basis for our struggle against social injustice. It also is the ultimate foundation for a philosophy of social justice.

This realization also has implications for the preceding findings about the dilemmas of fair compensation for natural handicaps.

These will affect man-made handicaps and compensation as well as natural compensatory justice. Realizing the limitations of both types of justice makes it urgent to transcend not only natural but also social justice rather than to worship it uncritically. Justice may be the first word in the struggle for social betterment. But it cannot be the last word. Ultimate justice between the handicapped and the nonhandicapped is essentially impossible. Hence the last word will have to be an amendment to compensatory justice. Its basis could be a covenant between fellow co-existers both caught in the mesh of the accident of birth, regardless of whether they are disadvantaged or advantaged. In this spirit they may find a solution based on mutual respect, empathetic understanding and active cooperation aimed at maximum possible harmony and conciliation.

This seems to me one of the possible meanings of fraternity, i.e., of brotherhood and sisterhood among the members of the human family. For in the family too the original position of the siblings is one of a common congenital fate based on moral accident. But our best chance to redeem it is a spirit of loving solidarity in overcoming the original accidents. This also could be the final compensation for the unfairness of an indifferent nature.

APPENDIX

Questionnaire for Persons Seriously Handicapped from Birth or Later by Accident

Purpose: Through the following questions I would like to enlist your help in my effort to find out how you, who have lived with a serious handicap, feel and think about it. I fear that my own attempt to imagine your experience vicariously, based on only minor and temporary handicaps of my own, badly needs checking by you. The ultimate goal of my study is to understand your situation better and to determine whether and how we, the less handicapped, can cooperate with you in relieving your problems. Don't hesitate to make suggestions which I would try to pass on. Unless released, I shall consider your answers confidential. You may give them anonymously.

PART I

1. What is your personal handicap? Circle and complete the pertinent label from the classification by the White House Conference on the Handicapped Individual of 1977:
(1) amputation (2) arthritis/rheumatism (3) blindness (4) visual impairment (5) cancer (6) cerebral palsy (7) congenital malformation (8) deafness/hardness of hearing/hearing impairment (9) deaf blindness (10) diabetes mellitus (11) epilepsy (12) heart disease (13) language disorder (14) learning disability (15) little person (16) mental retardation (17) mental/emotional disorder (18) multiple sclerosis (19) muscular dystrophy (20) myasthenia gravis (21) Parkinson's disease (22) polio (23) respiratory condition (24) speech impairment (25) spinal cord injury (26) stroke (27) multiple (specify:) (28) other (specify:)

2. Do you prefer the word 'handicap', 'disadvantage', 'impediment', 'impairment' or any other word for your condition? Circle the preferred word(s).
Have you any reasons for your preferences?   YES   NO
If yes, what are your reasons?

3. Are you conscious of your handicap?
    (a) always
    (b) most of the time
    (c) sometimes
    (d) rarely
    (e) never?
Circle one letter above.

4. What do you miss most as the result of your handicap?
    (a) that you ever had what you lost through your handicap?
    (b) that you still remember its presence?

5. Do you experience you handicap always as a loss? YES   NO
If not, when not?

6. Do you feel that your being handicapped is 'unfair'? YES NO
If so, in what does this unfairness consist?

7. How much does religion means in your life? Circle one letter on scale below.
   (a) much
   (b) little
   (c) nothing
   How does your religion or 'philosophy of life' help you in coping with your handicap?

8. Do you feel your life is worth living?   YES   NO
   If not, would you prefer not to have been born to living with your handicap?   YES   NO

9. How close do you feel to
   (a) persons with the same handicap?
       1. very close
       2. close
       3. same as to other handicapped
   (b) persons with different handicaps?
       1. very close
       2. close
       3. same as to any other people
   (c) all the handicapped in the world?
       1. very close
       2. close
       3. same as to any other people
Circle one number above.

10. Do you belong to organizations for the handicapped? YES NO
If yes, name them here:

11. What fraction of your friends are handicapped?
    (a) all
    (b) most
    (c) about half
    (d) a few
    (e) none
Circle one letter on the scale above.

PART II

12. What ways, if any, do you see for reducing or removing your handicaps?
   (a) by special services or aids?
   (b) by monetary compensation?
   (c) by other aids?

13. How do you feel when other people
   (a) never mention your handicaps?
   (b) inquire about them?
   (c) express compassion for you?

PART III

14. Do you feel that the nonhandicapped have a duty to remove or reduce your handicap or compensate you for it?   YES   NO
   If yes, for what reasons?

15. Do you think you have a civil or human right to assistance against the nonhandicapped?   YES   NO
   Why or why not?

16. If you feel you have a right to assistance, do you consider it
   (a) stronger
   (b) equal
   (c) weaker
compared with those of other minorities discriminated against for instance because of race or sex? Circle one letter on the scale above.

17. Do you ever feel embarrassed or hurt by accepting assistance?
    YES   NO
If so, why?

PART III

APPLICATIONS TO PROBLEMS OF THE NUCLEAR AGE

13. IS THERE A HUMAN RIGHT TO ONE'S NATIVE SOIL?

> In special memory of the Israeli and Palestinian child victims of Ma'alat and the Lebanese refugee camps and . . .

Nowhere, to my knowledge, has the moral impasse of claims and counterclaims in the Palestinian tragedy been summed up as concisely and poignantly as in the still valid report of the American Friends Service Committee, *Search for Peace in the Middle East*, of 1970.[208] The eleven points in this confrontation of the two cases begin with the Israeli claim that their ancestors controlled Palestine more than two thousand years ago matched by the Arab counterclaim that they had held this land for more than 1300 years without interruption.

I confess that I see no legal or moral basis for breaking this deadlock over the right to one's native soil by giving more weight to either priority or length of occupation as a way to a 'just' solution. What I would like to plead for here is not a facile compromise but something more radical: an attempt to undercut the whole controversy by questioning the alleged moral right to one's native soil. It is hardly accidental that even the Universal Declaration of Human Rights in its catalog of old and new rights has nothing to say about it.

My first question is: What moral right can be derived from the fact that a person was given birth by his mother at a particular spot on this earth? Specifically, does he have the right to remain there;

---

208. *Search for Peace in the Middle East*, Revised Edition. New York: Hill and Wang, 1970.

Reprinted by permission from *Friends Journal* 20(1974), no. 15.

to claim it for himself, his children and children's children, to exclude others not born there, and to control the vicinity, perhaps jointly with others born near the spot?

I submit that being born at a certain place is in itself nothing but an 'accident of birth', even more so than being born to certain parents, in a certain family, a certain society, nation, racial group or religion. If this is true —and the full meaning and truth of this phrase must be thought through and 'realized'— birth by itself does not constitute any claim to any privileges, and does not commit to the acceptance of any handicaps that go with it. In this light the right to one's specific place of birth is indeed one of the most dubious and precarious human rights. It is one of the unearned enrichments or deprivations subject to adjustment to those underprivileged without their fault by those privileged without having merited it.

However, in thus denying radically any native right to one's specific place of birth I am not rejecting a moral right to *some* such place. On the contrary: I want to plead the moral right of every person born into this world to some space where he can live his life as a human being in accordance with his basic needs and particularly the needs for his full development. This right would not be exclusive of, but equal to, those of others born in similar circumstances. It may include the equal right to the natural resources of this place, not only on the national but on the international level. For instance, the right to such resources merely on the basis of one's having been born in an oil-rich country is morally unwarranted. It is therefore indeed a moral revolution that in these days the 'common heritage of mankind' to the riches of the seabed is universally accepted. This is a first step in rethinking our attitude to the old resources already carved up according to principles not squared with moral requirements.

I realize that both the denial of the right to one's native soil and the assertion of a new right to some soil on this globe calls for a radical change in our moral-political thinking as well as in our national and international policy. It takes intellectual and moral courage to face it. But it is also important to realize that this change need not and cannot be implemented immediately. This would not only be self-defeating but entail new injustices to those who inherited their present status without their fault nor on the basis of per-

sonal merit, but who may have earned some merit by their steward-
ship. In case of free immigration there must be protection through
minority laws for those who thus may lose majority status. Moreover, there has to be an effective policy for discouraging, if not
preventing, irresponsible parenthood. Without a new ethics of birth
control a mere ethics of equal rights of all those already born to
equal shares in living space and resources would breed new injustices
not only for more responsible parents but for the victims of a continued population explosion. Ultimately, there would have to be
an international agency which would explore and arrange the most
suitable opportunities for the fairest distribution of the remaining
life-space.

What would such a new approach mean for the concrete tragedy
of the Palestinian conflict? Specifically, would it mean the acceptance of the present or an earlier status quo? Neither one. For primarily it calls for a fresh start, abandoning the morally indefensible
idea of 'natural' rights to the soil inherited from one's father (and
mother), forefathers or arch-ancestors. It calls for recognition that
on principle no one has more right to the contested soil than his
opponent. Both are victims of the accident of birth who must realize
that being born Palestinian or Israeli is an accident of birth as is
being born into a have or a have-not nation. Morally, both might
just as well have been born in each other's places. All are fellow-
victims of a history which has pitted them against each other. In
the plight of being the born enemies ('arch-enemies') of one another,
they might realize that even the villains are primarily victims of a
tragedy in which the innocents slaughter the innocents to avenge
the 'sins' of their forefathers. Such an approach may lead to credit-
ing one's 'enemy' at least with good faith, if not yet with good will.
And it may lay the ground for a new approach to the wreckage of
war, to an attempt to distribute losses and gains in a way which
makes a peaceful future possible. Beyond this wish outsiders who
are not in close touch with the facts and with both perspectives
upon them have no business meddling. But they should attempt to
understand both sides and be ready to help from a sense of having
been spared similar lots without having earned it.

I am aware of the difficulty of shaking up the complacent ideologies of those brought up to believe in fatherlands, motherlands,
'promised lands', promised not only to one's ancestors but to their

children and children's children ad infinitum. Instead let us consider the following 'truths':

1. The alleged right to one's native soil is a relative novelty in history of mankind suited to its agricultural stage. It makes little sense in a nomadic society of hunters, much as they may care for their special hunting grounds. It makes no sense to gypsies, who claim nothing but the freedom to migrate like birds and fish.

2. A rapidly increasing proportion of the inhabitants of the globe no longer lives in its birthplace and not even on native soil in the sense of their country of birth.

3. The more we multiply and fill the globe, the more it will be necessary to move people from their native soil to locations with more space and opportunities.

4. There are no 'autochthons', i.e., people 'sprung from the earth' and still living in the places where their history began.

5. Even those of us lucky enough to still live on the soil cultivated by our fathers and forefathers know that originally they were squatters or, worse, conquerors displacing the 'aborigines'.

6. Those living on 'native soil' will indeed be an increasingly privileged minority who can earn such a privilege only by some kind of compensation to the underprivileged.

7. History with its story of migrations, emigrations and immigrations is not the only reminder of our common precarious moral plight as squatters and their heirs. Most, if not all, religions and particularly early Christianity have fostered the sense of the transitoriness of man's earthly abode.

This is the spirit in which all of us, religious or not, must face a future which for all of us, not only for the Palestinians and Israelis, demands the full realization of both our equal illegitimacy in claiming an exclusive birthright to a native soil and of our more fundamental human right to an equal share in the soil and other resources of the globe, no matter where, as long as it does not interfere with the equal rights of other fellow humans.

Epiloque 1982: The 'Right to one's Native Soil' and the
Rights of the Have- and Have-not Nations

The dilemmas about the rights to one's place of birth are actually only samples of much vaster international problems. The case of the Israeli-Palestinian conflict is merely a particularly burning example of the alleged historic rights of any nation to its present territory. Ignoring the legends of autochthonous or soil-born nations, all have acquired their land from native predecessors like the American Indians, who in turn occupied countries held before by more 'native' aborigines. None can claim that they have an ultimate right to their soil by any higher right than squatting, conquest or inheritance.

Under these circumstances I see again no way of judging the rights and wrongs of each nation's case. The only way to overcome these moral impasses is to make a fresh start: the start by seeing the situation through the eyes of the new generations born into the opposing camps by the accident of their births as victims of a history which they did not make. The only salvation for them is to confront these impasses jointly in the spirit of fellowship in fate, in an attempt to achieve a genuine new conciliation (rather than a mere reconciliation).

The situation is similar also to that of the more urgent and spreading conflict between the present have and have-not nations. None of the 'haves' is guilty of a wrong in being born into this privileged position and having improved on it by the 'admixture' of his labor. On the other hand, the have-nots cannot be blamed for resenting the fact that they never had a chance to start from similar advantages and add to them by their efforts.

Here too I believe that only a fresh start by the new generations equally born into either advantaged or disadvantaged nations without their merit or fault can make the difference. By mutual self-transposal they should be able not only to understand better their different plights. They also could try to overcome the inequalities of this situation without mutual discrimination in the spirit of creating a new fellowship cooperating for a harmonization of the inherited inequalities of which they are the joint victims.

14. TOWARD GLOBAL SOLIDARITY

'Either the present policy of collective egoism will persist, and in a few de-
cades the overpopulated third world, confronted with a univeralized
famine will throw itself upon the have-notions, thus triggering off the
nuclear holocaust —or qualified voices will multiply their efforts to sound
the alarm and commit those responsible for our destinies to modify
their policies toward the third world by making the terms of the exchange
more equitable, by giving to each his just share on a globe with limited
resources, and by contributing to the development of all. Then, and only
then, mankind, having become solidaric on this spaceship named earth,
will be able to prepare for a better future.'[209]

To men like Albert Schweitzer's fellow Alsatian, though unknown
to him, Alfred Kastler the belief that, since 'modern "nationalist"
man' is obsolete (Norman Cousins), the future of post-modern
man depends on the development of planetary solidarity before it
is too late would be almost a truism.[210] But very few people have
come to think and feel in terms of 'we humans', rather than 'we
Americans' or 'we Soviet Russians', whenever a major international crisis arises. In expressing loyalties, the closest rather than the
most comprehensive community usually takes precedence, so
that world citizenship remains a vague idea as long as there is no
world city in which to practice it.

The mere intellectual conviction that 'it is time to grow up and

209. This quote is from Albert Kastler, Alsatian Nobel prize winner for physics ('grand-
father of the laser') 1966. Translated from his French Preface to *Rayonnements d'Albert
Schweitzer*, edited by Robert Minder. Colmar: Editions Alsatia, 1975, p. 10.
210. Norman Cousins, *Modern Man is Obsolete*, New York: Viking Press, 1945, p. 20.
Reprinted by permission from *Prioritas* I, 4 (1977), pp. 3-5.

to become a world citizen', because this is a 'sheer driving necessity' will not do. The appeal to common-sense reasoning or to the emotions of universal love and compassion for all men has not been effective. Bringing about such a conversion is the staggering task of international education, an education which must aim not only at achieving mutual understanding but at creating a sense of global solidarity among the passengers of spaceship earth. But the case for such an education presupposes an ethics which can show convincingly the primacy of world loyalty over local loyalties. Thus far very little, if anything, of this spirit can be found in our academic and nonacademic moral philosophies. Why, then, should we not remain national citizens first and foremost, if not exclusively?

How can the belief in the solidarity of all humans be vindicated and expected of everyone in the face of the ensconced and hallowed ethics of national man, the practicing good citizen of the hundreds of sovereign states? What follows is a first step to prepare the way for such an ethics by a consistent development through widening and deepening of our ordinary ethical consciousness, an attempt whose adequate justification I cannot yet offer in this context.

Usually we speak of fellowship only with regard to limited groups sharing the same situation. A first example of a widening of this conception could be seen in what Albert Schweitzer called the 'brotherhood of those marked by pain' and liberated from it by modern medicine as the foundation for their obligation to those still suffering from such pain.[211] What is needed is to make the sense of such fellowship universal and to think through its ethical implications.[212] There are such fellowships in fates other than sickness. We are all fellows in the fates of our history and, ultimately, the fate of existence itself. What is fate in this sense? Not merely what befalls us by way of external misfortunes. Basically everything that happens to us without our doing is fate. It begins with the 'accident of birth', a phrase whose full meaning has not yet been fathomed. For what is accidental in this sense is not merely the external fate of being born or the even more accidental one of

211. Albert Schweitzer, *On the Edge of the Primeval Forest,* New York, MacMillan, 1921, Chapter XI.

212. See my 'Ethics for Fellows in the Fate of Existence', this volume, number 9.

being conveived at the fertilization of an ovum by one in a million sperms. The same is true of other biological and social circumstances which are our lot. In this way we experience the natural facts of belonging to one sex rather than another, to a certain race or gener-ation, and our initial membership in a social class, nationality or religious group. Ultimately, even what we seem to owe to our own efforts and not merely to such accidents is possible only on the basis of 'gifts' to us, however different they may turn out for each one personally. But there are even more basic parallel fates which we share. Each one of us is born as a human and not merely as a living being. But the deepest common fate is that each one has the consciousness 'I am' and closely allied with it 'I am me'. This is what I chall call here *fellowship in existence.*

But what is the ethical significance of such fellowships in the accidents of 'fate'? Determinists hold that in nature there is really no such thing as accident, and that what we call so is merely the expression of our ignorance of the determining factors. However, the phrase 'accident of birth' has really nothing to do with the denial of causality and, particularly, of rigid causal determination. What is involved is rather the moral fact that we know of no ethical justification for such fates.[213] This is true of our existence, our identity, our humanhood, historical location, nationality, class, race, generation and sex. Ethics knows no privileges of birth.

What follows from this situation for our responsibilities toward one another? At first glance one might think that the mere fact of being thrown together by fate without our consent does not com-mit us to anything at all, especially if our common fates are merely parallel, and not based on direct sharing of 'the same boat'. How-ever, a closer look at the experience of our narrow personal escape from a catastrophe of which our neighbors have become victims can reveal to us a sense of collective responsibility, if not of guilt, toward those less fortunate than we. The prime example today is that of the survivors of the first atom bomb in Hiroshima, whose lives since then have been under the shadow of 'survivor guilt', as

213. See my 'Accidents of Birth — A Non-utilitarian Motif in Mill's Philosophy', this volume, number 6.

revealed in Robert J. Lifton's classic study.[214] A related experience is that of spontaneous indignation at the thoughtlessness and heartlessness of those who escaped other people's misfortunes by sheer luck, who take their better luck as a matter of course and even enjoy it without caring about their less fortunate fellows in fate.

Fellowship in fate calls for *solidarity* in fate. It includes the demand for a compensating 'existential' justice, meaning that all those favored and spared by mere fate have a debt of compensation toward those less fortunate. Such compensation does not mean leveling equalization but the best possible provision of equivalent benefits. Fellowship in fate calls especially for empathic self-transposal by imaginative understanding into the place of the less fortunate with their natural and artificial handicaps, which the more fortunate have been spared merely by 'accident'. But it also requires that the underprivileged exhibit understanding and patience toward the privileged, whose advantages might also have resulted from circumstances not of their own doing or fault.

This sounds simple enough if each one of us belonged only to one such fellowship. But the fact —and the problem— is that we belong to steadily increasing numbers of fellowships, natural and artificial, among which we have to choose whenever they make conflicting claims on us. Which one deserves preference in such a situation —the one closest, like the family, or the one most comprehensive, like mankind as a whole? This is not an easy question to settle, although it should be clear from the very start that the 'sovereign' nation-state, being an intermediate fellowship, cannot make any obvious claim to supreme and unlimited allegiance on the basis of its size alone.

I submit that the decisive consideration is the concrete need and urgency of the life problems to which each fellowship attends. Thus the family takes precedence whenever the primary needs of the baby for food and affection are involved, i.e., the first and most urgent biological needs. But the profile of these life needs and urgencies changes throughout our lives. Thus the urgency of international problems and solutions has increased and become paramount with the shrinking of the globe and the global threat

214. Robert J. Lifton, *Death in Life: Survivors of Hiroshima*, New York: Vintage, 1967.

of total extinction of all life through the all-powerfulness of nuclear radiation. It is for such reasons that in the present-day world our always potential responsibilities toward mankind as a whole acquire actual precedence. This is also why the need for global solidarity has now become the demand of the hour.

My plea can be restated in the following two theses:

1. The case for a new solidarity of humans, as expressed in the need for developing a global *we-consciousness,* can be based on the consistent development of our everyday awareness of fellowship in fate as experienced by ordinary moral consciousness.

2. Such solidarity calls for the compensation of native inequalities, including those between have- and have-not nations.

It is time to lay the foundations for the needed world revolution against nationalist social ethics, a revolution spearheaded by such supernational humane humans as Romain Rolland and his friend Albert Schweitzer, who remained above the melee in the two world wars.

15. THE NUCLEAR POWERS ARE FORFEITING THEIR CLAIM TO CIVIL OBEDIENCE

What can philosophers as philosophers contribute to the struggle against the specter of a nuclear holocaust? Their distinctive concern is clearly not only that of the pioneering scientists, physicians and lawyers for social responsibility but also that for humans as citizens of the world as a whole. And their primary mission is that of critical examination in the spirit of Socrates of all the claims made by them and on them.

One of the major claims with which they are confronted is that of unconditional obedience to the national powers that be. Can this claim pass the test of critical examination, especially in view of the nuclear predicament of humanity today? The growing restlessness of citizens of all nations as expressed in the unprecedented worldwide protest demonstrations, in acts of civil disobedience and in the refusal to register for the draft and to pay taxes are unmistakable signs of a crisis in which the moral legitimacy of the present political system is at stake.

The right to civil disobedience asserted and practiced by these conscientious objectors has to be examined in the wider context of a supposed unlimited obedience to the ruling powers. Yet such a duty is by no means self-evident. In fact, it implies one of the most extravagant expectations by limited historical authorities imposed on free and self-responsible persons subjected to them by an accident of birth. What could possibly justify such a disproportionate demand?

The following statement is an attempt to examine the moral foundations and the limitations of this claim. Specifically, what are the moral consequences of the continuing failure of the nuclear powers to abolish the atrocity of nuclear weapons for their demand of unquestioned loyalty of their citizens?

This is not the place to review all the historical attempts to justify political obligation. Suffice it to select some that have made the strongest impressions on modern humanity. For the ceremonial of allegiance 'pledges to the flag and the Republic for which it stands' exacted of so many American school children can hardly be considered as valid commitments to undefined political obligations. Yet this pledge acknowledges implicitly the need for such a special justification.

The first to raise explicitly the question of the grounds of political obligation was Socrates, who in Plato's *Crito* argued in his imaginary dialog with the personified laws of his native Athens that every person born into a historical society owed it (rather than his parents or God) by his very existence complete obedience, even if it condemned him unjustly to death. But earlier even he in his *Apology* had refused to obey the demand of his city to stop his philosophical teaching as violating his superior allegiance to his divine voice. Similarly, in spite of the apostle Paul's blanket endorsement of all existing authorities as divinely ordained, Peter, the 'vicar of Christ', refused to obey man rather than God.

The most appealing modern attempt to justify the sweeping demands of political obligation is the social contract theory as developed by John Locke.[215] Here the original members of the new commonwealth have turned over some of their natural rights to self-defense to the new artificial authority dependent on the effective protection of their security, but have retained the right to resist and to overturn a government that has failed to fulfill this obligation. To what extent can today's nuclear State still guarantee such

---

215. Personally I do not subscribe to the Social Contract theory either in its classical forms or in that of John Rawls' contractarianism with its fiction of what would be a rational commitment 'under the veil of ignorance' about concrete circumstances (when in fact in most cases we know very well about them).

However, I do agree with the contractarians that each fellow-exister born into this world by an 'accident of birth', which as such does not commit him to any loyalty to his native community (in contrast to cases of specific conscious and free commitments by a personal pledge in accepting public office or citizenship by naturalization), does commit himself gradually as he accepts freely benefits which he could have turned down, for instance by emigration to another hospitable foreign country — something which is insecurity? The plain fact is that the spiral of accelerating nuclear armament has only added to our ultimate insecurity. It can promise some semblance of security only by increasing threats of a holocaust that would inflict unimaginable suffering not only on the armed forces, most of them conscripted, but on countless civilian bystanders, on the surrounding neutrals and ultimately on all life on this planet.

But it is not only the growing inability of the nuclear powers to provide for the security promised under a social contract that undermines their claim to absolute obedience. This claim cannot survive the test of other major ethical standards as well.

Thus utilitarianism might suggest that civil obedience makes sense as long as its consequences would result in greater 'happiness' than would civil disobedience. Such reasoning could be invoked particularly by the strategists of nuclear deterrence. But unfortunately the chances that huge arsenals of nuclear warheads can add to such relative 'happiness' are rapidly vanishing as the balance of terror under the name of Mutual Assured Destruction (MAD) no longer works and even the advocates of nuclear deterrence admit that even a limited nuclear war could have no victor but only losers. This latest turn further weakens the case for civil obedience to the nuclear powers.

But there is an even stronger case against any support of nuclear armaments: Kant, in his *Foundations of the Metaphysics of Morals,* proclaimed the categorical imperative that human beings must always be treated as ends and never as means only. Now, when in destroying a nuclear target we have to disregard the inevitable side effects of its destruction, we also have to treat the innocent bystanders, human as well as nonhuman, as mere means to our goal. Never could such callous disregard of persons be reconciled with an ethics of respect for human beings. Inasmuch as the use of nuclear arms would commit us to such crimes against humanity, any obedience to the agents of such powers becomes morally indefensible, and would make those who obey accomplices in the crimes.

creasingly difficult in an overcrowded world. But such accepted benefits, if not obtruded, such as public assistance and advanced education entail only limited commitment to loyalty including the obligation to return 'unjust enrichments' obtained since such commitments.

This applies equally to the actual use of such means as to the threat to use them even if connected with the 'pious' hope that they will never have to be used. For such a threat is either self-contradictory if it does not include the readiness to push the fatal button or unbelievable bluff. In this light it is the atrocious inhumanity and irreverence for life that undermines and limits the duty to civil obedience and establishes the right to civil disobedience.

This then should be one of the messages of the concerned philosophers, concerned for the future of humanity and the fate of the earth: The enormity of the nuclear threat, and the apparent unwillingness or inability of the nuclear States to reduce it effectively undermine the duty to civil obedience and add to the right to disobey wherever and whenever they initiate or prepare a nuclear holocaust.

PART IV

PHENOMENOLOGICAL FOUNDATIONS

> In the little world in which children have their experience, whosoever brings them up, there is nothing so finely perceived and so finely felt, as injustice.
>
> Charles Dickens, *Great Expectations* (ch. 8)

16. UNFAIRNESS AND FAIRNESS: A PHENOMENOLOGICAL ANALYSIS

16.1 Introduction

A. Aims

The inverted title of this essay calls for an immediate explanation: Why does it put unfairness ahead of fairness? My main reason for this seeming paradox is that the experience of unfairness is a much more striking and stinging phenomenon than that of fairness, to which we respond much more calmly and unemotionally. Already Schopenhauer had asserted the priority of injustice *(Unrecht)* over justice *(Recht)*.[216] More recently Edmond Cahn has made this observation the starting point for his stimulating book-size study of *The Sense of Injustice*.[217]

But why not continue this approach with a more systematic investigation of injustice rather than switch from injustice to unfairness? One reason for this substitution is that today in everyday English 'unfairness' and 'fairness' are more common expressions than 'injustice' and 'justice'. Secondly, as even Webster's remark on 'synonyms' under FAIR states, 'fair' is the 'most general' of all the terms such as 'just' with which he compares FAIR.[218] But most important, thus far, to my knowledge, no explicit study of the

---

216. Arthur Schopenhauer, *Parerga und Paralipomena* I Chapter IX, 17 and passim.

217. Edmond Cahn, *The Sense of Injustice*, New York: New York University Press, 1949.

218. *Webster's Third New International Dictionary of the English Language*, Springfield, Mass.: Merriam, 1971; under FAIR, p. 815.

meaning of 'fairness', let alone 'unfairness', has been undertaken under this title. Hence a thorough investigation of unfairness as well as of fairness appears to be an urgent need, even more urgent than the continued exploration of injustice and justice.

However, I have also ulterior aims for the present enterprise. In my collection of essays on ethics in this volume,[219] I started out from the concept of 'accident of birth'. I tried to draw attention to it first indirectly by pointing out its unexpected role in the social philosophy of J.S. Mill.[220] In an attempt to determine the full meaning of this phrase, which Mill in his utiliatarian scheme did not bother to explain, I suggested that the concept of accident as here used was actually a moral concept related to a conception of justice not usually listed among the traditional types of social justice such as distributive and commutative justice, and which I called 'cosmic justice'.[221] At times I talked even of 'existential justice'. But I failed to clarify the meaning of these phrases sufficiently. I now want to defray some of this unpaid debt. In so doing I intend to show how coming to terms with this fundamental human situation involves overcoming the 'accidental' predicament of initial 'unfairness' with a 'fairer' order, replacing the original 'accident' by an 'essentializing' choice. Clearly this calls for an elucidation of the underlying ideas of unfairness and fairness.

This objective is at least a partial fulfillment of my promise in the Introduction to this collection to supply the 'phenomenological foundations' for my new perspective on social ethics. Specifically, I intend to provide the phenomenological evidence for my assertions about 'cosmic' justice and injustice. From the very start I want to make it clear that I do not mean to imply that the cosmos as such, i.e., the non-human universe is an agent capable of acting justly or unjustly. Contrary to the spirit of Promethean revolt against a personalized fate, I do not hold that there is any basis for asserting or postulating the existence of anthropo-

---

219. ''Accident of Birth': A Non-utilitarian Motif in Mill's Philosophy'; this volume, number 6.
220. This phrase in two different meanings is also used and discussed by Joel Feinberg in his 'Non-comparative Justice' (*Philosophic Review* 83 (1974), p. 308, note 7).
221. 'Justice and Fairness', *Philosophical Review* 67 (1958), 164-194.

morphic cosmic villains for whatever is going wrong with the universe. I am not looking for a superhuman or subhuman divine or devilish scapegoat who could be held responsible for our human fate. What I do mean is that our experience confronts us with the experienced fact of morally disproportionate or proportionate fates for their victims or beneficiaries. It can be recorded regardless of whether anyone is responsible for them. It occurs even beyond the personal and social range, i.e., in the cosmos. There is no good reason to postulate in such cases a 'proportioner' and even less a 'disproportioner'. In this sense cosmic justice is simply an impersonal circumstance obtaining in the relation between humans and their fates.

In talking about this conception I also referred to 'existential justice'. In so doing I wanted to avoid the pretentiousness implied in implicating the universe in some very concrete human problems. However, the term 'existence', especially in view of some of the meanings attached to this term by the existentialist philosophies, invites other misunderstandings. Thus it may mean what man makes of himself as a result of certain fundamental choices. Rather, I mean by it the basic fact that a human being exists prior and independent of any choice. By linking this conception with that of justice I want to bring out the fact that there is some justice and injustice about this very situation. It would be unfair to hold humans responsible for it. The fate of existence, i.e., of having been born into a world not of their own making is more than a mere neutral fact. It conveys to such beings a moral status in the universe, with certain basic claims, rights, responsibilities, obligations and duties. My hope is that the following explorations will at least lay more of a foundation for this assertion.

As I see it now, the most urgent need for this conception will be a fuller understanding of the nature and implications of unfairness and fairness. In pursuing this goal I shall first discuss the possibility that linguistic analyses (linguistic phenomenology) can provide the necessary clarification. Next, I shall proceed with a 'phenomenological analysis', determining first the locus for unfairness and fairness, then their carriers, and finally their structure in themselves. Then the way in which these phenomena appear to us can be investigated. Also the certainty of our knowledge about them can be appraised. On this basis the grounds that make things unfair or fair will be explored. And finally the implications of these insights, for instance for underpinning my earlier ethical papers, will be taken up briefly. A reflection on the nature and limits of phenomenological analysis as exemplified in the present study will conclude this essay.

I would like to direct the reader's attention at once to what I hope will be two of the more significant and novel results of my effort. The first concerns what I call the structural analysis of unfairness and fairness themselves. Thus far fairness, and by implication unfairness, have been often invoked as ultimate or 'primitive' concepts and standards to which to appeal, but tacitly assumed to be neither in need nor capable of any further analysis. I want to show that this has been a prejudice, not to say a counsel of premature intellectual despair or laziness. It is possible and urgent to show that fairness can be 'analyzed', not in the sense of being taken apart into pieces but be assigned its proper place in the framework of fundamental ideas of moral and legal philosophy and to point out some of its unique characteristics, especially its place in the social pattern. Being unfair and being fair mean being unfair or fair toward someone or something else, i.e., an object of unfairness or fairness.

Secondly, unfairness and fairness are properties that are not self-sufficient: they have 'grounds' on which they depend. The most important grounds for the respect so demanded are certain basic claims of the object of respect. What are these basic claims? I believe that by focusing on the grounds for unfairness and fairness we can clear a new and more direct access to the vexing problems of 'natural' rights and 'natural' laws in a more concrete and less dogmatic sense than hitherto.

B. Previous Discussions of Fairness

Most Anglo-American legal philosophers treat fairness simply as a synonym for justice, and the two terms are used interchangeably. Nevertheless, in a few noteworthy cases legal philosophers do make a distinction between the meanings of the two terms. Among them are John Rawls, John Chapman and Brian Barry. Rawls' *Theory of Justice* is based on the formula 'justice as fairness', which he had introduced first in an independent article.[222] To be sure, the sense of the particle 'as' in this combination is not unambiguous. It does not mean that justice coincides with fairness. That this is not the case is stated explicitly in *A Theory of Justice*.[223] But I cannot find any exact account of their positive relation. What is clearly not meant is that justice is here considered only insofar as it coincides with fairness. However, in other contexts it becomes clear that 'the fundamental idea *in* the concept of justice is fairness'.[224] Elsewhere, the 'principles of justice' are not identical with fairness but are based on an 'initial situation that is fair'.[225] This would of course suggest that these principles are only indirectly fair because of their basis in a fair 'original position'. However, what is clear is that for Rawls, fairness is the necessary basis for all social justice.

But then, what is this distinct fundamental fairness? Later on, i.e., after developing the 'Principles of Justice' (section 11), Rawls introduces a 'Principle of Fairness' (singular) as one of two 'principles for individuals' (rather than institutions) to the effect that 'a person is required to do his part as defined by the rules of an institution when two conditions are met: first the institution is just (or fair), that it satisfies the two principles of justice; and second, one has voluntarily accepted the benefits of the arrangement or taken advantage of the opportunities it offers to further one's interests'.[226] Now this formulation and its context make it clear that the fairness here defined is actually secondary to the principles of justice for institutions discussed before. This leaves the fairness predicated of the original position, which underlies the principles of justice, unaccounted for. Apparently Rawls does not think that this fundamental fairness is in need of any further analysis or definition. Is this tacit assumption justified?

John W. Chapman, in his contribution to the symposium on justice,[226] in distinguishing between 'Justice' and 'Fairness' made at least a careful attempt to determine their relationship. In criticiz-

---

222. John Rawls, *A Theory of Justice*, Harvard University Press, 1971, p. 12-13.
223. 'Justice and Fairness', p. 164.
224. *A Theory of Justice*, p. 12.
225. *Ibid.*, section 18, pp. 112-113.
226. 'Justice and Fairness', *NOMOS* VI (1962), pp. 147-169.

ing Rawls' earlier article on 'Justice as Fairness' on 'historical, linguistic and metaethical grounds', he asserts a complete difference between justice and fairness. Linguistic evidence in particular is supposed to show that we apply the word 'fair' with reference to a process, for instance a trial, and the word 'unfair' with reference to its outcome, for instance a verdict (p. 155). Besides, he stresses the complexity of the considerations that go into finding justice in a given case compared with the relative simplicity of considerations needed to make sure that a case has been handled fairly. Eventually he separates fairness from justice as two distinct principles, fairness being concerned merely with 'reciprocity' in the procedure of fair dealing, justice with 'equality' of treatment, i.e., with a solution which takes account of the total situation, as does a just verdict compared with a merely fair trial. Justice cannot be interpreted simply as a kind of fairness. Whether or not this result is ultimately satisfactory need not be decided here. But again there is no final analysis of what fairness is in terms of a definition.

A significant and potentially very important distinction in the context of the theory of justice and fairness can be found in Brian Barry's *Political Argument*. [227] Here, in his chapter on 'Justice and Fairness', he introduces, in addition to 'procedural fairness' and what he calls 'legal justice', a special 'background of fairness'. In the absence of a definition one can only infer from the examples added on less than a page and from the name that what is involved is a kind of secondary fairness in comparison with the 'foreground' procedural fairness. It concerns the necessary foundations of a fair competition, making sure that no 'unfair advantages' are granted or overlooked, e.g., unequal weight in a boxing match. This kind of fairness is thus preprocedural. But beyond that it is not clear what are the underlying principles of such fairness. Is it related to Rawls' intent to 'nullify the accidents of natural endowment and the contingencies of social circumstances'? [228] [229]

227. Brian Barry, *Political Argument,* London: Kegan-Paul, 1965.

228. *A Theory of Justice,* p. 15.

229. For some perceptive remarks on differences between fairness and justice see also Walter Kaufmann, *Without Guilt and Justice.* New York: Peter H. Wyden, Inc., 1973, pp. 69, 90, 242.

C. A Start from Ordinary Language:
Linguistic Phenomenology

In view of the absence of a full-scale treatment of the topic of fairness, let alone unfairness, it would seem to make good sense to make a fresh start by consulting first the wisdom of ordinary language by what has been called 'linguistic phenomenology'. Indeed, apart from John W. Chapman's incidental observation about different usages of the words 'justice' and 'fairness', no systematic study of this relationship in English or any other language seems to exist. To undertake it thoroughly would clearly call for teamwork. It is certainly beyond my own competence and resources. But even a sample of what is needed might be sufficient to determine how far such an effort could pay off.

What I intend to do here is to explore primarily English usage in typical situations in which the two pairs, unfair-fair and unjust-just, occur but cannot be used interchangeably, as possible indications for differences in their meanings. I shall begin with cases where only one of the pairs, unfair-fair or unjust-just, can be applied. Omitting here the clearly unrelated uses of 'fair guess' and 'fair warning' I distinguish three groups:

(i) Advantage, bargaining, chance, deal, examination, grade, play, profit, share admit only the adjectives 'unfair' or 'fair', but not 'unjust' or 'just'.

(ii) Enrichment, peace, penalty, society, verdict, war allow only the adjectives 'unjust' or 'just', but not 'unfair' or 'fair'.

(iii) Action, compensation, decision, distribution, person, price, reward, settlement, wage accept both the adjectives 'unfair-fair' and 'unjust-just'. However, it may well be the case that they point at different aspects of the referents. For instance, 'fair' in the example of compensation points at the way in which the act of compensating is carried out, while 'just' points at the result achieved.

At first sight one may well think that it is merely a matter of historical convention what combinations between nouns and adjectives are required, forbidden or allowed. But on closer examination it would seem that the combination of the nouns with unfair-fair refers only to processes, that with unjust-just refers only to results.

Yet the combination with unfair-fair would not refer to processes in the cases of advantage, chance, profit and share, that with unjust-just in the case of war (in contrast to peace as a process, not as a result).

As far as current English is concerned, my tentative conclusion is therefore that unfair-fair and unjust-just are not simply synonyms even in those cases where we can use both pairs of adjectives for the same noun. But this does not mean that the difference in meaning is that between focussing on the procedure and on the outcome of the procedure. In particular, the distinction between unfair and fair has a much wider range than that between unjust and just. This is in accordance with the observation of the *Websters New Dictionary of Synonyms*[230] according to which FAIR, among the synonyms FAIR, JUST, EQUITABLE, IMPARTIAL, UNBIASED, DISPASIONATE, UNCOLORED, OJBECTIVE, is 'the most general term, which 'implies the disposition or intention to regard other persons or things without reference to one's own interest, feelings, or prejudices, often even to the point of conceding every reasonable claim of the weaker side or giving oneself or the stronger side no undue advantage...' In any case, what the preceding preliminary survey of English seems to show is that unfair-fair and unjust-just are not merely synonyms in the sense that they have the same denotations and connotations and can be interchanged (with care). Yet the usual interpretation of the difference as based on the difference between procedure and outcome does not cover some important cases. Hence, an alternative interpretation, also suggested by Chapman, seems to me worth considering, namely that judgments of unjust-just concern matters of much graver significance than those of unfair-fair. In everyday situations we are much more inclined to complain that we have been treated unfairly than that our treatment has been unjust. Being denied one's place in a line at a counter will hardly be called unjust, but certainly unfair. But a trial in which the defendent is denied the right to a hearing and a defense might very well be called an injustice, even a 'flagrant' injustice. And we would hardly talk about a 'flagrant unfairness', but very well about 'clearly unfair treatment'. In such cases the difference between the two judgments may be expressive largely

230. Springfield, MA: G. & C. Merriam Company, 1968, p. 319.

of the degree of 'moral indignation' felt about a violation of some-one's interests. But there cannot be an injustice without a primary unfairness. In this sense unfairness is the more fundamental pheno-menon to be investigated first.

All the same, I am very doubtful that on the basis of current us-age it will be possible to find a sharp distinction between the mean-ings 'unfair-fair' and 'unjust-just'. At this point it seems to me ur-gent to consider the historical and geographical relativity of present English usage, particularly of its Oxford variety. There is hardly any good reason for assuming that the present stage in the development of the Queen's English has reached absolute perfection and that there will not be further shifts after the ones recorded in the New English Dictionary and its supplements and parallel American enterprises. We know already enough about the changes from the obsolete sense of 'fair' as antithetical to 'foul' to its present prolifer-ation. And indications seem to be that the present expansion of its use and meaning may further reduce the range of the language of injustice-justice. I also seem to notice an increasing tendency to talk about the suffering of the naturally and socially handicapped as unfair, something which I doubt was the case before the rise of social legislation with its interest in welfare rights.

An even more important reason for caution in using linguistic phenomenology as evidence of, or at least as a reliable clue to, dif-ferences in the phenomena meant is the questionable trust in the superiority of one particular language like English. A comparison with German ordinary language (with which I am most familiar) could serve as a warning. Here the adjective *gerecht* and the noun *Gerechtigkeit* in their current, though no in their past, meanings may be considered as approximate equivalents to 'just' and 'jus-tice'. But their is no German equivalent to 'fair'. To be sure, the words *unfair* (pronounced *oonfar*) and *fair* has actually invaded the German language, especially in the areas of sports and busi-ness, not only as loanwords, but as parts of the German language in phrases like *fair play* and *unfaires Benehmen* (conduct). But the connotation attached to *fair* is primarily that of 'decent' and 'proper',[231] whereas to talk about an *unfairer Prozess* (= trial)

---

231. See *Wörterbuch der deutschen Gegenwartssprache*, Berlin: Akademie Verlag, 1976, II, p. 1199.

or *faires Verhör* (hearing) would be very forced (for: *ungerechtes Verfahren* or *ungerechtes Verhör*). In other words, the German *gerecht* comprises both English 'just' and 'fair'.

There is, however, another German word which is used often as a companion to *gerecht,* namely *billig.* At times it functions as an exact synonym for *gerecht* or rather *recht*, as in the saying *'Was dem einen recht ist, ist dem anderen billig'.* But, in general, *Billigkeit* in the context of *Gerechtigkeit* stands for Aristotle's *epieikia* or English 'equity', i.e., a corrective of strict moral and especially legal justice, not of fairness. Moreover, in common usage *billig* has acquired the connotation of 'cheap' and 'trivial'. Hence, there is no special German term corresponding to the common English usage of unfair-fair. In other words, in German the field of unfairness-fairness and injustice-justice is structured quite differently from that in English, as it makes use of both Latin and Anglo-Saxon ingredients. It is also instructive that the English unfair-fair has entered German, filling a gap, as it were, but not exactly corresponding to its English connotation.

The situation is even more different in French. Here 'fair' is used only as a loanword, and so is the phrase 'fair play'. As an equivalent for English 'unfair' only the word *équitable* and the opposite combination *pas équitable* can be used. But the English word 'equitable' is hardly identical in meaning with 'fair' (one cannot talk about 'equitable play' or an 'equitable trial'). Apparently the undifferentiated *unjuste-juste* has to serve as the equivalent of both 'unfair-fair' and 'unjust-just'.

Under these circumstances it would hardly be wise to use present-day English as a faithful reflection of the articulation of the phenomena and as more than a preliminary guide to the phenomena, like the linguistig phenomenology of J.L. Austin.[232] This does not exclude the study of the ordinary meanings of everyday language as a point of departure for a direct investigation of the corresponding phenomena. But it should serve as a warning against blind confidence in the wisdom of the historical languages. I would certainly favor and welcome a much more thorough study of the linguistic phenomenology of unfairness-fairness and of injustice-justice on

232. See J.L. Austin, *Philosophical Papers,* Oxford, 1962, p. 130; see also my *The Context of the Phenomenological Movement,* The Hague, 1981, p. 89.

historical and comparative grounds. But in the context of the present enterprise, I do not think such an investment would be justified. At best it would be a detour to the phenomena which would still have to provide the final validation of the linguistic distinctions.

(d) The Phenomenological Approach

A phenomenological approach to unfairness and fairness would clearly mean as direct as possible an investigation of the phenomena without intermediary preliminaries. While this means that it would bypass a prior analysis of ordinary language, it does not mean that it can do without paying any attention to language. No phenomenology makes sense without the '-ology' of language, which is a basic tool for as social an enterprise as science for purposes of communication. This includes the staking out of the area of investigation by definition and other linguistic devices as well as the description of its findings for their efficient transmission. This indispensability of language calls for careful study and utilization of the linguistic tools of the phenomenological enterprise. But it does not require a preliminary investigation of the entire language which can be used in talking about the phenomena.

What then does it mean to go as directly as possible to the phenomena? And first, what do I mean by the term 'phenomenon' in this context? There is clearly an experience in which we are confronted, 'struck' as it were,[233] by the unfairness of discrimination, e.g. seeing that people differing only by hair or skin color are not admitted to public facilities. Even before expressing our indignation by protest in linguistic form, we experience a characteristic shock, which we may not even be able to 'articulate' except by inarticulate 'outcries'. It is these experiences which are the major concern of a phenomenological approach to the 'phenomena' to be investigated and analyzed. Thus the term 'phenomenon' in this context does not mean what it does in everyday life when we refer to an exceptional event like the appearance of the northern lights or of similar natural occurrences as a phenomenon (German: *ein Phänomen*). Nor do I mean by it appearances in contrast to things-

---

233. 'Three Types of the Given', *Husserl Studies* I (1984), pp. 69-78.

in-themselves in Kant's sense. Phenomena in the sense in which I shall use the term here means whatever makes its appearances in our immediate experience regardless of whether such appearances correspond to real facts or merely to what seem to be facts (illusions).

However, even a phenomenological phenomenon in this sense is not a simple matter. It has a structure which requires explication. It appears in an experiencing 'act', which is part and parcel of the total experience. In this experience one has to distinguish between *what* appears, i.e., the experienced 'object' or content to which the experience refers and the experiencing process or event *in which* it appears. This double aspect of the phenomenal situation calls for parallel attention to both these aspects, i.e., to the experienced phenomenon and to the experiencing 'act' which appears at the same time as the phenomenon. In more technical language, they have been called the intentional or intended object and the intending act (Husserl's *noema* and *noesis*). In addition to these poles of the experience one also has to consider the different ways in which the phenomenon appears to the experiencer, e.g., clearly or dimly, in different 'perspective', etc. Phenomenology in the widest sense here used has to pay attention to all these 'aspects'. More specifically the study of the objective phenomenon, i.e., of what appears as it appears, can be called phenomenological ontology; that of the corresponding acts, 'act-phenomenology'; and that of the different ways of appearance as phenomenology in the narrower sense or 'phenomenology proper'.

On the basis of this conception (which is incidentally not shared by all phenomenologists), I shall first deal with what appears when we have experiences of unfairness and fairness, trying to explore the structures which present themselves as they are meant and experienced. Next, I shall analyze and describe our experiencing of these 'objective' aspects in an act-phenomenology. Finally, I shall try to show how the 'objective' phenomena constitute themselves as we become conscious (aware) of them.

16.2 An Analysis of Unfairness and Fairness

(Phenomenological Ontology)

(a) Where Unfairness and Fairness Appear: Their Locus

In what 'region' of the universe can unfairness and fairness make their appearance? The best way to approach an answer to this question is to determine toward whom and toward what we can be unfair or fair.

At first sight one may think that it is only persons in the fully developed sense of the term who can be the locus for the appearance of unfairness and fairness. Certainly they are the only ones who can protest about unfairness and appreciate fairness. But unless one makes this ability the decisive criterion for possible unfairness and fairness, cannot something very similar also occur when we owe some debt to a nonpersonal being? For instance, can we not be unfair even to animals when we expect them to suffer the kind of 'indignity' meted out to them, when pigs and chicken are cooped up in 'meat-factories' for fattening? How about unfairness to plants when we destroy them wantonly to no purpose? Can we not also be unfair to nature as a whole by the kind of wholesale indictment expressed, for instance, in Tennyson's reference to 'Nature, red in tooth and claw[234] and Matthew Arnold's lines

'Nature is cruel, man is sick of blood:
Nature is stubborn, man would fain adore . . .'[235]

The new attitude toward nature expressed in environmental ethics can also be interpreted as an attempt to be fair to nature for its own sake, not only for our own, as 'human chauvinism' would see it in its lack of reverence for life, including wild life and even for non-living parts of the universe such as crystals, mountains, rivers, for their own sake. What else is the meaning of vandalism in national parks but such irreverence?

But can there also be unfairness and fairness to the background media of time and space? I am inclined to deny this, although I

234. Tennyson 'In Memoriam, LVI'.
235. 'In Harmony with Nature'.

share Augustine's wonder in his inability to tell what time is once he is asked to describe what it is. Denying or affirming the reality of time is hardly being unfair or fair to it.

(b) What Can Be Unfair and Fair: Their Carriers

What sort of 'things' can carry unfairness and fairness? In what kind of entities can they 'inhere'? Here two cases have to be distinguished: (1) that of actions, personal conduct and its agents and (2) that of impersonal situations.

(1) The most obvious 'carriers' of unfairness and fairness are persons and personal conduct. Actually, it is through conduct that persons manifest their unfairness and fairness. In order to obtain a first survey of these personal carriers it may therefore be best to line up representative types of unfair and fair conduct such as:

1. unfair thinking, e.g., considering only fortunate individuals, compared with fair thinking, which considers also the unfortunate ones;

2. unfair imagining, which imagines only utopian possibilities, but not the dystopian ones, as fairness demands;

3. unfair remembering, which recalls only successes but not failures;

4. unfair judging, which considers only one side of an argument;

5. unfair decision-making, which decides haphazardly by casting lots;

6. unfair questioning, which intrudes into the other's 'privacy';

7. unfair replying, which evades the issue;

8. unfair distributing, which favors one side over others;

9. unfair punishing, which is motivated by revengefulness.

In fact, any conduct affecting other people can be unfair or fair in this sense, even loving and hating, as far as they are not beyond our control.

By performing such unfair or fair acts on a sustained scale the performing person herself becomes unfair or fair, as unfairness and fairness become persistent dispositions.

(2) 'Unfair' and 'fair' are predicates which can also be applied

to situations, natural or man-made, if only in a slightly modified sense. Thus a person may find himself without any fault of his own at an 'unfair' disadvantage or advantage compared with others. Such unfairness may affect not only the individual but also groups and whole countries. Thus an underdeveloped nation or a land-locked country may be 'naturally disadvantaged' if it has no outlet to the sea, one of the new problems in international ethics. Again as in the case of conduct I shall line up some representative cases of typical unfair and fair situations:

1. with regard to natural starting conditions (Brian Barry's 'background' fairness);

   a. unfair conditions affecting a baby's conception;

   b. unfair conditions at birth (injuries);

   c. unfair disadvantages at birth (heredity, ill health, poor intelligence);

   d. social disadvantages (family and historical setting within a nation, class, religion);

2. with regard to postnatal conditions (food, health care, parental and social acceptance (rejection versus 'love'), education (authoritarian versus permissive), social support versus neglect, equalization versus individualization;

3. with regard to conditions at maturity;

   a. access to opportunities;

   b. credit for achievements;

   c. consideration of headstarts and handicaps;

4. with regard to conditions after maturity;

   a. old age care;

   b. dying and death care.

This is clearly only one dimension in the lineup of natural situations in which questions of unfairness and fairness can arise. Theoretically they can occur in connection with any circumstances not controlled by humans. Thus all kinds of historical changes, climatic and economic catastrophes and windfalls raise questions of unfairness and fairness with regard to their victims or beneficiaries.

The ethical implication of these situations are enormous. For questions of unfairness and fairness arise not only in the dealings of personal beings with one another but also in the relation between them and their natural situations.

(c) Unfairness and Fairness Themselves

Now that we have a first denotative idea of where and on what kind of carriers unfairness and fairness occur, it makes sense to try to determine what they are in themselves connotatively. Again I shall focus on the phenomena of unfairness and fairness in that order. Depending on whether or not these terms are used interchangeably with 'injustice' and 'justice' the following analysis would apply to both pairs insofar as the range of 'unfairness' and 'fairness' includes the narrower one of 'injustice' and 'justice' too.

There is a strong temptation to assert from the very start that unfairness and fairness are indefinable and unanalyzable, as are, according to Bishop Butler, G.E. Moore and their followers, the fundamental concepts of moral philosophy, notably good and bad, and leave it at that. But even if this assumption should ultimately prove to be correct, this is no excuse for not trying to examine carefully the evidence for and against. At least their relations to other phenomena should be explored in order to establish their uniqueness. In any case, the class or genus for these phenomena, if not their specific differences, ought to be determined in order to assign them their proper places in the framework of a comprehensive ontology.

At the start of such an analysis, I would like to state that in using the nouns 'unfairness' and 'fairness', I do not imply that they refer to independent entities after the model of Platonic Ideas. As far as I use them at all, they are to serve merely as convenient abstractions for concrete phenomena in our experience. These concrete phenomena are referred to best by the adjectives 'unfair' and 'fair'.

1. What these adjectives stand for are dependent properties of certain acts, persons or situations as identified in the preceding section. If thus being unfair and being fair are in their ontological structure primarily properties, what kind of properties are they? Obviously they are not the kind of natural properties ob-

servable by sense perception, properties such as being round or
yellow. How can they be characterized positively? In our ordinary languages there are no words that would point at a common distinguishing characteristic for them such as 'physical' or
'psychic'. The best approach to answering the question would
be from the distinctive way in which we become aware of them.
Thus, we might say that we 'feel' the unfairness of a decision or
situation. But this verb is applicable also to a choice or to a pre-
monition. It also does not always signify a clear awareness of
'unfair' or 'fair', but merely a preliminary impression. Fur such
an awareness we will have to resort to the visual language of
'seeing'. But to 'see' the unfairness or fairness of a decision is
certainly very different from visual seeing, and more related to
'insight'. What distinguishes 'seeing unfairness' from 'seeing
yellow' is something for which ordinary language is not differ-
entiated enough. All we can do is to point at the peculiarity of
this seeing by looking first at our typical responses and then
pointing at what feature in the object it responds to. Such responses would be in the case of the unfair outrage, indignation,
and the like, in the case of the fair being approval, satisfaction,
or pleasure. This is clearly a case where we might think of coining a new term or phrase that would indicate the sui-generis
character of this experience and particularly the source of these
responses in their objects. At this point I can suggest only the
combinations 'seeing-feeling' or 'feeling-seeing'. As to the unfair
and fair to which such seeing is directed, they could only be designated as (intended) objects or origins of such feeling or seeing.

2. Unfair and fair in the context of social relations are not merely
   simple unstructured properties like round and yellow, and not
   even like the original referents of the word 'fair' in the sense of
   (moderately) beautiful (as in 'fair looks', 'fair sex', 'fair weather')
   or blond (as in 'fair hair'). 'Fair' in the sense on which I am focusing is what is unfair or fair *to* someone or something. It is
   therefore a relational property comparable to such properties
   as equal to, different from. More specifically, two such relations
   have to be distinguished: (a) fair in relation to parallel cases and
   (b) fair to a standard criterion. (a) Unfair and fair to parallel
   cases implies that one could not judge about them, for instance,

about the fairness of prices, wages or profits, without knowing about other prices, wages, and profits. Also, such properties would be not only relational but relative in the sense that they vary with the shifting differences in the economic conditions. What is a fair price at a city market will be unfair in a rural setting. (b) It is different in cases where the referent of unfair and fair is an objective standard. Joel Feinberg has made an impressive case for the consideration of a type of justice thus far overlooked which he calls 'non-comparative justice'.[235] One major example is the 'justice' or 'injustice' we do to a work of art or a book when we judge it, e.g., in a review, by itself without paying attention to other reviews. What decides or should decide are the intrinsic merits or demerits of the book itself. While Feinberg refers to this new standard as a kind of justice, he also very often uses the words 'unfair' and 'fair'. Since he does not distinguish sharply between justice and fairness, it seems to me perfectly justified to introduce also a 'non-comparative unfairness and fairness'. While they are relational properties too, they are not relative in the sense of comparative unfairness and fairness and in this limited sense even 'absolute'.

It is of course also possible to compare a review of a book with those of other reviewers and judge it as comparatively unfair or fair. In this sense the same 'carrier' may have the relational property of unfairness and fairness at the same time, i.e., be comparatively fair and non-comparatively unfair or vice versa.

3. If thus being unfair and being fair are both relational properties of carriers of either comparative or noncomparative nature, are there still other common characteristics of them? Thus one might think of unfairness and fairness as *gestalt*-qualities, as they occur in connection with the physical entities described by *gestalt* psychology. There seems to be indeed a case for looking at being fair and being unfair as characteristics that attach to total conduct or total situations. But the *gestalt* characteristics of unfair and fair clearly differ from those of merely theoretical wholes like geometric shapes that can be perceived by our senses.

235. Joel Feinberg, 'Non-comparative Justice', *Philosophical Review* 83 (1974), pp. 297-338.

Another similarity of unfair-fair properties is to value qualities. Indeed, unfairness has essentially negative value and fairness positive value. But this does not imply that in themselves they are nothing but value qualities. To establish this would require a complete phenomenology of value qualities, which I cannot offer at this point. Nevertheless, the unfair-fair properties have a distinct affinity to such properties as beauty or goodness, as suggested by the etymology and history of the word 'fair'. But unfair-to and fair-to are relational properties which differ structurally from simple value qualities. Thus they would certainly have to be value qualities sui generis.

The preceding account of the structures of unfair and fair seems to apply to both of them. There are, however, also characteristics which differ for each of them. I shall try to identify them here separately.

A. Being unfair:

As pointed out at the start, unfairness differs sharply from fairness in the more intense and striking personal experience through which it is given to its victim. It is now time to identify this difference more directly. This can be done best by focusing on the unfairness of discrimination. It could be described by such metaphors as suffering a sudden mental pain or a hurt affecting the inner balance of the victim, endangering her moral self-esteem. This is obviously only the *effect* of experiencing an unfairness. How far is it possible also to characterize the cause of this effect in the carrier of unfairness, i.e., the act, person or situation? Metaphorically one could again refer to a certain intent or tendency to injure or hurt the victim. But such language would be clearly too 'anthropomorphic'. Nevertheless, one might say that it is characteristic of discriminating unfairness to be unconcerned about the possible effects on the victim, if not downright aggressive against it. In other words, unfairness implies a tendency to inflict moral injury on its victim.

B. Being fair:

By contrast fairness implies no such tendency, aggressive or defensive, toward a possible beneficiary of it. One might therefore think that it could be characterized as the negation of unfairness.

But such a double negation would certainly not do justice to the positive, if not obtrusive, property of being fair. This experience could be described as a peculiar sense of satisfaction with being the beneficiary of fair treatment or with witnessing fair treatment enjoyed by others. Usually, however, we do not experience it as vividly as unfairness, and then only when our attention is drawn to it. Being treated fairly, especially after having been subjected to unfairness, may also be accompanied by a sense of gratitude or thankfulness for a benefit that cannot be taken for granted.

How far is it possible to trace these characteristic responses back to properties of what is fair, i.e., to acts, persons, or situations? I submit that the source of this experience is a peculiar consonance between the situation of the beneficiary of fairness and the solution of his problem. The content of this experience is definitely positive. Being fair in the case of an act, a person or a situation means their relational property of being in a peculiar felt harmony with, appropriateness to, the requirements of the total situation.

There is still another aspect of unfairness and fairness that can lead to a better understanding of their significance. Unfair conduct in relation to others is always a sign of disrespect, or lack of respect for them. What does 'respect' mean in this context? At least a special consideration for the peculiar nature of the others and ultimately for their basic claims to be acknowledged.

In mentioning such a basic claim as the ultimate target of respect in the case of fairness and disrespect in the case of unfairness, I am introducing an entirely new aspect into the structure of the phenomenon. To explore it adequately would be a formidable task which I cannot and will not undertake in this context. Suffice it to mention some of its dimensions which are particularly pertinent for a better understanding of unfairness and fairness.

In addition to the traditional claims of life, liberty and security, there are for instance: (1) the claim to recognition of one's separate existence on equal terms with that of anyone else. It would be unfair to claim special deals merely because of factual inequalities; (2) the claim to respect for one's right to dissent from and consent to decisions affecting one's life; (3) the claim to respect for one's right to secede from or to join groups relevant to one's life; (4) the claim to respect for one's privacy or one's right to communicate; (5) the claim to sympathetic understanding of one's social or natural predicament.

What do I mean in this context by 'claim'? Very often today, especially for supporters of Wesley Hohfeld's *Fundamental Legal Conceptions* a claim occurs only in persons if and only if another person has a legal duty toward the first person. However, I understand by 'claim' an underlying phenomenon which is not yet related to any such duty. This is the kind of claim advocated by Joel Feinberg in his essay on 'Duties, Rights and Claims',[236] a right to have rather than a right against someone else. Feinberg in his note 13 admits: 'No doubt this is an extended sense of 'right'. I insist only that it is a proper and important one.' I would like to second the implication of a need for an extrapolation to this wider use of 'claim' paralleled by the use of the German word *Anspruch*, which I have explored elsewhere.[237] The 'clamor' which according to the etymological sense of the word 'claim' issues from the claimant is primarily one for the fulfillment of a legitimate need even before the search for a possible 'fulfiller' of such a claim can begin.[238] While the term 'claim', as distinguished from 'right', does not occur in the 'Universal Declaration of Human Rights', the phrase 'entitled to all the rights . . . set forth in this Declaration' in Article Two comes at least close to it, since a right, rather than a claim, to a right would hardly make sense. Such a claim 'precedes' even the possibility of a claimant who can claim, i.e., assert and defend this claim.

(d) Is the Relation Between Unfair and Fair Disjuctive?

At first sight it may seem that there can be no middle ground between being unfair and fair. This would indeed be obvious if 'unfair' were merely the contradictory opposite of 'fair', i.e., not fair. But

236. *Rights, Justice, and the Bounds of Liberty*, Princeton University Press, 1980, pp. 189-241.

237. In a special chapter (VIII) of my unpublished German book of 1937 on *Sollen und Dürfen: Grundlagen einer Philosophie der ethischen Rechte und Pflichten.*

238. See my *The Phenomenological Movement*. Third revised and enlarged edition. The Hague: Martinus Nijhoff, 1982, pp. 704-706; and 'Three Types of the Given', *Husserl Studies* I, 1964, p. 71.

is this really the case? My analyses, by stressing the disruptive character of unfairness and the harmonizing character of fairness seem to leave a good deal of neutral ground between them.

Is whatever is not unfair necessarily fair? This would be the case if 'fair' is understood in a nonemphatic sense, in which 'fair' also represents a 'middling' grade, way below what is really good, let alone excellent, and halfway down the scale to poor and failing. But if 'fair' is taken as what after careful appraisal represents the most perfect solution of a problem, for instance resulting in perfectly fair distribution, then there are plenty of intermediate alternatives which are neither unfair nor fair. Mere noninterference in other people's affairs is hardly a case of fairness in the emphatic sense.

Another aspect of this problem appears in the following situations: (i) A treatment can be partially fair (to one party) and partially unfair (to the other party). The result would be that the treatment is mixed, both unfair and fair. (ii) There can be degrees of unfairness and fairness. In the case of unfairness this seems to be implied when we speak of an unfairness as flagrant or outrageous versus what may be called a minor or mild unfairness. Can one decision also be fairer than another? If it should be correct that unfair and fair can have degrees, then it would hardly be surprising if there could be a zero degree of both unfair and fair.

16.3 How Unfairness and Fairness Appear

(Phenomenology Proper)

As in the case of all other 'phenomena' unfairness and fairness are given through different ways of appearance (*Gegebenheitsweisen*). Thus, they can be given either directly or indirectly, e.g., through different aspects in different perspectives, thematically or marginally, adequately or inadequately, clearly or dimly. Of particular interest in connection with the givenness of unfairness and fairness are the different perspectives through which an unfair or fair situation appears to us.

These differences in their appearance depend largely on the standpoint of the experiencer, i.e., in the case of the appearance of the unfairness of discrimination on the perspectives of (1) the victim, (2) outside witnesses, (3) an umpire, (4) an impartial judge, (5) a partial attorney in an adversary procedure.

1. Appearances of Unfairness

(i) The most direct shock of unfairness is experienced by the immediate victim of discrimination when she is told point-blank that someone else is to receive preferred treatment. In this case the sting or wound may even precede full realization of what precisely the discrimination consists in. Only subsequently, as the victim finds out about the nature and the degree of the injury inflicted on her and reflects on it, can she fully realize the unfairness of her plight, thus obtaining an intuitive fulfillment of what before was still largely an empty anticipation of what had happened to her. Even so, the victim is always too close to the scene to focus on it.

(ii) Outside witnesses of the event will be in a position to see the event in much better perspective, although they too may be too close to, or too far from, it unless they take proper precautions against bias. For they too may be affected by vicarious indignation at the unfairness and its perpetrators. The impartial observer is not necessarily the one who observes best. Critical observation requires often imaginary self-transposal into the place of the victim and of other witnesses.[239] Only the cautious synthesis of several (how many?) such outside perspectives can approximate, but never reach, the fullest possible visualization of the unfairness.

(iii) The role of the umpire in competitive games such as baseball, football, boxing (but not racing or tennis) offers perhaps the best chance to see unfairness directly in optimum perspective by considering all the relevant perspectives impartially. He needs it not only in order to keep the competitors in line, to declare 'fouls' and to assign 'penalties', but also to assign proper head-starts and handicaps.

239. 'Putting Ourselves into the Place of Others', *Human Studies* 3 (1980), pp. 169-173, also this volume no. 5.

(iv) By contrast, an impartial judge is not allowed to be in direct touch with the events and parties he judges. Otherwise he has to disqualify himself and can act at best as one of the witnesses. Instead, the judge's evidence has to be derived from third persons, i.e., the direct observations of the victim and other more or less critical witnesses and from other indirect evidence plus perhaps the direct perception of 'exhibits'. Thus his judgment has to be based essentially on 'hearsay' evidence. But it is hearsay evidence of witnesses who themselves have to be direct eye- or ear witnesses and are not allowed to rely on subwitnesses. The judge has to remain at a distance, but a fair distance in order to be impartial.

(v) The case is different with a private, as distinguished from the state, attorney, especially under an adversary system, who is supposed to search out and to present only the evidence in favor of her client. Such an arrangement is defensible only on the assumption that someone biased for one side will have the chance to avoid bias for or against the other side. To this extent the service of a partial attorney can be an aid not only to the victim of unfairness but also to the impartial judge.

2. Appearances of Fairness

From my occasional comparisons between the greater impact of unfairness to that of fairness it is to be expected that the way fairness appears differs somewhat from the appearances of unfairness. Again we should distinguish between the different perspectives for different experiencers of this property.

(i) As to the beneficiary of fairness, e.g., of fair treatment, she will as a rule not be 'struck' by her advantage in the same way as the victim of unfairness was by her disadvantage. But she will most likely notice and appreciate it after having been subjected to unfair treatment before. But most of the time she will simply take it for granted. When she does notice it, she is likely to be unemotionally appreciative of it, although she is of course involved. Such 'objectivity' may be combined with special gratitude toward the dispenser of fairness.

(ii) Outside witnesses of fair treatment will presumably experience it not differently from those witnessing unfairness, though they may also experience some vicarious satisfaction and relief, once fair treatment is administered or restored.

(iii) For the umpire, fairness in his adjudications is presumably experienced dimly as the obverse of his avoiding and preventing unfairness. But one or the other may be in the foreground, depending on the differences in the situation when either unfairness has been prevalent before or the general atmosphere has been one of good will and harmony.

(iv) The judge, in dispensing fairness, for instance in a fair trial or a fair hearing, will experience fairness presumably in weighing her decision while trying to avoid unfairness in a process where the cases for the two parties are pitted against each other in her weighing imagination until she reaches a decision in which fairness gets the upper hand. Usually such a test may not be necessary, but it may be quite prominent where it is difficult for the judge to be fair.

(v) The partial attorney, in trying to achieve fairness for his client, may at first be less concerned about being fair, especially fair to his adversary. Yet ultimately his intentional bias is to be a means for reaching objective fairness in a synthesis of his and his opponents' biased pleas.

16.4 How Certain is Our Knowledge of Unfairness and Fairness: Epistemology

Knowing about the ways unfairness and fairness are given in our experience will also enable us to some extent to determine how much we really know about them, and how reliable such knowledge is. It can also be a reminder of the needs for caution by keeping down one's claims to have the final word about them and against the arrogance of self-righteousness.

For a complete evaluation of these claims we would of course have to examine all the general circumstances that go into the appraisal of human knowledge. For knowledge about unfairness and fairness is only a special case of knowledge in general. Also, inasmuch as unfairness and fairness are value qualities or at least very similar to them, the particular problems of value knowledge have to be considered. For these much greater problems I shall have to refer to general and axiological epistemology. I shall simply assume that in general some knowledge is possible and actual, even though

I would not claim absolute certainty for areas outside the epistemological minimum of Cartesian indubitability.

At this place I merely want to discuss the implications of our preceding phenomenological explorations. In general it should be clear that empty reference (the mere or signitive intentions of Husserl) without intuitive fulfillment is not valid proof of the actual presence of a thing. This is even more true for unfairness and fairness. Only when we are confronted with some concrete intuitive evidence is there a case for claiming some knowledge, subject to confirmation or invalidation. Recalling the different perspectives in which unfairness may present itself, I maintain:

1. The primary shock suffered by a victim of an unfairness may be so overwhelming that she cannot properly appraise the meaning and validity of it. Her very closeness to the phenomenon may block access to it, much as it does in the case of close-up vision excluding intermediate light from the object before us. Once she has overcome this shock, some 'fairer' estimate is at least possible. But the danger of partiality is always present and pardonable. However, the victim's experience of unfairness is one of the least certain types of knowledge of unfairness.

2. Outside observers, once they can free themselves of all bias for or against the victim, may be in a much better position to reach valid knowledge about the unfairness of the treatment she has undergone. But this position alone is not yet a guarantee for the reliability of this knowledge. It requires a sustained effort to 'do justice' to the case. Insofar as this presupposes knowledge of other minds and imaginative self-transposal into their places, these are further factors suggesting moderating any claims. However, pooling such knowledge with that of other outside observers may lead to increased assurance, but also to a diminution of it in case of disagreement among them.

3. An umpire given direct access to all sides of a conflict and even the chance of stopping a contest by blowing the whistle should be able to achieve the most objective appraisal of a situation. But even he is not beyond criticism, and his ruling may often be contested and appealed. To credit him with infallible judgment, even if no further appeal is possible, would be anything but safe, especially when he has to make a ruling on the spur of the

moment. Clearly, the validity of his judgment of an unfairness depends on his chance to observe carefully and to reflect without pressure and especially without emotionalism which may bias him as he watches and has to settle violent arguments.

4. Supposedly the judge in a court of law has the best chance to reach the facts of the case, particularly in the case of unfairness. And clearly under normal circumstances, as distinguished from abnormal states of emergency under 'martial' law, she will not be under the time pressure under which the umpire has to operate. On the other hand, the 'evidence' of the judge is primarily indirect, based on reports of witnesses on the witness stand, whose testimonies are notoriously fallible, if not biased, even if purged by the filter of an oath or solemn affirmation. Under these circumstances her verdict on matters of fact, and on unfairness in particular, is anything but unchallengeable. This is even more true of the verdict of an inexperienced jury, in spite of the requirement of unanimity. At least the judge's verdict can be appealed, in the case of certain errors, up to a 'supreme court'. Thus, the judge's verdict, although given from a distance may well be the best possible approximation to knowledge about fairness. But it is anything but infallible.

5. Obviously the case stated by an attorney for one party in a trial cannot and does not claim to contain reliable knowledge about unfairness. At best its role is that of an aid in preparing for a less one-sided and more penetrating appraisal of the case by a judge through introducing new evidence in favor of his client that would otherwise be overlooked.

   And what about the certainty of our knowledge of *fairness*? In general it may be expected that in accordance with its smaller emotional impact our awareness of fairness will be less obtrusive than that of unfairness. But that does not mean that our knowledge of fairness will be less certain and reliable. Here again a closer look at different perspectives of fairness as we experience it is indicated.

6. The beneficiary of fairness is usually not aware, and rarely fully aware, of his benefits. But at least he will not be diverted as much as the victim of unfairness by his emotional response. This does not mean that he will not enjoy and appreciate fair-

ness, especially after having been the victim of unfairness. In any case, once he focuses on such fairness he may be fully aware, and he may claim to know that he is being treated fairly. But his closeness to this situation may make him over- or under-sensitive to these benefits.

7. This handicap will not affect outside observers. Their chances of obtaining reliable knowledge of fairness is much the same as that of observers of unfairness.

8. The same may be asserted of the umpire who is in direct contact with the fairness of handling a situation. Only that again the pressure of the concrete situation in which he has to act may affect his own subjective sureness and the objective certainty of his perspective.

9. This is also true of the judge's perspective. While based on more indirect evidence, his greater distance from the emotionalism of the immediate scene should enable him to give a more considered verdict on fairness with a greater claim to being valid knowledge. Yet its dependence on unreliable evidence makes it far from infallible and liable to appeals and reversals.

10. Obviously, the knowledge claim of an attorney's consciously one-sided plea for his client's fairness cannot be defended. Its epistemological value is at best that of providing grounds for a better verdict by a judge based on a deeper understanding of the situation because of the consideration of additional partial evidence from one side and preferably from both.

There is no sufficient reason for asserting absolute or 'apodictic' certainty of our knowledge of unfairness as well as fairness. With our limited knowledge of the general and especially the social circumstances, based largely on hearsay, a definitive verdict about unfairness and fairness is 'certainly' beyond our reach. Caution and epistemological humility are clearly what is called for, but not despair and sweeping scepticism.

16.5 Grounds of Unfairness and Fairness

Thus far I have explored only what being unfair and being fair are in and by themselves, their ways of appearance and the certainty of our knowledge about them. What remains to be investigated is on what factors the occurrence of these properties depends or what are their 'grounds', understanding by 'grounds' of unfairness and fairness the unfair- and fair-making characteristics, in analogy to what in general ethics is called good- (and bad-)making characteristics. Such grounds are also to help us understand as far as possible why certain acts, persons and situations are unfair or fair.

According to my analysis of unfairness, the victim of unfair treatment has certain claims, which in the case of unfair treatment are violated and, in that of the beneficiary of fairness, respected. I have tried to list some of these claims at the end of section 16.2 as implied in the essential structure of unfairness and fairness, e.g., the claims to life, liberty and security, or to recognition of one's separate existence on equal terms.

What then can make unfair treatment, persons and situations unfair and their fair equivalents fair? A first answer to this question could be that it is the violation of, or respect for, the basic claims.

However, such a first-level reply to the question cannot yet be considered final, inasmuch as the violated or respected claims themselves are by no means ultimate, but are dependent on 'claim-making' factors or grounds. These would then at the same time be the ultimate grounds for unfairness and fairness. This is not the place for a thorough exploration and discussion of possible grounds for claims. I have tried to supply them in the larger context of a philosophy of human rights and duties which I cannot present or presuppose in the present contect.[240]

240. *Sollen und Dürfen. Philosophie der ethischen Rechte und Pflichten,* Ch. VII.

Instead I would like to introduce a possible answer based on a more easily accessible and current idea: that of human dignity as the ground for basic human claims and through them for what is unfair or fair. One way of approaching such a solution could be to study what is involved in the 'striking' experience of the phenomenon of 'indignities'. As a first attempt to describe it I suggest the interpretation of indignities as sufferings that are incompatible with the upholding of (human) dignity. This means that the decisive concept behind indignities is (human) dignity. What, then, is human dignity? In contrast to the still growing popularity of this phrase, which has been awakened by the 'indignities' of totalitarianism, and especially by the fascist and Nazi atrocities, I have tried to show that this idea is anything but clear and unambiguous and challenges contemporary philosophy to clarify and buttress it.[241] But I cannot claim to have met this challenge. All I intend to do here is to outline one possible answer not based on the traditional theological interpretation of man as the image of God. Instead of this and other theological and philosophical answers. What I propose to do here is to suggest an answer hinted at by Kant, who in his *Foundation of Moral Philosophy* had based his categorical imperatives on 'the idea of the dignity of a rational being who obeys no law except that which he himself also gives (autonomy) . . . and which does not have mere relative worth, i.e., a price, but an intrinsic worth, i.e., 'dignity'.'[242] However, he also introduced close to the start of his *Anthropologie in pragmatischer Hinsicht*[243] the following additional ground:

> That man can have the idea of an 'I' elevates him immeasurably above all other beings on this earth. This is what makes him a person. He is a being completely different in rank and dignity from things, the like of which are animals without reason . . . even when he cannot yet say 'I'.[244]

I maintain that this fact, expressed also on a more phenomenolo-

---

241. See my 'Human Dignity: a Challenge to Contemporary Philosophy, New York: Gordon and Breach, 1971, and above no. 9.

242. *Foundations of the Metaphysics of Morals* (1785), translated by Lewis White Beck, The Library of Liberal Arts, 1959, p. 53.

243. *Anthropologie in pragmatischer Hinsicht* (1798) Akademie Edition V, p. 127. Translated with an introduction and notes by Mary J. Gregor, The Hague: Nijhoff, p. 197.

244. 'On the I-am-Me Experience in Childhood and Adolescence', *Review of Existential Psychology and Psychiatry* 4 (1964), pp. 3-21 and above no. 1.

gical basis in what I call the 'I-am-me' experience is one of the most telling reasons for meeting personal beings with a special respect and for meeting them fairly and not treating them unfairly. Unfairness is ultimately an attack on human dignity (and other 'dignities'), fairness a way of preserving and promoting it.

16.6 Implications of the Phenomenology of Unfairness and Fairness

The preceding analyses have considerable significance for ethics and other fields. In the present context I shall single out those (a) for a specific theory of justice, namely Rawls' idea of the 'Veil of Ignorance'; (b) for normative ethics in general; (c) for other fields; (d) for the foundations of my *Steppingstones Toward an Ethics for Fellow Existers*.

(a) Implications for the Theory of Justice: Rawls' 'Veil of Ignorance'

One of the most original and fruitful but also most paradoxical doctrines in Rawls' theory of justice is that of the 'veil of ignorance' as the prerequisite for choosing his two 'principles of justice'.[245] Instead of a detailed discussion I shall point out here simply my agreements, reservations and corrective suggestions:

1. In principle I agree wholeheartedly with Rawls' attempt to 'nullify the accidents of natural endowment and the contingencies of social circumstance' (p. 15).

2. Yet from the very start I felt puzzled and even repulsed by his insistence on the need for a 'veil of ignorance' as needed before his 'principles of justice' could be agreed upon.

3. As far as I have been able to make out there is no precedent in ethics or legal philosophy for this conception. Nor does Rawls give an explicit explanation for the abrupt introduction of his

---

245. *A Theory of Justice* (1971), pp. 12, 19 and section 24.

metaphorical innovation.

4. Specifically, I wonder what the metaphor of a 'veil' in this phrase is supposed to convey. Veils may be more or less transparent from the inside and even from the outside, e.g., brides' veils. But there are also completely nontransparent veils, e.g., veils that conceal an object, e.g., veils hiding a new statue before 'unveiling', cloaks, or curtains. To what extent is the veil of ignorance supposed to be one or the other? Indications are that this veil is to conceal from its users certain facts so completely that they can no longer penetrate it.

5. This veil is to consist of 'ignorance'. How literally is the word 'ignorance' to be taken here? Ignorance means properly a state of not knowing and never having known before, in contrast to the case of forgetting. Ignorance in this sense therefore cannot descend on a situation like a veil or a curtain. At best an act of ignoring can do that, i.e., overlooking some circumstance while knowing it exists, i.e., in bad faith.

6. Assuming, then, that what is involved is dropping the veil of ignorance in the sense of ignoring, my first question would be: Can such an operation be carried out successfully? Can a person be honest with and to himself pretending that he does not know, e.g., his class or social rank, his share of natural assets and abilities, his intelligence and strength and presumably all other individual differences from other individuals including his sex (which is strangely never mentioned by Rawls) as he is instructed to do, while he is allowed to hold on to his general information, i.e., his knowledge of general laws and theories without limitation, which can remain unveiled? Is such a separation even remotely possible? How can a person black out all his individual knowledge about himself? Would he not be fooling himself by pretending that he does not know what he obviously does? Would he not have to resort to negative autosuggestion to blind himself to the irrepressible facts?

7. If so, how could one assert an obligation to carry out such an impossible operation, when clearly no one can be obligated to an impossible performance *(ultra posse nemo obligatur)*? In other words, would such an imposition be fair in the sense in which Rawls asserts the fairness of the 'original' position rather

than the ultimate in unfairness?

8. Nevertheless, I agree with Rawls' demand that we must disregard the original differences between us in order to arrive at a hypothetical consensus about this or some other principles of justice. But I would deny that in order to accept this principle it is necessary to undergo the preposterous phase of self-blinding implied by the metaphor of the veil of ignorance. Would it not be equally possible to reach the same conclusion as Rawls does without it? Why not honestly admit one's individual differences and face them squarely? Even then one could refuse to attach any weight to them in designing the principle of justice.

9. Such an open-eyed discounting of individual differences could actually be defended in the name of fairness with the argument that it would be unfair to let 'accidents of birth' enter our ethical thinking. Such discounting does not mean concealing by a veil. On the contrary, in order to discount them, we have first to disqualify them in an open contest, and even to compensate for them in the case of the handicapped and to 'handicap' those with a natural headstart.[246] Rawls is right that ultimately it is fairness which requires such a 'nullifying' operation. But that can be accomplished directly and above board without the disingenuous fiction of concealing the accidents of birth and individual circumstances rather than by attending to them directly in our deliberations. Unfairness and fairness are actually the decisive criteria at the ground level of a satisfactory theory of justice. But they do not require the dropping of a veil of ignorance but rather the illumination of daylight or intuitive reason in order to identify some, if not all, individual differences as irrelevant to the search for the principle of justice.

---

246. See my 'Why Compensate the Naturally Handicapped?', see above no. 12.

(b) Implications for Normative Ethics

Ethics does not coincide with normative ethics, i.e., the ethics of what ought to be and what ought not be done, and what may be and may not be done. There is also the ethics of what is good and bad in general. And there is the ethics of supererogatory ideal 'oughts', whose foundations are primarily what is ideally desirable in general and specifically by way of human conduct, based primarily on the demands of love in the sense of charity. But this order of supererogatory desirabilities is based on an underlying order of minimal requirements whose fulfillment can be expected ('erogatory' requirements). What about the grounds for these strict requirements?

In the present context, I cannot examine all the possible foundations for their buttress. Yet, I do not think that a utilitarian theory can support the unconditional or 'categorical', or better the apodictic tenor of these fundamental requirements. Nor can Kant's autonomism ultimately account for the 'objective' obligatoriness of these requirements, if the legislation by the autonomous subject is to be understood in the ordinary sense of a freedom to take it or leave it, rather than some 'Pickwickian' sense.

What seems to me the decisive consideration in support of this part of ethics is the fairness or unfairness of the fundamental requirements prior to all considerations of ideal requirements. I submit that the ground for such fundamental requirements, obligations, duties and responsibilities is their fairness in terms of what can be expected as a minimum of ethical conduct, and the unfairness of its violation. Thus the question of unfairness and fairness is at the root of all questions of fundamental requirements and thus of all normative ethics.

(c) Implications for Metaphysics and Philosophical Anthropology

Clearly the boldest use of the preceding analyses of unfairness and fairness would be to show their implications for 'metaphysics'. If one understands by metaphysics the study of 'ultimate reality', one might ask, for instance, what role unfairness and fairness play in the pattern of the cosmos. The answer would then presumably have to be: 'not very much of a role'. Beyond the inhabited part of the earth, the solar system, our galaxy and the millions of galaxies beyond, composed of myriads of stars, unfairness and fairness have no place. And once life on earth has died off, either in the normal course of the 'running down' of the universe due to entropy or to the insanity of human 'omnicide' in a total nuclear holocaust, there would no longer be any scope for unfairness and fairness at all. Would this mean the insignificance of the two in the total frame of things?

If size and permanence alone mattered, I see no escape from such a melancholy conclusion. But do they? I submit that they are not the only dimensions according to which 'ultimate reality' could and should be appraised. There is, for instance, the dimension of qualitative abundance. And here evolution in whatever small a corner of the universe has added something completely new to the empty vastness of the cosmos. That it occupies only an infinitesimally small part of it, and even that eventually it will disappear is no reason to write if off as meaningless. No subsequent annihilation can undo its having happened at some unique point of time in the continuum of time-space. Quantity and endless duration is not all. In fact, sheer bigness by itself is meaningless. By contrast, the entrance of unfairness and fairness into the universe represents a turning point in its evolution. The engineer of this turn is no one else but man. She is the principle who injects into an indifferent universe a new dimension by raising the question of unfairness and fairness. By sponsoring the cause of fairness and by trying to reduce, if not to abolish unfairness she makes a cosmic difference. This too may be one of the major grounds of human dignity. Whether or not this fight is ultimately doomed to failure amounting to a cosmic Quixotism does not invalidate it.

(d) Implications for the 'Steppingstones Toward an Ethics for Fellow Existers'

In presenting in this collection of essays on what I consider to be new 'ethical dimensions' or fulcrums for a new ethics, I admitted that they were still in need of a philosophical and especially of a phenomenological foundation. I now would like to furnish at least a beginning of the promised leverage by showing the significance of the present phenomenology of unfairness and fairness for the main ingredients or stepping stones which I have presented. As to particular essays:

1. 'Accident of Birth': The unacceptability of the accident of birth and of similar circumstances rests at least indirectly on the unfairness of conditions not supported by autonomous consent, and hence requiring its 'nullification' by 'fair' 'essential' compensation.

2. 'A Defense of Human Equality' is based on the fact that natural inequalities are based directly on an accident of birth and indirectly on the unfairness of this 'accident'.

3. 'Human Dignity', based ultimately on the uniqueness of the I-am-me experience, also has roots in man's role as a protagonist of fairness versus the unfairnesses surrounding us.

4. 'Fellowship in the Fate of Existence' is rooted in the common accident of existence and the demands of fairness in sharing this accident and in 'de-accidentalizing' or 'essentializing' it by conscious choices.

5. 'Good Fortune Obligates' is a principle, launched first by Albert Schweitzer, which is an expression of the experience of unfairness in the congenital headstarts of the fortunate few over the unfortunate many.

6. 'Why Compensate the Naturally Handicapped?' My answer to this question has its ground in the attempt to make up for the glaring unfairness in the fates of the naturally disadvantaged.

7. 'Is There a Human Right to One's Native Soil?' bases its denial of such a right on the unfairness of the accident of being born at a privileged place and time compared with those without it.

8. 'Toward Global Solidarity' states the case for a global ethics on the basis of the unfairness of putting accidental allegiance to parochial states over the essential global solidarity.

9. 'The Nuclear Powers are Forfeiting Their Claims to Civil Obedience' grounds the right to civil disobedience on the failure of the accidental national states to fulfill their *raison d'être*: providing international security.

16.7 Summary and Conclusion: The Meaning of
Phenomenological Analysis

First, a brief and incomplete summary of my main findings:

1. An analysis of unfairness and fairness has to go beyond a linguistic analysis to a phenomenological investigation.

2. Unfairness and fairness as they occur in actions, persons and situations can occur in any kind of personal acts and social situations.

3. Unfairness and fairness are relational properties encountered in a peculiar feeling, related to other persons or impersonal standards, paying respect to or violating certain basic claims.

4. They appear in different ways and different perspectives more or less adequately.

5. There are degrees of certainty in our knowledge of unfairness and fairness, but there is no absolute certainty.

6. The ultimate ground for claims issuing from unfairness and fairness is the 'human dignity' from which these claims to respect derive.

7. Unfairness and fairness are important buttresses for 'Stepping Stones Toward an Ethics for Fellow Existers'.

In what sense can the preceding investigations of and findings about unfairness and fairness be considered 'analyses' of these phenomena? Certainly they are not analyses in the literal sense of a dissection of the phenomena into their component parts comparable to an analysis in chemistry. Nor can they be considered as analyses in the sense of complete descriptions leading to connotative definitions in terms of proximate genus and specific difference. Least of all, are they analyses in the sense of 'analytic philosophy' which would be able to put them together again à la Humpty Dumpty from the ingredients even of my own account. What then has been accomplished? I submit at least a better understanding of the uniquesness of the phenomena by plotting them against the background of adjacent phenomena. This analysis can also convey some idea of the general structure of unfairness and fairness as properties closely related to *gestalt* phenomena. It can direct the search for them. And it can remove from them the aura of inscrutable mystery beyond possible understanding and communication. But it cannot spare us the effort of making their direct acquaintance in depth by the intuitive 'fulfillment' of merely verbal meanings.

Phenomenological analysis is not an end in itself. It is a device for facilitating our direct encounter with the phenomena themselves.

INDEX OF NAMES

INDEX OF SUBJECTS
not sufficiently covered in the Table of Contents